p 16817 — exactly the situation
in 2016!

TOMORROW'S WAR

The Threat of High-Technology Weapons

DAVID SHUKMAN

HARCOURT BRACE & COMPANY

NEW YORK SAN DIEGO LONDON

Requests for permission to make copies of
any part of the work should be mailed to:
Permissions Department
Harcourt Brace & Company
6277 Sea Harbor Drive
Orlando, Florida 32887-6777.

Library of Congress Cataloging-in-Publication Data
Shukman, David.
[Sorcerer's challenge]
Tomorrow's war: the threat of high-technology weapons/
David Shukman.—1st ed.
p.   cm.
Originally published: The sorcerer's challenge.
London: Hodder & Stoughton, 1995.
Includes bibliographical references and index.
ISBN 0-15-100198-7

1. Weapons systems—Technological innovations.
2. Military research. 3. Arms race.   I. Title.
UF500.S55   1996
355'.07—dc20   95-47575

Printed in the United States of America
First U.S. edition
A C E D B

For Jessica

CONTENTS

AUTHOR'S NOTE

The armed forces of Britain and the United States – and the scientists who support them – continue to use a mixture of Imperial and Metric measurements. Soldiers, for example, describe distances in kilometres and the calibre of their weapons in millimetres while pilots refer to altitude in feet and the weight of their bombs in pounds. This book reflects that inconsistency.

ACKNOWLEDGEMENTS

Many of the people who provided the most help in this project –
by agreeing to be interviewed or introducing me to other experts or
offering to share private correspondence and early drafts of papers
– are identified and quoted during the course of the book; their
contributions are self-evident. I am very grateful to all of them for
their kindness and patience. Sam Gardiner deserves to be singled
out in this regard. His friendship and unstinting support opened
new doors for me in the often secretive world of the military and
generated much of the material included here.

Others offered crucial assistance and guidance but chose to remain
anonymous because of the sensitivity of their positions in or association with the armed forces or the intelligence services; I thank them
for their frankness and trust.

I am indebted to Liz Peace, Company Secretary of the Defence
Research Agency, who arranged the interviews with the DRA's
scientists. Despite the difficulties of this task, she was invariably
optimistic and encouraging. Other senior figures in the DRA, including Bill Clifford, Director of the Weapons Systems Sector, were
generous with their help and time. The only condition attached to
interviews with DRA personnel was that I should submit the relevant
parts of the manuscript for screening on three counts: technical accuracy, the inadvertent use of classified information and operational
security. I agreed to make some minor changes to the text as a result;
most involved points of technical detail.

I am grateful to Colonel Michael Dewar, Deputy Director of the
International Institute for Strategic Studies, Michael Clark, Director
of the Centre for Defence Studies at King's College, London, and
others for reading the manuscript; the responsibility for any faults,
factual or otherwise, is of course mine.

Little of this work would have been possible were I not fortunate
enough to have been engaged as Defence Correspondent for BBC

News and Current Affairs from 1987 to 1995. In particular, a series of filming trips to weapons laboratories in Russia and the United States for Television News and for the current affairs programmes, *Newsnight* and *Assignment*, made me realise how privileged and varied a journalist's access can be – and how readily these experiences might be included in a book. Although all additional research and the writing were undertaken entirely in my own time, I am grateful to the colleagues who provided help at various stages along the way.

It is no exaggeration to say that without Julian Alexander, my literary agent, the project would never have been started. Richard Cohen, the book's original editor, must be thanked for proposing its shape. Roland Philipps, who later took over as editor, offered tremendous encouragement and suggested numerous improvements.

My greatest debt of gratitude is to my wife, Jessica. Not only did she endure the long hours of my absence in the study at home – in addition to my absence during assignments abroad – but also she found time in her own busy life as a psychology student and mother of our three children, Jack, Harry and Kitty, to provide invaluable criticism and constant support.

PREFACE

The arms race has not stopped. Instead, with the passing of the Cold War, it has lurched in new and potentially more dangerous directions. At the same time, the pace of research in certain key areas is quickening. Technologies of a bewildering variety – from nuclear energy to miniature computers to robotics to biological engineering to space-flight – are suddenly on the loose and the competition to find new ways of putting them to military use is no longer the preserve of the most advanced industrial nations. There is now a free-for-all to acquire weapons which may allow even relatively weak countries the chance to leap-frog their way to battlefield superiority – at what could hardly be a more uncertain or unstable time.

This book explores the strange and often disturbing course of weapons research. It asks the scientists in the leading military laboratories to share their secret ideas for armaments thirty to forty years ahead. It finds their imagination undimmed by the widespread cuts in military spending. Some of their concepts are startling: robot-soldiers the size of ants, genetically modified algae to store computer data, electronic eyes programmed to identify friend from foe, automated missiles accurate enough to hit a particularly vulnerable point on an aircraft or tank, squadrons of near-invisible solar-powered gliders poised to shoot down Scud missiles, laser-beams and super-bugs to immobilise enemy soldiers rather than kill them, microchips which see in the dark.

The book finds a world inhabited by future projects with bizarrely evocative names like Raptor-Talon, Midas and Excalibur. It is a world in which scientists, in their quest for perfect weapons, seemingly adopt the ancient role of the sorcerer by offering soldiers near-magic powers with which to defeat their enemies: an invincible sword, an impenetrable shield, unfailing sight, an unerring aim, a trusted aide and the ultimate triumph of bloodless victory. Their belief is that science is on the brink of yielding yet another revolution in weaponry and that these powers have never been so achievable. They also believe that since so much of the technological progress making these breakthroughs possible has derived from commercial rather than purely military research, any nation with a reasonably advanced industrial base will be able to share its fruits. It is therefore vital, they warn, to keep ahead. It means that, however distasteful the suggestion, there may be no option but to stay in the race.

TOMORROW'S WAR

A FORBIDDING CHALLENGE

Although the world has changed, it remains a deeply turbulent and dangerous place.
> Douglas Hurd, Foreign Secretary, speaking in the House of
> Commons, 22 February 1994

The commander of the most powerful air force in the world was looking for help. Like every other western military official, General Merrill 'Tony' McPeak was troubled by the bewildering and hazardous new circumstances that had emerged from the Cold War. He wanted assistance to try to understand them. Every six weeks, on a Friday evening, General McPeak, a gaunt figure with a quiet, friendly manner, who retired as Chief of Staff of the United States Air Force in late 1994, cleared his busy diary and left his office in the Pentagon building to travel by limousine to join a private group of military experts for an unpublicised brainstorming session over dinner. The conversations and arguments would often run long into the night; they were always off-the-record, McPeak's presence kept confidential. They were a chance for the general to speak his mind and to hear fresh views on how to cope with an increasingly unpredictable future. Though he had the latest high-technology weapons from Stealth fighter-bombers to spy-planes to smart missiles under his command, these had been bought to fight a Soviet Union which had since vanished and were now arrayed against a completely new and different set of enemies. The ending of the stand-off with the East had wrenched open a can of hostile worms – the spread of nuclear weapons, the instability of Russia, the eruption of nationalist and ethnic conflict. It had also left the United States in a unique position of responsibility: it had become the only superpower able to respond.

One of the sessions, held in December 1993 in a private dining-room at the Marriott Hotel overlooking Key Bridge in Washington, began with all the appearance of a corporate meeting out-of-hours. General McPeak and the other participants were casually dressed in sweaters and open shirts, amiably exchanging anecdotes and looking as if the evening ahead of them might have been to tackle the launch of a new product or to thrash out the latest advertising strategy. The only rule was laid down half-jokingly by the organiser of the group, Sam Gardiner, a jovial and free-thinking consultant to the Pentagon, the CIA and the Ford motor company: 'you have to be willing to say when you think someone is full of crap'. The participants were indeed fond of spearing each other's arguments with witty jibes and gentle abuse. Yet their subject matter was thoroughly menacing. It was 'the business of war', as one of them had declared at an earlier gathering, and the talk was quickly brought round to it. Their hunger was for novel insights into the post-Cold War world. There was much to discuss: so much had changed even since the last session, just one and a half months before.

For all the fearful words about the old Soviet Union from the Pentagon and the military think-tanks and the weapons laboratories during the Cold War, the threat from Moscow had proved to be a comfortable resource, ironically an ally, compared to the multiplying complexities faced today. The armed services had had little trouble arguing the case for new arms and equipment and, especially under the administration of Ronald Reagan in the 1980s, maintaining large or sometimes expanding forces. They knew where to point their guns and they could rehearse the battles of the Third World War that were to be fought in the submarine-lanes of the north Norwegian Sea and over the invasion routes across Germany. There was a single adversary, easily contemplated – and readily exploited. The defence contractors constantly sought orders for new weapons and the politicians in Congress, eager to see work placed with the factories in their home states, were happy to oblige. It was a profitable system dubbed 'The Iron Triangle' and Moscow, no doubt unintentionally, served it well. The triangle and the threat that oiled it have both now suddenly disappeared. General McPeak and the rest of the western military have had to start thinking again.

They talk about the changes taking place in the world as a 'moving target' – an inaccurate description because it implies a degree of confidence about making accurate judgements at a time when forecasts have become impossible. The difficulty is that the pace of history has been accelerating. Institutions have been struggling to keep up; the military have been among the slowest. From the moment the Berlin Wall fell in November 1989, the first of the old certainties in military planning was lost. But no sooner had the Warsaw Pact disintegrated in the summer of 1990, giving substance to talk of a 'Common European Home' and of dialogue replacing conflict, than Saddam Hussein ordered Iraqi forces into Kuwait. Then, within months of the emirate's liberation by the largest American-led coalition since Vietnam twenty years earlier, Slovenia and Croatia broke away from Yugoslavia and triggered the worst fighting in Europe since the defeat of Nazi Germany in 1945. Even as the battles moved south to Croatia, a still more significant event was to come: the collapse of the Soviet Union in late 1991 and with it the birth of several new, nuclear-armed countries. In the demise of the old Kremlin empire, economic hardship combined with angry disputes between the former Soviet republics over borders and the sharing of Moscow's weaponry to raise the spectre of massive civil war or 'Yugoslavia with nukes', as one American official put it.

But history, once suggested to have ended with the Cold War, was unrelenting. Not all of it was bad. The peace accord signed by the Israeli Prime Minister, Yitzhak Rabin, and the Palestine Liberation Organisation's Chairman, Yasser Arafat, was one 'magic moment', as President Clinton called it. But, for the military, the collapse of agreements and the failures of diplomacy attract the keenest interest: their whole purpose is to prepare for the worst, and there has been plenty of need for that. Russia, tottering between reform and reversion to its old ways, has proved to be constantly unnerving. In October 1993, Boris Yeltsin used force to crush renegade members of the Russian Parliament only to see the subsequent elections that December introduce even more hostile voices against him. That of Vladimir Zhirinovsky, an ultra-nationalist urging the government to reclaim Russia's 'rightful' territories, seemed to capture a disturbing trend of public opinion, especially in the military, in favour of a far more assertive foreign policy. One of Zhirinovsky's eeriest taunts to the West was that Russia had a secret weapon called 'Elipton' which was far more dangerous than nuclear weapons and with which 'the entire world could be destroyed'. By March 1994, the new American Defence Secretary, William Perry, had to admit publicly that it was possible Russia 'could emerge from her turbulence as an authoritarian, militaristic, imperialistic nation hostile to the West'.

By this time Bosnia had descended into a nightmare of Serb-led 'ethnic cleansing', mass rape and concentration camps; the war threatened to spread and the outside world was left looking unwilling or unable to stop it. Other conflicts, such as those in Georgia and Nagorno-Karabakh in the Caucasus, produced their share of horrors too but attracted less international attention. Somalia, where clan warfare had caused widespread starvation, did catch Washington's eye but was assisted by an American-inspired military aid operation which later lapsed into open combat. By contrast, the massacres in Rwanda in April 1994 prompted little discussion about outside intervention. Yet these were mainly crises of conscience; crises of national interest had emerged as well.

Nuclear weapons, the most destructive arms ever invented, were suspected of having been developed by one of the most bellicose, isolated and economically backward countries on earth: North Korea. The fear was that, unlike successive Politburos in Moscow, the secretive North Korean leadership might be rash enough to do more than issue threats with a nuclear arsenal – but to use it as well. South Korea and the American forces stationed there are within range of North Korea's bombers and missiles; so is the powerhouse of the global economy, Japan. Other countries, including Iran, were suspected of trying to acquire the Bomb as well but curbing their ambitions was proving harder than ever. Nuclear components and nuclear scientists were on the loose. In August 1994, the authorities in Germany seized several samples of smuggled plutonium; none was sufficient to make a weapon but the trade was seen nonetheless as the tip of a future iceberg of nuclear dealing made possible by Russia's instability.

The Cold War had made way, not for the 'New World Order' promised by the last American President, George Bush, but for an era of limitless uncertainty and incalculable dangers. As Les Aspin, a former American Defence Secretary, put it: 'The world is looking a little long on "new" and a little short on "order".'

As if these global changes were not challenging enough, western military forces have faced two profound internal developments themselves as well. The first is that they have seen their budgets slashed dramatically, leaving them, in the opinion of one analyst, 'in a state of trauma – they're worried about the next meal'. The American defence budget, which provides the backbone of the western military alliance, was scheduled to fall from around $300 billion in 1993 to about $240 billion by 1997. It was not alone. Britain's defence budget which began the 1990s standing at about £24 billion slipped to about £23 billion during the middle of the decade. Governments throughout NATO had declared the Cold War over and, having decided that budget deficits were now more important than preserving defence spending, implemented a lengthy and inexorable cut-back. In 1993, the latest American review decided that the cuts planned by the previous administration should be even deeper: the Army would keep only ten active divisions not twelve; the Air Force would have twenty air wings not twenty-six and a half; the Navy would shrink to 345 warships from 450; only the Marines Corps was to grow, by 15,000 to 174,000. With the British armed forces being cut by one-fifth on average – though much more deeply in particular areas – many commentators and backbench politicians condemned the reductions as foolhardy at a time of danger. Sir Nicholas Bonsor, Chairman of the influential Commons Select Committee on Defence, described the cuts as 'disastrously wrong' and the optimism on which they were based as 'wildly misplaced'. Senior officers, unable to speak publicly, would tend to agree.

But the military are in the grip of more than budget paralysis. A second profound change, a technological one, is beginning to affect them as well. New feats of scientific ingenuity are producing startling possibilities for the transformation of weaponry. And new doctrines and strategies and skills are required as a result. The performance of precision-guided bombs, the use of satellites and the advent of battlefield computers in the Gulf War had caused gasps of amazement and claims that a military revolution was under way. 'Revolution' has since gone on to become one of the most overworked words in military circles; commentators, arms manufacturers and generals alike are fond of using it at almost every opportunity. Yet the word is being applied prematurely. The reality is that in the Gulf War no single piece of hardware worked so sensationally that it can be claimed to have been responsible for the freeing of Kuwait. Some individual technologies – such as cruise-missile guidance, night-vision goggles and satellite navigation – provided breakthroughs in limited areas but, as ever in warfare, were only as effective as the personnel who operated them and as the system into which they were integrated. One example of this (as Chapter 5 will explain) is that despite having high-technology spy-planes like

5

J-STARS to track down Iraq's mobile Scud-missile launchers, the allies never managed to pass the relevant information quickly enough to the fighter-bombers which were supposed to attack them.

That fundamental changes in warfare afforded by technology are on the horizon is not doubted. Huge advances in electronics, computing, miniaturisation, automation and genetic engineering are under way, with profound implications for the military. It may take another ten or even thirty years for the latest of these technologies to be fielded -- even longer for their full integration into the armed forces to yield their true worth. History shows that it is not so much new weapons themselves which provide a breakthrough as the way in which they are used: though the tank first appeared on the battlefields of the First World War, it did not prove to be a decisive technology until the *Wehrmacht* exploited it as the hammer-blow of their blitzkrieg manoeuvres two decades later. Nevertheless, in the case of the tank, as with weapons ranging from the machine-gun to the submarine to the jet-fighter, it was the technology that made new strategies for warfare possible in the first place. As the military historian John Keegan has observed, weapons made of copper and stone soon gave way to those made of bronze, 'as man bent to the almost universal rule that a superior technology obliterates an inferior one as fast as the necessary techniques and materials can be acquired'.[1] Technology itself cannot represent a revolution but it can be the cause of one – and that is starting to happen now.

The next generation of weaponry will signal the arrival of an entirely new approach in warfare: information rather than brute force will win the day. The potency of modern electronics will be the key -- not for its own sake but for its ability to handle and process information. For weapons to become faster, more accurate and more 'intelligent', they must be able to handle vast amounts of data at fantastically high speeds with ever-smaller computers. With the ability to see an enemy's moves in the minutest detail, to analyse the information instantly and to transmit it to a weapon which then makes unerring use of it, warfare will be transformed; information will be its determining factor. The technology at the heart of this change is the microchip. With each passing year, computer processors are more agile, lighter and less power hungry. 'There'll be chips with everything,' one British military scientist is fond of saying.

It means weapons will become more robotic, doing more for themselves, and far more accurate, aiming not just for a tank or plane but for a particularly vulnerable part of it. It also means weapons may be able to replace personnel in many of the most hazardous military tasks. One idea is for automated sentries; another is for an unmanned artillery piece; a third, more extravagant plan, is for solar-powered gliders armed with smart rockets to offer round-the-clock defence against missile attack. Tiny computers and sensors will also allow cheap mini-satellites to spy from space or even 'robot-ants' to act as scouts or to eat their way through electric cables. The lowliest soldier will be enabled to see in the dark and, for the first time in the history of warfare, know precisely where he is and what is going on around him. But all this will depend not just on the technologies themselves actually working (and bitter experience shows that many weapons take years or even decades to perfect) but on decisions to provide adequate funding for their development and on the military grasping how best to employ them. Neither factor is guaranteed in a period of dwindling finance. The choices are awkward – deciding between spending precious money on future weapons or on politically sensitive regiments or shipyards in areas of high unemployment.

But the nature of technological progress has changed and that in itself may force a decision in favour of futuristic research. Many of the most recent advances, making the next generation of weapons possible, have been the result of commercial investment in research. Genetic engineering, for example, with its potential for biological manipulation has become a multi-billion-dollar industry, yielding new medicines, new methods of preserving food and even, with a protein derived from algae, new substances in which to store computer information. Yet this burgeoning field of interest has a darker, military side too. If individual molecules can be manhandled for the benefit of civilian life, it follows that they can also be rearranged to create new biological weapons in the form of disease-inducing bacteria. One analyst has suggested that it would be scientifically possible to 'plant' the ingredients of snake venom in an ordinary flu virus, turning the flu into a killer. Another has warned that lethal germs could be engineered to target only the members of particular ethnic groups – tailor-made for a twenty-first-century version of the Nazi death camps and the Serbs' ethnic cleansing. To make matters worse, future germ weapons of this sort are within the grasp of any newly industrialised country with facilities – which may be perfectly legitimate – for manufacturing vaccines. No longer the province of the major powers (Russia, for example, maintained a highly secret biological

7

weapons research programme long after it claimed to have abandoned it under the terms of the 1972 Biological Weapons Convention), this avenue is now being pursued by an estimated twelve countries including China, India and Taiwan. Iraq's biological warfare programme was only discovered after the Gulf War and may, even now, have evaded full UN scrutiny.

The danger is that the advances in this field and those of information technology are available to all: not just to commercial firms but also to potential adversaries. There is a serious risk that others, such as newly industrialising countries, could leap-frog ahead of the West by developing novel weapons systems first. General Colin Powell, the former Chairman of the US Joint Chiefs of Staff, warned of this in 1993: the 'information revolution', he said, was making it possible for some countries to develop new weapons 'that might look rather sophisticated in a few years'. Not only that: those weapons could well come into service in such countries before they do in the West. The reason is that the new powers offered by computers are increasingly widely available. And, with the most advanced computers, the performance of future weapons can now be simulated with a high degree of realism. Different computers and design characteristics can be 'tried out' in a mock battlefield and adjusted until an adequate technological edge is achieved. The resulting data can then be passed directly to a computer-controlled plant for manufacture. While the western military struggle for a decade on average to acquire new weapons, a country with commercially available computer equipment and less rigorous democratic and accounting processes could field new systems within a few years. It is the stuff of military nightmares.

'I am your next enemy.'

So begins a privately circulated article written by a senior American military intelligence officer, who asked to remain anonymous. His job is to watch the ebb and flow of technology – to see which weapons are being bought and developed by other countries. He wrote his article as a warning, similar to General Powell's, to show his superiors how easily a future adversary might exploit technological advance to America's disadvantage. It could provide no clearer indication of the military's current nervousness. For all the talk of winning the Cold War and then the Gulf War, there is deep unease about the future.

'My officers,' the article continues, in the assumed voice of a

8

potential opponent, 'have gone to your combat arms schools, your military intelligence schools, your command and general staff school, your War College, your Air War College.

'We were a minor participant in Desert Storm.

'We have been building slowly and quietly over this decade. Thank God you are too busy to read. Otherwise you would have found out from *Jane's Defence Weekly* and *Aviation Week & Space Technology* what we were buying. Our purchases of obsolete Soviet equipment were made through the open market – our real purchases have been made through Japan or the drug cartels. But we were your "friends" so it wouldn't matter anyway.

'Now we are ready.

'I will be facing you soon.'

The author, a tall, clean-cut Texan, was in the US Special Forces' Green Berets; he led one of the FBI's 'SWAT' anti-terrorist teams; he is cleared to high levels of secrecy. 'I know what I'm talking about,' he insists. He also knows how to scare himself. He believes that the West is on the brink of disaster by underestimating how rapidly emerging technology could be seized by other countries. His paper outlines a scenario similar to that of the Gulf War, set at the turn of the century. All of the weapons he describes are plausible even if they have the ring of science fiction: most exist either in fact or on the drawing-board, a few are more distant concepts which are nevertheless taken seriously. The story starts with an invasion.

'We have taken over a neighbouring country for its mineral wealth.

'We allow you to build up your Rapid Deployment Forces. We anticipated that – we have had our Special Forces in place for over a year.

'What do you have to worry about? We have no chemical or nuclear capability – WE WON'T NEED THEM.'

This putative enemy is armed with the most sophisticated conventional weapons. Its missiles are guided by beams of light rather than by radio signals which are vulnerable to jamming. They will be 'intelligent', which means their on-board computers can recognise and select appropriate targets for themselves. Its communications will be virtually impossible to intercept or block because the transmission frequency will 'hop' as many as 2,000 times per second. The enemy will then stage a massive deception plan. There will be fake communications traffic on the very frequencies the allies expect will be used. Mock-ups of tanks and other vehicles will fit the allies'

9

understanding of the enemy's forces. All mock-ups will be heated to give off the same infra-red signature as a real version; they will have metal coatings to do the same for radar.

'You will then start with an air attack.

'You will be successful in knocking out all of my mock-ups. Movie special effects will confirm every hit with graphic explosions.

'One thing we count on is how cocky you Americans get from easy success.

'Your commanding officer tells the press how well his equipment and tactics are working. He assures the American public that most of the troops will be home soon. How right he is – home in body-bags.

'Now the ground war is launched at night since you "know" that we have no night-fighting capability.

'But as your forces cross the line, strange things start happening . . .'

The enemy uses huge guns powered by electromagnetic energy to fire cheap satellites into low-earth orbit; the guns work by massive surges of reverse magnetism rather than by gunpowder. They leave no trace, no launch plume to be detected and attacked. The satellites are 'killers', small space-bombs. They manoeuvre themselves close to America's satellites and explode, destroying themselves and their targets. The allies lose their best sources of intelligence, communications and navigation.

Again without trace, more electromagnetic guns fire 'dazzlers', shells whose brightness overwhelms the allies' night-vision devices. They also launch electromagnetic 'pulse' weapons. These explode with a blast of electrical power that shatters computer software, communications and the radar of the vital AWACS control planes. The allies are suddenly blinded. Just as they claimed to have 'conquered the electromagnetic spectrum' in the Gulf War, they now find themselves denied the very medium on which they most depend.

Their staging areas are bombed with fuel-air munitions. The shells scatter a dense cloud of fuel vapour and then ignite it, triggering a shock wave with much of the force of a small nuclear weapon. 'Eighty per cent nuke for size and no international outrage.'

Allied fighter-planes, stranded without communications or guidance, fall victim to High Energy Lasers. Or fly through specially generated smoke containing tiny particles of superglue: their engines quickly jam and stall. The same happens to cruise missiles.

The headquarters staff are suddenly violently sick. Even in full chemical and biological suits and masks, they become too ill to work. A new enemy toxin has penetrated even the most advanced protection. Once it has taken effect, enemy Special Forces teams arrive and kill everyone dressed in uniform. They spare news correspondents who soon recover and report the carnage.

'In 100 minutes we have turned your force into a farce.

'We will ask your State Department for peace terms . . . and warn that any strikes at our homeland will result in in-kind bombs within the United States.'

The scenario comes to a humiliating and alarming end.

'Let us stay ahead of future weapons developments,' the author pleads in conclusion, 'not become their test bed. We have a new threat that our current disciplines do not readily address. Our failure in this will prove disastrous.'

Though this analysis is no doubt overplayed – many in the military are innately pessimistic and arguably need to dream up new threats to keep themselves employed – it does reflect a danger which cannot be readily dismissed. But just as high technology is spreading with discomforting speed, so too is another problem: the inability of the western military to cope with low-technology conflict on a smaller scale as well. Nasty, old-fashioned, limited wars have become the scourge of the 1990s. The British Army's Conflict Studies Research Centre at Sandhurst has identified thirty-five active or potential disputes over borders and ethnic divisions throughout post-Communist Europe – so a rash of so-called 'small' conflicts is possible.[2] The conflicts which have already erupted in a great swathe of territory from the Balkans through the Caucasus to central Asia involve relatively crude forms of combat, fought with simple weapons. Yet the state-of-the-art arsenals of the major powers seem curiously inappropriate, even inadequate, for dealing with them. For all the decades of military investment to prevent world war in Europe, the weapons laboratories have apparently failed to come up with any technological solutions for the regional wars which have burst open there instead.

The evening sunshine was turning the wooded hills a golden-green as we approached the base of the British United Nations contingent on the edge of Vitez in central Bosnia; the well-watered countryside of the Lasva Valley was the picture of idyllic rural calm. It had been a relatively quiet day in this chocolate-box war zone: only sporadic fire from mortars and snipers had been exchanged along the tangled front line dividing the forces of the Bosnian Croats and those of the mainly Muslim Bosnian government. For the British troops, the usual duty of escorting aid convoys had continued as normal. It was August 1993 and the digestion of the latest of many peace plans had brought a certain lull in the fighting. But it had not stopped it altogether.

Right beside the British base, we turned off the main road into a Croat-held lane in which the BBC and other news organisations rented houses. Just beyond the base, less than 400 yards away, was a steep hill held by the Muslims: the lane was in full view of the Muslim soldiers who spent their days lounging bored in the fox-holes, a green Islamic flag prominent above them. Usually the Croat civilians who used the lane had little trouble. Not this evening. We found the lane teeming with agitated people, their faces drawn, their gestures frantic. Two young people were being helped into a car, their eyes empty. Blood stained the tarmac, a girl's shoes lay nearby. Dobroslava Cutovic, aged eighteen, and her brother, Mladic, aged twelve, had been shot in the legs.

A Muslim sniper, from his vantage-point on the hill, had fired over the heads of the British UN troops and had found two targets. In a twenty-four-hour period he and his colleagues were to wound another ten Croat civilians, including a priest, the local baker and a middle-aged mother, and to kill one, all within sight of the British base. Males tended to be hit in the upper body – to cause the greatest chance of death – females and children in the lower body. Dobroslava and Mladic were driven to the Croats' makeshift hospital which had been set up in a church nearby at Nova Bila, the pews lashed together to form beds, the crypt used for operations with minimal anaesthetic. The consultant showed us the X-rays. Dobroslava, the worst hit of the pair, would probably have to lose a leg.

By Bosnian standards, her tragedy was small-scale and the newsroom in London accordingly showed little interest. But the shooting represented a more fundamental issue: the outside world was unwilling to force itself on this Balkan battlefield to smother the fighting, however relentless the suffering. Even when shots had been fired across a United Nations base – established to assist a humanitarian relief effort which was meant to benefit Bosnia's civilians – nothing had been done in this or other, often worse, cases. Not that this was in any way the fault of the UN soldiers themselves, many of whom were profoundly upset and spoke privately about wanting 'to sort this lot out'. Their actions were governed by a Security Council mandate which authorised them to focus solely on the aid operation; the mandate in turn was strictly interpreted by the British and other governments which had committed troops to Bosnia under it. The politicians' view was that there was to be no attempt at enforcing a peace, even if civilian children were being wounded at the very gates; it had been decided that this was not a war which outsiders could ever win.

That evening, a pair of NATO fighters roared noisily but ineffectively overhead. 'Little use them being here,' said a corporal, adding a few expletives.

Part of the problem was that the only option available to western governments for ending the war was to despatch tens of thousands of troops to occupy the country. Such an operation would have had to have been open-ended and large numbers of casualties would no doubt have resulted. No government, least of all that of the United States, the one country with the resources to manage it, wanted any part of that. And, since there were no 'silver bullets' or magical technological fixes which would offer a solution overnight, the only alternative was to offer support from the margins instead. For the future though, it is possible that new options will become available.

Bosnia quickly became a source of agonised self-recrimination among many in the military. Here was the first major conflict on European soil since the Second World War and the massive armoury at the disposal of the NATO alliance was irrelevant to it. At the same time the United Nations, heralded as a central force for peace after the multinational victory over Iraq in the Gulf War, appeared weak in the face of the aggression of the Bosnian Serbs and their one-time patron, the Serbian president, Slobodan Milosevic; weak too in the face of aggression by the Bosnian Muslims, the principal victims of the war, who by the summer of 1993 had learned that it was better to keep fighting while talking rather than to rely on negotiations to produce a satisfactory outcome. If ever there was a test case of the world's ability to provide a collective police force after the four decades of hostility between East and West, this was it; the world was evidently failing.

Much as the American armed forces were relieved not to be committed to a Balkan version of Vietnam, the constant barrage of television images from Bosnia kept its war on their agenda and on that of Sam Gardiner's discussion group meeting over dinner in

December 1993 in Washington. Bosnia tugged at their consciences and unnerved them with its potential for escalation. A guest of the group that evening, I was pressed for my own impressions of the war: there was particular interest in firsthand detail about the extent of the suffering, with General McPeak asking about the effectiveness of the parachuting of aid supplies from his Hercules transport planes. There were questions too about the risks of the war engulfing neighbouring areas of the Balkans as well.

The fact that the United States was not as involved as it could have been had frequently divided opinion in the group, much as it has in the western military generally. After one session, Sam Gardiner, always eager to break the mould of established textbook thinking, had summarised the two opposing points of view in a memorandum. One camp had said: 'The chaos in the world is an important interest to the United States. Chaos in central Europe is intolerable. We must be involved. It will spread. By what we do, we will define ourselves in the post-Cold War alignment of nations. Leadership demands a greater involvement.' But the other camp had argued the opposite: 'We have no interest there. Stay away. It has been going on for a thousand years. The American people won't support getting involved. Let it burn itself out. We don't want a single American to die in this quagmire.' At this point Gardiner had urged the group not to become stuck on that fundamental question of interests – one which seemed to paralyse President Clinton's administration as well – but to think around it, beyond it.

That is very much his style. A man who prides himself on dreaming up novel approaches to military problems, Gardiner, who left the US Air Force after becoming one of its youngest colonels, has long been dismissive of the quality of analysis by middle-ranking and senior officers and, with an engaging smile on his face, he does not mind saying so. Indeed it was criticism of a particular US Air Force plan which had brought him to General McPeak's attention and later led to McPeak joining the discussion group. His formative experience, he says, came in Vietnam. When Gardiner had served as a planner at a bomber base and his commanders had announced plans for a major new campaign meant 'to bring the North Vietnamese to their knees', Gardiner realised, when he saw the reconnaissance photographs of the targets, that the plan would never work. In his view, the targets which had been chosen would not influence North Vietnam at all; one was even the transmitter station broadcasting radio propaganda to the American servicemen, hardly critical to the North Vietnamese. He was proved right but the affair confirmed to him the intellectual limitations of his former colleagues. 'We go into each war thinking we're fighting the last one again; we can't get away with that any more, the world won't be so kind to us.' Bosnia has shown that.

The group's discussions about Bosnia mirrored that of the US administration. As recently as April 1994, as the Bosnian Serbs resumed their shelling of the Muslim enclave of Gorazde, Washington was openly divided on whether American interests demanded some form of intervention. While the Pentagon declared that the US 'would not enter the war', the State Department argued that that response was an 'open invitation' to the Serbs to continue their aggression. It meant there was stalemate while Muslim civilians suffered; two small-scale NATO air-strikes changed little on the ground. In the discussion group though, once they had agreed to side-step the question of America's interests in former Yugoslavia, Gardiner and his friends found themselves led towards ideas for an entirely new approach to warfare. They agreed that whether or not the United States needed to be involved, there were common principles of humanity at stake which meant that it probably ought to be – and that that should still be possible without taking the politically contentious step of committing American soldiers on the ground. A new version of the Hippocratic Oath sworn by doctors was to be their guide: any intervention should be calculated to do more good than harm (a highly pertinent question for the generation involved in Vietnam). Assuming that that condition was met, the overriding objective was to prevent the deaths of women and children. With that goal established, the group then faced the question of how technically to achieve it. It was here that a need for some futuristic technology became evident.

One idea was to maximise the publicity surrounding each atrocity and every manoeuvre: to televise the entire conflict. The full range of intelligence-gathering techniques would locate all the main forces of the warring parties and then broadcast that information 'to show who was doing the violence' in the hope of shaming them into stopping. Another suggestion was to use radio signals and microwave beams to disrupt and disable the combatants' heavy weapons by triggering their fusing devices prematurely – without killing the troops themselves. Such 'non-lethal' systems are feasible if not fully developed and may be pressed into service soon. The point that

15

emerges from this is that although the only way to settle the conflict is by political means, there is now a demand for a whole new category of weaponry – arms with which to keep a peace or even to make one. In the words of one of the participants, John Rothrock, 'we must do something and . . . credible, non-lethal attempts' such as these might be the way to help 'a tragic and potentially explosive situation'.

John Rothrock spends his time trying to predict the trends of events for the future. A consultant like Sam Gardiner, he also left the US Air Force as a colonel, his last post being that of chief of intelligence planning and he is now director of the Stanford Research Institute's Global Security Planning Center. He has a tendency, when describing the awfulness of what is likely to happen, to bow his head as if in pain. He even began one presentation to the NATO Defence College admitting that he had found the paper difficult to prepare 'because of the pessimism I found myself succumbing to as I brought it together, one menacing piece after the other'; security for individuals and for nations, he said, would be a much rarer commodity in the next century than it was in this one.

In a briefing paper for the military, which he calls 'Fault Lines of the Future', Rothrock highlights the key factors which will determine – and no doubt plague – the decades ahead. The first is economic: the gulf between the 'haves' and the 'have-nots' is growing inexorably. In 1990, the 247 richest people in the world had a combined annual income equal to that of the incomes of all households in China and Indonesia – a quarter of the world's population – while more than 80 per cent of people have to survive on 20 per cent of its wealth. At the same time, improvements in information technology with television, telephone and fax mean that the 'have-nots' are better able to see what the 'haves' are enjoying. They are also increasingly able to act on it. With extremely potent weapons more readily available – such as missiles and nuclear, chemical and biological warheads – the have-nots could win concessions from the liberal democracies simply by threatening to use them. 'Imagine Germany during the Gulf War,' Rothrock says, 'if there'd been even a hint of a direct threat by missiles against Europe proper.'

The next ten to fifteen years, he predicts, will see increasing instability and violence. And underlying it all and adding new possibilities for tension every year will be the relentless drumbeat of the population explosion, which is expanding at a rate three times faster in the underdeveloped world than in the developed world. The global population was 2.5 billion in 1950, 5.3 billion in 1990, and could reach 6.3 billion by the turn of the century and 8.2 billion by 2020. By the year 2000, the world will have two billion males under the age of fifteen, the vast majority of them 'have-nots'. This is what really disturbs Rothrock. Once, as he drove me to lunch, he talked about the potential for unrestrained aggression from youths of the underdeveloped world: 'Just think of all that testosterone.' He winced as he spoke.

Carl Builder paints a similarly disturbing picture of the future. Another mainstay of Sam Gardiner's discussion group, Builder, a tall, schoolmasterly type, is one of a rare breed of futurologists or professional soothsayers. 'Most people call me a maverick, an oddball,' he admits. Employed by the RAND corporation, one of the largest and most influential military think-tanks, he has a reputation, despite a warm-hearted demeanour and a gentle manner of speaking, for making uncomfortable predictions which prove uncannily accurate. In a scenario for a war-game which he wrote in 1985, he surmised that the two halves of Germany would be united by 1991. And in May 1990, in an internal electronic message to a RAND colleague specialising in the Soviet Union, he offered this: 'my estimate for systemic collapse is six months to two years'.

Much of what Builder predicts is unpopular. Military institutions in particular, he says, are 'wishing about the future' and sometimes resent his suggestions. They think 'about a future they'd like to see not the one they might well have to entertain, namely a United States in decline and a world that is far more chaotic. They're afraid of looking into abysses or breaking sacred idols.' The military have yet to realise that the United States' power is diminishing, Builder believes. If America had been stronger, it could have carried out Operation Desert Storm without needing the political support of coalition partners or the financial backing of the Saudis and the Japanese.

Builder sees the reduction in America's global power as part of a general trend in which nation-states are suffering an erosion in their ability to influence events. The more individual nations want to shape their own destinies, the less they are able to – and the less the armed forces of any one country can be decisive. Ethnic groups and terrorist gangs within nations, and the multinational corporations (even unofficial ones like the drug cartels) which straddle borders, are emerging as the new powers of the coming age. Communications are becoming so accessible and instantaneous that national frontiers and sovereignty are being undermined. Computer networks, 'E-mail' and fax machines are yielding new forms of contact and of alliance in which the location of each participant is irrelevant, creating possibilities for economic and political influence regardless of geography. And it is a development which is only just beginning.

An information age is upon us, according to Builder, and it will last at least half a century. It is the latest in a series of 'intellectual frontiers', each replacing the other at intervals of about fifty years. Builder's research has found that fifty-four-year cycles are commonly observed in human activity: one analysis from 1500 to 1869 showed that English wheat prices, for example, fluctuated on that cycle; interest rates, sunspots and tree-rings have been seen to alter over a similar period as well. In the case of America, Builder says, a 'governmental frontier' in which collective interest was focused on the Constitution and new forms of administration peaked in about 1750. Fifty years later, a 'land frontier' began to emerge, with land-grabbing in the central and western United States reaching a frenzied maximum in about 1850. That soon gave way to an 'industrial frontier' which by 1900 had gripped the nation in a fever of interest in the potential of mass production. A 'technological frontier' followed, peaking in about 1950, in which the public consciousness was seized with the joys of gadgets such as cars, radios, televisions and helicopters which owed more to ingenuity in the laboratory than in the factory.

This frontier was to be replaced by an 'information frontier'. The gadgets are no longer as important as the data they can handle, receive and exchange and the level of investment in information technology is evidence of that. Whereas in 1950 only about 6 per cent of total US spending on plant and equipment was on communications, that figure had leaped to 20 per cent by 1978 and 40 per cent by 1988. It is a shift gradually becoming evident in military thinking as well: it is no longer technology which wins wars but the information which can be handled by that technology. But in Builder's view the cycles of development will not stop here. As the information frontier peaks at around the turn of the century, a 'genetic frontier' will emerge to replace it by the year 2050. Genetic engineering should lead to the eradication of disease, the development of new forms of biologically generated power and the invention of new forms of food production. Although it will be 'a more crowded, meaner world', global

18

population will be fed on algal soup. Beyond that, taking advantage of unlimited bio-power and better adaptation to new conditions, long-distance space travel will 'finally become feasible on a practical scale'. The year 3000 will bring genuine exploration of the heavens.

But not all Builder's soothsaying involves the distant future; he has immediate concerns as well. While the military are still thinking of buying new fighter-planes and tanks – evidence of 'their mid-twentieth-century minds' – new threats demand totally new approaches. The greatest danger in his view comes from nuclear weapons, not only in the possession of trigger-happy dictatorships but also becoming available to individual regions within a nation or, worse still, to terrorists or rootless organisations with nothing to lose. He talks of the possibility of 'kitchen-table nukes', crude nuclear devices assembled with components which are increasingly available on the open market: 'they are more easily made than the public realise – an apple-pie recipe is challenging unless someone lays out the ingredients for you'. As the first director of the US Nuclear Regulatory Commission, responsible for the security of civilian nuclear material, he was in a position to learn firsthand just how simple it can be to build a Bomb.

The prospect of such a device, 'the equivalent of an AK-47 assault rifle in the hands of a madman', reaching the wrong people is one of the few which Builder finds frightening. He is generally optimistic that mankind will somehow pull through and manage its affairs successfully. But he cannot avoid making another of his all-too-reliable predictions: that the next decade or two will see nuclear weapons actually used.

Carl Builder was invited to run through his ideas for the future faced by the armed forces at a meeting of the discussion group at Sam Gardiner's home in Arlington, Virginia in June 1993. He left everyone worried, and with little hope that he would be proved wrong.

It was 2 a.m. General McPeak rose to leave. 'I'm bailing out of this mess,' he said.

AN INVINCIBLE SWORD

Would it not ... be an abominable crime to send any future Foreign Secretary naked, as it were – that is, if we had no nuclear weapons – into any conference chamber?
Lord Molloy, House of Lords debate, 28 June 1993

A state with nuclear bombs has a decisive voice in world affairs.
Scitkazy Matayev, spokesman for the President of Kazakhstan, 19 April 1992

There is now a highway to the birthplace of the nuclear bomb. Los Alamos is easily reached, even if the spread of its nuclear knowledge is impossible to reverse. Smooth asphalt leads along the desert valley of the Rio Grande, past the pueblos and mobile homes of New Mexico's impoverished Indians, towards a junction complete with a flyover where a sign marks the turn-off for Route 502. The road climbs into the Jemez Mountains, twisting through white cliffs and forests of spindly aspens, scenery so spectacular it inspired the state slogan, 'Land of Enchantment'. At 7,200 feet, the road reaches a mesa or plateau, split by a deep canyon, and, as it enters the small town and complex of laboratories of Los Alamos, it turns into Trinity Drive, named after the first test explosion of an atomic device. It was here in this rarefied, pine-scented atmosphere that the most costly, secret and ingenious research effort of twentieth-century science was undertaken, providing America with the most powerful weapons in the world – but, in so doing, letting the nuclear genie out of the bottle.

Los Alamos was chosen as the site for this work for its remoteness, ease of protection and beauty. On a visit on 16 November 1942, Leslie Groves, an irascible but effective general, and Robert

Oppenheimer, a melancholic but brilliant physicist, had selected it at first sight; the only inhabitants, the owners of a boys' school, were happy to sell. Under Groves's command and Oppenheimer's scientific direction, Project Y, otherwise known as the Manhattan Project, got under way within a few months and achieved its aim within three years, building what one of the scientists involved was later to call 'a terrible, swift sword' with which to end the Second World War, even 'all wars'. Harnessing the energy released by the splitting of the atom, two Los Alamos bombs, 'Little Boy' and 'Fat Man', devastated Hiroshima and Nagasaki with unprecedented savagery and gave the United States unassailable global power. It was not to last: others had the secret too, or would have it soon. The demands of achieving victory in one war in this century had created a burgeoning nightmare about future wars for the next. In 1992, Les Aspin, President Clinton's first Defence Secretary, was even moved to declare: 'If we now had the opportunity to ban all nuclear weapons, we would.'

Even before the first nuclear weapons had been used, many insiders had realised that knowledge about 'the most compact, efficient, inexpensive, inexorable mechanisms of total death' would spread by fair means or foul.[1] They were right. One member of the British contingent at Los Alamos, the German-born Klaus Fuchs, later admitted passing secrets of the designs to the Soviet Union, meeting his KGB handler amid the pink adobe buildings of nearby Santa Fe to hand over the crucial technical details. It has even been suggested that Robert Oppenheimer himself, known to be a Communist sympathiser, ensured that Moscow was provided with the key details; a book by the former KGB officer Pavel Sudoplatov claimed that the Los Alamos director handed over crucial information no fewer than five times.[2] In any event, by September 1949, a Soviet copy of the first Los Alamos device was successfully detonated; tests of Soviet-designed warheads came later. Britain, whose early discoveries in physics had encouraged the initiation of the Manhattan Project in the first place and whose scientists' contributions at Los Alamos had been highly valued, exploded its first device in 1952. France, without outside help, followed suit in 1960; China, dependent on Soviet assistance, in 1964. It did not stop with these five original nuclear powers: a chain reaction of proliferation, not unlike the process which made atomic weapons themselves so potent, was under way.

France helped Israel to become a nuclear power. Along with Britain, Canada and the United States, it also helped India. The Soviet Union got North Korea started, as did China with Pakistan, and a number of western and former Warsaw Pact countries with Iraq (which, by some estimates, would have had a nuclear device by May 1993 had it not been for the Gulf War and the intervention of the United Nations). Israel in turn probably gave South Africa the expertise it needed to acquire a nuclear arsenal. When the Soviet Union fragmented in 1991, three new countries, Ukraine, Kazakhstan and Belarus, inherited the nuclear weapons which Moscow had stationed on their soil; since then, other nations in the Middle East and Asia have stood to gain by hiring former Soviet scientists or buying surplus nuclear material. Some countries, including Sweden, South Korea, Brazil and Argentina, began to develop nuclear weapons but stopped short, nevertheless retaining the expertise required to reinstate their programmes in the future, earning them the status of 'virtual' nuclear powers. The ambitions of others, including Iran, Taiwan and Japan, remain too secretive or uncertain to fathom.

Robert Oppenheimer, as director of the Manhattan Project, was among those who had warned that the Bomb would not remain America's alone. An elegant, cultured man, his soulful eyes, as caught in photographs, masking an intellectual sharpness which was frequently perceived as arrogance, he had long been tortured by the ghastly implications of his work. He had captured the ambivalence felt by many of his colleagues when, after the first nuclear test in 1945, he had quoted lines from the *Bhagavad-Gita* of Hindu scripture which provoke a mixture of awe and dread: 'If the radiance of a thousand suns were to burst at once into the sky . . . I am become Death, the Destroyer of worlds.' Even at a ceremony in October 1945 to mark the nation's appreciation for the achievements of those at Los Alamos – intended to be an occasion for celebration – Oppenheimer spoke of how everyone's pride must be 'tempered with profound concern'. If atomic bombs were to become new weapons for a warring world, or for nations preparing to fight, he said, 'then the time will come when mankind will curse the names of Los Alamos and Hiroshima'. It was a concern he shared at the highest levels. President Truman, recalling a meeting with Oppenheimer the following year, described him in private correspondence as wringing his hands 'and telling me they had blood on them because of the discovery of atomic energy'.[3]

Truman thought Oppenheimer 'a cry baby'. But the scientist was not deterred. In November 1945, in a speech to 800 members of the Association of Los Alamos Scientists, gathered in the local cinema, Oppenheimer sought to explain why he feared 'the fix we are in'. His observations remain as pertinent now as they were prescient then. The job of building the Bomb, he said, had been done because 'if you are a scientist you cannot stop such a thing . . . you believe it is good to turn over to mankind at large the greatest possible power to control the world.' Yet at the same time the facts of nuclear weapons would inevitably become more generally available: 'that they are not too hard to make, that they will be universal if people wish to make them universal, that they will not constitute a real drain on the economy of any strong nation and that their power of destruction will grow and is already incomparably greater than that of any other weapon . . .'

The only solution, he suggested, was world unity. Since nuclear weapons were a peril affecting the whole world, all nations must unite to prevent the wars in which the weapons may be used. International co-operation would be for the general good. It would allow the benefits of nuclear research to be shared. Most importantly, it would support a system of strict controls on the proliferation of nuclear weapons. It was idealist thinking which could perhaps explain Oppenheimer's decision – if the recent allegations against him are true – to pass the Los Alamos secrets to the Soviet Union; the logic being that the world would be made safer if nuclear knowledge was quickly shared. Yet other influential voices, in the State Department, for example, gave the idea of international co-operation great credence too -- not so much the concept of a happily united world but that of international regulation of the nuclear genie. But in his speech Oppenheimer warned that Americans were slow to grasp the implication of nuclear weapons – that monopoly was impossible, that once the secret was out, everyone was threatened, regardless of who had the Bomb first. Other countries, he said, may take even longer 'to understand what this is all about'. A year later, he was proved correct: an American proposal for United Nations controls, inspired in part by Oppenheimer's pressure, collapsed in the face of Soviet suspicion and Pentagon unwillingness to surrender an advantage. His old boss at Los Alamos, General Groves, set the tone: 'If there are to be atomic weapons in the world, we must have the best, the biggest and the most.' The course of the Cold War nuclear arms race was set.

Nuclear devices in vast numbers were fitted to bombs, missiles, torpedoes, depth-charges, artillery shells and even land-mines to be carried in an infantryman's backpack. Between 1945 and 1992, the United States went on to manufacture a total of 70,000 nuclear weapons, some 10,500 of which are still in service. The Soviet Union produced 55,000, of which 15,000 are currently active. Britain reportedly made 834 nuclear warheads, France 1,110 and China 600. According to various reports of unknown reliability, Israel may have made 200, India twenty, Pakistan between four and seven. South Africa admitted it had produced six devices before giving up its programme; North Korea may have one or two. Each type of weapon varies in destructive power but most are at least ten times as potent as the bomb dropped on Hiroshima which, in an instant, killed 100,000 men, women and children.

The Hiroshima weapon represented the first generation of nuclear device. It relied on a conventional explosion to crush a radioactive core so violently that a fission reaction ensued, splitting a suddenly increasing number of atoms and, in the process, releasing vast amounts of energy. Though the technique is regarded as crude and inefficient by standards of the latest designs, it is now believed to form the basis of the nuclear arsenals of nations such as Israel, India and Pakistan. The second generation of development introduced the thermonuclear weapon, the far more powerful hydrogen bomb. An initial fission explosion is used to trigger a vastly larger fusion reaction which can readily yield energy one million times greater than that achieved at Hiroshima. A further step has been to take this design and miniaturise it, scaling down each component so that the weapon as a whole became sufficiently small and light to fit inside the nose-cone of a missile. Thus the lightning speed of a rocket was harnessed to the staggering power of an H-bomb and, with flight-times of less than thirty minutes between the United States and the Soviet Union, the nuclear hair-trigger of the Cold War was established.

There have been attempts to contain or even to reverse the nuclear arms race. In the Strategic Arms Limitations Treaties (the SALT deals) of the 1970s, Moscow and Washington agreed to set limits on their nuclear arsenals (though these had the effect of freezing the huge number of weapons deployed by either side and spurring efforts to add to their sophistication). The Intermediate-range Nuclear Forces Treaty of 1987 went further by banning all Soviet and American ground-launched missiles with a range of between 300–3,000 miles. And the Strategic Arms Reduction Talks, finalised as the START-1 and START-2 treaties in 1991 and 1992, slashed the superpowers' arsenals of long-range weapons by about two-thirds, Washington being allowed to keep about 3,500, Moscow about 3,000 (though the process of reducing the forces to these levels will last well into the next century). At the same time, the two governments agreed to 'detarget' their missiles away from each other – for the weapons' guidance computers no longer to be programmed with the co-ordinates of targets in the other country. Later, similar deals involved Russia and Britain, and Russia and China.

The only formal attempt to involve other countries and to stop the spread of the Bomb around the world has been the Nuclear Non-Proliferation Treaty (NPT), signed in 1968. This effectively legitimised the position of the original five nuclear powers while forbidding all other nations from developing nuclear weapons. At the same time, as an incentive to those nations denied nuclear arsenals, the treaty stated that the nuclear powers would never take advantage of this position by using their weapons against them; it also helped non-nuclear weapons states to pursue civil nuclear power programmes while mounting regular inspections to check that these were not being turned to military use. The scheme cannot be said to have worked as planned. Some countries, including Israel, were immediately distrustful and have refused to sign on. Others which did join the process, like Iraq, then successfully hoodwinked it; inspectors, who were sent by the International Atomic Energy Agency and were received politely enough, failed to spot that Saddam Hussein had set about obtaining the Bomb. In addition, powerful accusations of anti-Third World bias came from India and Mexico. They persistently attacked the original nuclear powers for using the treaty to justify keeping their own arsenals while preaching that others should remain without them. Mexico's chief UN negotiator in Geneva, Miguel Marin-Bosch, once told me: 'There is a general feeling that they do apply double standards – one for themselves and one for the rest of the world.' Due for review in 1995, the NPT, the one bastion against nuclear proliferation, has long been under potentially fatal strain.

As the current American administration confronts the legacy of Los Alamos, it has found that Oppenheimer's prediction continues to be eerily accurate. More and more countries are seeking to acquire nuclear weapons in the belief that they will become more secure as a result, when in fact the weapons serve only to unnerve neighbouring states and create greater insecurity than existed before. Just as Oppenheimer feared, the world is now caught in a dangerous paradox: the more the Bomb spreads, the more countries will feel the need to get it, the greater the danger of global annihilation. As a result, nuclear proliferation, long ignored as a problem during the obsessive stand-off of the Cold War, has emerged as one of the most hazardous global challenges. *Iran, N Korea*

The auditorium was full and the chatter was excited. It was June 1993, the fiftieth anniversary of the start of work at Los Alamos, and one of the key events in a week of commemoration was about to begin. The laboratory's pet slogan for the year was 'Proud past . . . exciting future'; in-house literature was full of talk of the 'second fifty years'. But it was an undeniably uncertain time for the 9,000 staff. With some lay-offs under way already and more in prospect, no one could be sure why their future should be exciting, or even if they would have a future at the laboratory at all. The Los Alamos director, Sig Hecker, writing in an internal magazine, began an article with a question which unintentionally seemed to sum up much of the confusion amongst his staff: 'Where do we go from here?'

The unpalatable truth is that the Cold War served them well, as it had their counterparts in nuclear laboratories world-wide. Orders for new types of nuclear weapons and demands for ever more novel ways of delivering them never stopped. Each new generation of warhead was designed to be more accurate, more manoeuvrable and more effective than the last. There was the enhanced radiation 'neutron' bomb, which would kill people but spare buildings; there were 'bunker busters' to burrow hundreds of feet underground to reach the Soviet command posts before exploding; and then there were the plans for Star Wars space weapons, nuclear devices to take the Third World War to the heavens. Each project entailed theoretical physical work, warhead design, engineering, fissile materials handling, administrative back-up, catering, supplies – and an army of scientists, technicians and support staff.

This army in turn required accommodation, shops, recreation, sports facilities and the town of Los Alamos grew to provide them. A far cry from the hurriedly built huts and muddy lanes endured by the original Manhattan pioneers, Los Alamos now offers rows of neat houses, a modest collection of shops and handfuls of motels and petrol stations in a model of litter-free, comfortable Middle America. The green-clad mountains above the mesa and the customary blue skies contribute to a life which has, for many, been prosperous and enjoyable. Several of the scientists, when asked why they have stayed at Los Alamos, isolated from the rest of academic and research life by secrecy and distance, replied simply by gesturing at the stunning surroundings and by breathing deeply in the clear, dry air.

Now, without fresh orders from the Pentagon, the laboratory as a whole is fighting to justify its existence, each department squabbling over a dwindling financial cake from Washington. The survival strategy adopted by Los Alamos has been to stress its strengths in general science, above all in fields relevant to civilian technological activity for which it has generated over 100 partnerships with industry. Officials are fond of repeating the claim that with 250 post-doctorate staff – 'more Ph.Ds per capita than anywhere else on earth' – Los Alamos is a national resource with a role stretching far beyond the original nuclear one. On a visit to the laboratory in May 1993, President Clinton was shown a sample of the work which almost exclusively had non-military applications: oil recovery, environmental clean-up, machine-tool improvements, computer simulations of global climate change. The Los Alamos staff knew those projects would be well received; the company newsletter's report on the visit makes hardly any reference to the fact that the laboratory was the powerhouse of the Domesday arsenal and could still be. It was as if the Bomb had been air-brushed from the corporate record.

Indeed, President Clinton himself chose to emphasise a non-military future for the laboratory. In a speech to a crowd of employees and their families, he described how Los Alamos had been the leading edge of America's security for its first fifty years. 'Now, as we go into the next half century, Los Alamos will be . . . the leading edge of our prosperity.' It would develop technology 'that will put all these young Americans who are here today at the front of a new race, the race to compete and to co-operate in a world that is getting smaller, richer, more diverse . . .' Only in the closing part of his speech did Mr Clinton mention the 'national defence mission', the need to maintain the nation's existing nuclear weapons and to counter the threat of proliferation. Yet he did not elaborate on either of these points. It was easy rhetoric but, without explanation, lacked any meaning. Key questions remained unanswered. Simply minding America's shrinking nuclear arsenal would surely not be demanding enough to maintain a pool of trained nuclear experts at the laboratory. And, if Los Alamos was able to do anything about the spread of the weapons first invented here, presumably there needed to be a major government initiative in that direction. Above all, there seemed to be no thought given to the future of nuclear weapons themselves. With so many countries now acquiring them, would it be better, as Oppenheimer had suggested in 1945 and Les Aspin in 1992, to ban the lot? Would that even be possible?

The next month, the 800 present and former Los Alamos scientists who had gathered in the laboratory's main auditorium during anniversary week had these problems in mind. Their predecessors had gathered in the same numbers and in an equivalent place to hear Robert Oppenheimer's thoughts on the future. Now they were to hear the predictions of one of the colleagues who had survived him, one of the most controversial and influential figures in the American nuclear world: Edward Teller, 'father of the hydrogen bomb', the role-model for the mad scientist in the film *Dr Strangelove*. 'If evil walks this earth,' one anti-nuclear campaigner once told me, 'it's Teller.' He has a contradictory reputation: one of the many East European *émigré* physicists to escape the Nazis, his technical judgement has frequently been called into question while at the same time he has remained prominent in all the major disputes and decisions of the nuclear age. He has enjoyed the ear of most post-War presidents; Teller's opinions are not lightly ignored.

A murmur that he had arrived swept the room and a hush fell. Edward Teller knew how to make an entrance. Battered, aged eighty-five, dressed in a crumpled suit which hung limply off his twisted shoulders, he shuffled down the aisle with the help of a vast wooden stave of medieval-battlefield proportions, his watery eyes holding the gaze of people near him. There was an air of defiance about him, as if declaring his right to command this level of interest. He of all people would have known that his cantankerous manner, extreme hawkishness and public confrontations with Robert Oppenheimer had made him numerous enemies at Los Alamos; some officials were even surprised he had the gall to turn up. For most of the four previous decades, he had been director of a rival nuclear laboratory, Lawrence Livermore in California. Even before that though, during the Manhattan Project, Teller sulked and left when Oppenheimer refused him a key post; later, when the two clashed over whether the United States should develop the H-bomb, Teller implied to a congressional committee that Oppenheimer was a security risk, testimony which led to the latter losing his security clearances and to his subsequent ostracism from the nuclear community. It was a move which created lingering bitterness towards Teller. The previous evening I had asked one group of veterans, who had returned for the commemoration, whether they would attend the Teller speech. 'No,' came the answer. 'I'll be out walking,' declared Professor Ernest Klema, a tall, slightly stooped figure with the darkened glasses of someone with failing sight. 'I won't have anything to do with him because of what he did to Oppie.'

Nevertheless, Teller had returned and, at a time of widespread unease about the future, many felt this 'ugly old Hungarian', as one veteran described him, might offer some useful ideas. Up on the stage, he rejected the chair set aside for him and chose to perch on a small table instead and swing his thin, bony legs beneath him. The microphone became tangled in his tie but his large expressive hands waved away the attentions of his minders. He spoke logically and cogently without notes for one and a half hours.

'I am an optimist,' he announced, his guttural accent somehow adding force to his delivery. 'I-ee . . . am . . . an . . . optimeest. The future ees uncertain . . . BUT . . . vee can do sumting about it.'

The table creaked beneath him, the sudden noise filling the silent, dark chamber. It added to the feeling that this wizened, belligerent figure – a man accused of claiming other people's work as his own, of shifting allegiances with changing political fashions and of wasting huge sums of public money because of a cavalier approach to scientific facts – was the first pirate of the nuclear age. The wooden stave never left his side.

His opening remarks were music to the ears of the current generation of nuclear scientists. He pretended the year was 2043, not 1993, and that it was the 100th anniversary of Los Alamos, the immediate implication being that the laboratory would remain in business for at least another fifty years. Technology remained the most natural of things, he reassured them. Mankind had to know what could be done; whether that knowledge was used or not was not up to the scientists. In other words, there was no need to feel any guilt. Nor was it possible to un-invent the Bomb, he said. 'Atomic bombs are a reality, they are a part of the human experience, and the important thing is not to throw them away, but to know how to use them rightly – how to improve them and develop them further in the right way.'

It was at this point that he paid homage to his old enemy Robert Oppenheimer and his proposals in the aftermath of the Second World War. 'The solution to atomic bombs,' Teller said, lay in the original American attempt, initiated at Oppenheimer's suggestion, to bring nuclear weapons under United Nations control. In 1946, he said, the administration had understood that the Bomb ended America's isolation; it would now always be open to attack in the same way 'as Poland' in 1939. But the American proposal for international controls, known as the Baruch plan, presented to the UN by a presidential adviser, Bernard Baruch, had run into the sand. Stalin vetoed it, Teller said; he had objected to the requirement for inspections to verify the controls. (Teller did not mention that the United States had stopped short of offering the one concession that may have convinced Stalin: the handing over of America's nuclear arsenal to the United Nations.)

The solution now, Teller suggested, was for a new Baruch plan. Looking back from his supposed vantage-point of the year 2043, he said the new plan had taken 'many years' to develop through several different presidents and changes of public opinion – in other words, he was predicting that it was not to be accepted at least until the early years of the next century. The first stage involved handing over control of all the world's weapons-grade plutonium to the United Nations. That would limit the scope for the production of new weapons. Los Alamos, he said, continuing the theme of his false retrospective, had set a precedent by handing over its plutonium stockpile first.

The next stage of Teller's plan would not have met with Oppenheimer's approval. He suggested establishing a system which would seek to impose some order on the chaos of nuclear proliferation rather than to reverse it. There would be three tiers of nuclear ownership: the smallest weapons would be in the hands of the nations which had only recently become nuclear powers; the next largest should be under UN command and used to curb the activities of the smaller, illegal nuclear states; and the biggest and most powerful weapons should remain with the original five nuclear states, above all the United States. Arming the UN would give it new authority as proliferation continued, Teller argued, while the fact that the original nuclear powers retained the most potent weapons would ensure that the change towards world order was 'evolutionary and gradual'. Eventually, there would be no more need for wars because countries had so many interests in common, not least the prevention of nuclear conflict.

There was prolonged applause, probably as much in relief as anything else: Teller's awkward diction had been hard to follow. A greater problem though was that Teller's 'solution' was immediately recognisable as being inadequate. It was a tidy proposal which had no chance of being accepted. The suggestion that the United Nations might have its own nuclear force flies in the face of political reality. It has proved difficult enough securing common agreement on the use of conventional force, however benignly, even in cases of dire humanitarian hardship; achieving unanimity on the need to drop a UN-labelled bomb which would kill thousands of uninvolved civilians beggars belief. Yet in a period of frantic searching for new approaches to the horror of nuclear proliferation, Teller's contribution was valuable in that it emphasised the need for radical thinking. His speech highlighted another need as well: for scientists themselves to join the debate about the future of nuclear weapons, much as Oppenheimer and his troubled colleagues had done fifty years before.

The awkward fact is that, at Los Alamos at least, that kind of politically aware scientific leadership appears to be lacking. The intellectual giants of nuclear science, with breadth of vision and profound understanding of the global impact of their work, seem to belong to another age. The current director of Los Alamos, Siegfried H. Hecker – 'but please call me Sig' – is a slight, likeable man with a bandit's moustache, wiry glasses and a diffident manner which does not command the immediate respect of his staff. When I put it to one Los Alamos official that Hecker might be in the same mould as Oppenheimer or his successor, Norris Bradbury, the reply was emphatic: 'Definitely not!' Hecker's strength – and presumably the reason for his selection – seems to be a calm administrative skill, a bureaucratic savvy that might prove more effective at ensuring the laboratory's survival than a more flamboyant, less conscientious leader. Yet this scientist, with the proverbial pen in his shirt pocket and a cautious approach to outsiders like me, only sounded enthusiastic about points of detail. It was hard to detect vision.

'Plutonium is the world's most fascinating element,' he declared, using his hands as if playing with the stuff. We were sitting on the lawn outside the laboratory cafeteria, the Jemez peaks brilliantly lit around us, and he was unaware of the image he was portraying. He cannot have realised that few people outside the nuclear weapons industry would even think of plutonium as anything other than frightening, not 'fascinating'; the same material had, after all, served as the radioactive core of the bomb which had killed 140,000 people at Nagasaki. It was rather like describing chlorine gas as a fascinating chemical after the First World War.

Hecker had begun his career as a materials scientist but soon found that 'nuclear weapons were my most exciting work' because of the scientific challenge and 'a sense of patriotism'. Like many of his predecessors, Hecker is a product of the darkest moments of Europe's recent history, born in 1943 in Poland in a German army camp, the son of an Austrian conscripted into the *Wehrmacht*. His father was sent to the Russian front from which he never returned and Hecker's mother moved the family back to her birthplace, a village near Banja Luka in Bosnia-Hercegovina. Then came a move after the war to the American sector in Austria. A visit to the summer camp in Vienna in 1953 took Hecker, then aged ten, through the Russian sector of the capital. The sight of 'Cossack hats and rifles', together with the 'terrible stories told by my mother and stepfather' and the loss of his father to the Russians, left a deep and disturbed impression.

It underlies Hecker's faith, shared by his colleagues, in nuclear weapons as the ultimate safeguard of America's security, the reverse of the Oppenheimer approach. In their view, nuclear weapons helped win the Cold War and will continue to protect the United States long after it. There seems little place in their thinking for ideas about international controls and the deliberate sharing of nuclear knowledge. One Los Alamos scientist told me a story which revealed his gut feeling about nuclear weapons. During a visit to Munich, a neo-Nazi demonstrator had approached him and had screamed abuse from close up. The incident had apparently prompted an instinctive reaction: 'Thank God we've got the W88 on our side.' (The W88, the warhead carried by the US Navy's Trident submarines, is the most accurate warhead ever designed.) The idea of using such a weapon against a resurgent Germany came naturally. Yet that view, that blunt and politically embarrassing statement about what nuclear weapons might be for, is not aired, let alone debated, publicly.

Certainly not by Hecker. His quiet confidence in the validity of nuclear weapons goes unchallenged. He speaks, as President Clinton did, about the need to dismantle America's surplus weapons and to fight proliferation but without offering a coherent plan for achieving those aims. Nor does he suggest a rationale with which to justify America maintaining nuclear weapons while at the same time urging others not to acquire them. Less still does he acknowledge Oppenheimer's original warning that the Bomb would continue to spread until everyone understood the meaning of its existence: the ability to build nuclear weapons was never likely to be the preserve of one nation and therefore all nations had to co-operate to limit the potential for their own destruction. Others do not seem to have acknowledged the point either, and now may never do so.

As dusk fell, floodlights cast a silvery sheen over the vast, black hulk of HMS *Vanguard* as she lay on the dockside at Barrow-in-Furness in Cumbria. It was March 1992 and *Vanguard*, the first of Britain's new Trident-missile submarines, had been unveiled to the accompaniment of band music at a grand ceremony earlier that day. The minister and his officials had left by helicopter, most journalists were on the train back to London and the anti-nuclear campaigners had collected their banners and gone too. Now it was the turn of the shipyard workers to bring their families to gawp at the size and sinister potency of this awesome new weapon system. Young couples with babies in push-chairs, gangs of boys on bikes and old men in cloth caps leaned against the railings of a bridge, the nearest vantage-point, to chat and laugh, their voices carrying on the cool evening breeze. One father pointed out the submarine's features to his children: the large wooden box masking the propulsion system at the back (so the Russians could not learn its secrets and work out how to track the vessel by the note of its propeller underwater), the conning tower and, just behind it, a flat-topped section of the hull in which the nuclear missiles were to be stored. His tone was one of pride; it was not the time to reflect on the submarine's purpose as Britain's future nuclear deterrent.

In rotation with three other submarines of the same type, *Vanguard*, due into service in 1995, is designed to be armed with sixteen Trident D5 missiles. Each missile is likely to carry up

34

to six warheads, making a maximum total of ninety-six nuclear weapons per submarine. Each warhead will probably have ten times the destructive power of the bomb dropped on Hiroshima. Each submarine, on patrol beneath the Atlantic with its crew of 200 sailors, will therefore be able to destroy an area equivalent in size to 960 Hiroshimas. *Vanguard* and her sister ships, gradually taking over from the current Polaris fleet, will be in service at least until the year 2030. Britain will remain a force to be reckoned with.

It is that devastating power which remains the key to the policy of deterrence. Any enemy will have to bear in mind that there is a chance, however remote, that the missiles might be unleashed on them. As the Defence Secretary, Malcolm Rifkind, put it in a more formal statement, deterrence was about 'sustaining in the mind of a potential aggressor a belief that our use of the weapons could not prudently be altogether discounted'.[4] That threat, he argued, had helped preserve peace in Europe for nearly fifty years and continued to serve a positive purpose, not just for Britain and the rest of the NATO alliance, but for other non-nuclear states in Europe as well. Any state that had signed the Nuclear Non-Proliferation Treaty and, in so doing, had given up the right to possess nuclear weapons, had automatically earned a promise from the nuclear powers that nuclear coercion would never be used against them. With that principle, the West's nuclear deterrent had prevented war and had helped create stability. So it should not be thrown away now, Mr Rifkind claimed. In other words, Britain and the other original nuclear powers have a right to the Bomb; other countries do not.

Yet he must have known he was on thin ice, just as Edward Teller had been with his nukes-for-the-UN plan a few months before. The reality is that the very reasons that encouraged Britain to become a nuclear power – and to stay as one – have influenced other countries in the same way as well. With the Cold War over, Britain's justification for its nuclear arsenal and its simultaneous protests about others following the same path, are looking increasingly contradictory. For the post-War government in London, nuclear weapons were an obvious choice: they served as a hedge against Moscow and as a ticket to global status to compensate for the collapse of the Empire. Margaret Gowing, who first chronicled the development of the British Bomb, said the decision to go nuclear was 'almost instinctive'. There was '. . . a feeling that Britain must possess so climacteric a weapon in order to deter an atomically armed enemy, a feeling that Britain as a great power must acquire all major new weapons, a feeling that atomic weapons were a manifestation of the scientific and technological superiority on which Britain's strength, so deficient if measured in sheer numbers of men, must depend.'

Those feelings – the need to match nuclear adversaries like-for-like, to stay at the top table and to rely on nuclear weapons to make up for inferior numbers – have been identified in other countries as well, and no doubt will be in many more in the future. As Professor Lawrence Freedman of King's College, London observed in a speech in February 1994, nuclear weapons 'are attractive to countries with a chronic sense of inferiority'. In the case of France, for example, the decision to develop an atomic bomb was taken within six months of the humiliating defeat of French forces by the Vietnamese at Dien Bien Phu in 1954; a powerful element of Gallic pride was also evident in the desire not to become dependent on the protection offered by American nuclear weapons. Josef Stalin, anxious to catch up with America's nuclear lead, chose to use a copy of the stolen Los Alamos design, rather than a Soviet one, for the first test to avoid the risk of a flop. The director of the Soviet nuclear programme, Igor Kurchatov, remembered Stalin demanding immediate progress 'on a broad front, on a Russian scale' and offering prizes to the scientists and 'everything that was needed' to speed up the work 'for solving our problem' (the problem being that the Americans had got there first).[5] China too took the decision to acquire nuclear weapons because of a perceived need to achieve equal status. The Chinese leader, Deng Xiaoping, was quoted in 1957 as observing that the western 'imperialist' powers were afraid of the Soviet Union because it had the Bomb. 'Are the imperialists afraid of us? I think not . . .'[6] Later, the director of China's nuclear programme declared that the weapons were needed 'to get rid of imperialist bullying . . .'

This perception that nuclear weapons were the panacea to each country's security fears spread across the Himalayas. When India exploded a nuclear device in 1974, official sources claimed the test was for 'peaceful purposes'. Behind the scenes though, some Indian experts justified the development of nuclear weapons as a means of deterring China, the giant neighbour to the north and by now nuclear-armed. But if China's nuclear status lay behind India's, the Indian nuclear test was itself seen as a threat and as an incentive to other countries. A secret American memorandum, now declassified, assessed the implications of the event.[7] For Japan, Argentina and other nations described in the document as 'near nuclears' (because they were and are still able to develop nuclear weapons), the Indian test 'could make it easier . . . to follow suit, claiming that they too are following the route of "peaceful" accession to nuclear power status'. More significant was the document's assessment that 'the impact has been hardest on Pakistan'; its 'fears of India have intensified'. Three lines of text in the paragraph dealing with Pakistan's reaction remain blacked out by the censor: they probably referred to US intelligence on the likely acceleration of Pakistan's own nuclear programme.

Pakistan's response materialised over a decade later. According to General Aslam Beg, retired chief of the Pakistani Army and a supervisor of its nuclear programme, his country has been able to assemble a nuclear weapon since 1987.[8] Although Washington long suspected Pakistani nuclear ambitions, it turned a blind eye while Pakistan served as a vital staging-post for American aid to the mujahedin fighting the Soviet Army in Afghanistan. 'We were merrily making nuclear weapons' during this period, General Beg has been quoted as saying. His rationale for possessing the Bomb was the same as that used by India in relation to China, and by China in relation to the Soviet Union: it was a means of achieving equality. Pakistan would not hesitate to use its Bomb, said General Beg, 'to prevent the collapse of its conventional forces' if attacked by the far larger armies of India (just what the British government had felt about the Soviet Union in weighing up its decision to go nuclear). The Pakistani Prime Minister, Benazir Bhutto, confirmed that view in a more diplomatic way. 'So long as there is no threat to our security,' she said, 'our nuclear programme will continue to be peaceful.'[9] Usually, the word 'peaceful' is associated with a nuclear project meant to generate power for civilian use; in this context, it probably means that the warheads are prepared but not finally assembled. 'Just a screwdriver away,' according to one expert, they are therefore meant to be used in response to an attack rather than to launch one.[10]

The result is that India, having initially sought a nuclear option to counter China, now faces a nuclear Pakistan as well and the risks of war between the two countries are immense. At one stage in 1990, during an angry diplomatic confrontation between New Delhi and Islamabad, US intelligence satellites spotted the tell-tale signs of preparations for nuclear war: certain types of vehicles moving between bunkers at an airbase, certain types of fighter-bomber being readied for use. The United States was worried enough to despatch Robert Gates, then a senior official, later director of the CIA, to act as a mediator. The crisis subsided. But the religious antagonism between the two countries, their dispute over the ownership of Kashmir, the fact that their proximity means warning times are virtually non-existent and a history of conflict which has brought them to war three times in the last fifty years combine to keep concerns at a high level.

The best hope is that, by being nuclear-armed, India and Pakistan may be able to copy the Cold War balance of terror which existed between the United States and the Soviet Union. The superpowers, though close to conflict on several occasions, especially over Cuba, nevertheless developed a unique, unwritten code of diplomatic nuances and military signals with which to keep their confrontations from escalating. Both sides knew the consequences of misunderstanding each other, of failing to climb down at the crucial moment after 'nods and winks', as one analyst put it. Yet it is far from clear that this carefully evolved death-dance of mutual deterrence will apply on the Indian subcontinent, let alone in other regions of the world. More likely, the presence of nuclear weapons will exacerbate periods of tension and will provide a dangerous source of instability. Each side will fear that its few nuclear weapons may be an inviting target for the other. It may feel pressured into using them first in preference to losing them in a sudden attack. It may easily over-react, catastrophically. A study for the US Congress identified the danger when it noted that in Third World countries 'warning and command and control systems may not be adequate . . .'[11] One US official was quoted in February 1994 as warning more starkly: 'If a nuclear weapon is detonated in anger in the next five years, the most likely place that could happen is South Asia.'[12]

The United States is working hard to limit the risk – even to undo the cause of it – by playing up the drawbacks of acquiring a nuclear arsenal. One leading Pentagon official, speaking to me privately, likened the possession of nuclear weapons to progressing to 'long pants' after wearing the shorts of boyhood. 'But what do they do for you? Nothing. It's like showing your parents you can take heroin – and then becoming a drug addict. It's stupid hubris with a long-term price.' The price is the imposition of sanctions and trade restrictions. Pakistan has been denied American military equipment because of congressional objections to its nuclear programme. According to the Pentagon official, Pakistan has found that its navy and air force have suffered, its relations with the United States have been weakened and 'it's made itself less safe against India'.

Yet in spite of these warnings and of the risks of war, there is no sign that Pakistan or India will change their policies: politicians and military leaders alike seem to believe their security is still best served by possessing nuclear weapons. One reason is that they have no allies to depend on, no superpower offering to provide nuclear cover, only their own strength to defend themselves. Israel, denied American military support for most of the 1950s, felt similarly isolated at its inception – and continues to do so. David Ben-Gurion, its prime minister at the time, doubted that the United States would threaten nuclear force against other countries on Israel's behalf and sanctioned early work on a nuclear weapons programme. The work was always kept secret but clues to its existence emerged early on. Ben-Gurion told the Knesset in 1955 that Israel's security and independence required more young people to enter 'science and research, atomic and electronic research . . .' Ernst Bergmann, the first chairman of Israel's Atomic Energy Commission and a scientist described as its 'Robert Oppenheimer', said in 1957 that he was convinced that 'the state of Israel needs a defence research programme of its own'.[13] Nuclear weapons were the key. No longer would the Israeli mentality derive from Masada, the desert bastion where 900 Jewish zealots committed suicide rather than surrender to the Romans. Now the example would be Samson who, captured and faced with humiliation, brought down the temple, killing not only himself but also his enemies. Israel, vastly outnumbered but armed with nuclear weapons assembled at its underground plant at Dimona in the Negev desert, would by itself ensure that it was never to be overrun.

South Africa, ostracised for its apartheid policy, took similar steps to safeguard itself. Dr André Buys, head of planning for Armscor, South Africa's armaments corporation, which ran the country's secret nuclear programme, has said that the decisive period was in the early 1970s. South Africa was 'threatened by Soviet expansionism throughout Southern Africa' and 'it was clear that it could not rely on external help should it be attacked'.[14] Its weapons were meant to be a Domesday lever with which to coerce the United States to come to South Africa's rescue.

Military planners and politicians in Ukraine or Kazakhstan would understand that. Both countries inherited strategic nuclear forces from the old Soviet Union and have several times pledged to hand them over to Russia. Yet the louder the international clamour for the weapons to be given up, the more the two governments involved have realised that this otherwise unwanted Soviet legacy has value; one Kazakh official noted, probably correctly, that a flurry of visits by leading western ministers including the British Foreign Secretary would never have happened had Kazakhstan not been a nuclear power. One by one the various agreements to surrender the weapons have been stalled. Ukraine in particular, increasingly in dispute with Russia over the division of the Black Sea Fleet, trade and ethnic Russians within the country, has sought to keep its arsenal. One commentator, writing in a Kiev newspaper in February 1994, angrily pointed out that most other countries were trying to acquire nuclear weapons, not give them up, and that their worth to Ukraine was 'colossal' as the only 'sure protection against aggression' by Russia. In Kazakhstan too the fear of Russia reasserting itself within the old Soviet Union has led to a hardening of opinion. One report by two leading advisers to the Kazakh government warned that leaving Russia as the only post-Soviet nuclear power could allow it to carry out 'nuclear blackmail'. The result would be that 'people would curse the nuclear pacifism of their leaders'.[15]

Even countries protected by military alliance with the United States and its nuclear weapons can feel vulnerable. South Korea is in this position. Despite the presence of tens of thousands of American troops guarding the border, the very threat that their numbers might be cut in the 1970s triggered immediate work on a nuclear weapons programme. It had been thought that the research had stopped once the planned force cuts were shelved. Yet even when Washington made it palpably clear that South Korea would be defended vigorously, the Seoul government commissioned renewed nuclear work in response to another perceived threat – the fear that its hostile neighbour North Korea was acquiring the Bomb.[16] American persuasion reportedly brought the work to an end in 1991 – but there is little reason to believe that it has stopped for good. The reality is that South Korea's faith in the American nuclear umbrella is slipping.

The principle on which it is meant to operate is that the United States' deterrent power – its nuclear threat to potential enemies – is extended to cover allies. The system of so-called 'extended deterrence' has worked with NATO in Europe (in that only Britain and France have felt the need to acquire their own nuclear arsenals, the others trusting in America). But the example of South Korea shows that there are growing doubts that America's nuclear cover will be there when it is needed; the weaker America looks, the greater the incentive for its allies to go nuclear. Some observers have, as a result, criticised President Clinton for apparently limiting the conditions under which America will intervene in crises abroad. In his speech to the United Nations General Assembly on 27 September 1993, he insisted that America would only help if there were 'a clear threat to international peace', clear objectives and an identifiable way out – hardly a reassuring signal to countries nervous about their security.

Nowhere is that more the case than in the Far East. Amid the deep reductions in the size of the US Pacific Fleet, a three-way stand-off has developed between North Korea, South Korea and Japan. Each is a potential nuclear weapons state, each is watching the others' moves. North Korea is known to have nuclear facilities capable of producing weapons-grade plutonium and, according to one estimate, may already have manufactured one or two nuclear warheads. South Korea, fearful of North Korea's motives, remains poised to go nuclear. Japan, denied by its current constitution the right to possess nuclear weapons, has nevertheless built up a ten-ton stockpile of plutonium from its civil reactors which could be adapted for use in crude weapons; it has also developed its own sophisticated H2 rocket. The Japanese government denies it is maintaining a nuclear option but the scientific evidence indicates the opposite. As the threats from North Korea grow ever more belligerent – and North Korea's home-grown rockets bring Japan within range – Tokyo's political antipathy to nuclear weapons may well change. Japan, faced with a nuclear North Korea, a nuclear South Korea and, eventually, a nuclear united Korea, will probably feel the same 'chronic inferiority' which has driven so many other countries to pursue atomic arms. That pressure can only grow – and spread. Opposition leaders in Taiwan, for example, are pressing for nuclear weapons to be developed as a counter to Communist China.[17]

In Europe too a similar process may unfold. Germany, caught between a rapidly diminishing American presence in Europe and an increasingly unpredictable Russia, may come to the same conclusions as Britain in the 1950s or South Korea, India and Pakistan in the 1970s: that independently owned nuclear weapons are the only guarantee of security. For the time being, Germany, as a member of NATO, already enjoys the promise of nuclear protection from the

United States. But doubts will inevitably grow about whether that promise is credible – it involves America putting herself at risk from nuclear attack for the sake of defending Germany. For states outside NATO the value of nuclear weapons may be even greater. Poland is one example. Denied membership of the western alliance and vulnerable to the turmoil of the former Soviet Union on its border (and the territorial threats of ultra-nationalist Russian politicians like Vladimir Zhirinovsky), Warsaw may find the nuclear option has great appeal. In the absence of firm pledges of help from outside powers, it may see, as South Africa did in the 1970s, that a small nuclear force could be sufficiently frightening to forestall invasion.

In an age of fearsome unpredictability and universal technology, the list of potential nuclear powers is endless. Thirty-two countries have civilian nuclear power programmes and are therefore on the road to nuclear weapons, should they choose that step. Nuclear anarchy may be the result. One analyst has likened this prospect to the Wild West where 'everyone thought they needed a six-gun' to defend themselves. 'We may be moving into an era of the nuclear six-gun.' And we have yet to see the consequences.

In the warmth of a small conference room in a commercial office-block on M Street in the heart of Washington, a nuclear war was under way. The conflict was set six years in the future in 1999. A horseshoe-shaped table was draped with maps of the Persian Gulf and the Korean peninsula. There was an atmosphere of agonised crisis. Paper coffee cups and cans of Diet Coke jostled for space with thick sets of documents explaining each stage of a complicated war-game. Ten military experts, eight men and two women, were assuming the role of the President's top security advisers. They were faced with Robert Oppenheimer's nightmare vision of a world in which efforts to stop proliferation had failed. It was an exercise, organised by the RAND corporation, a leading military think-tank, and sponsored by an anxious Pentagon, to explore the implications of the Bomb spreading. As one participant wrote later: 'We have seen a future. It is not particularly pleasant.'

The scenario begins in the late summer of 1999 with two crises unfolding, in the Gulf and in Asia. Iran has emerged as the dominant power in the Gulf region: it conquered Iraq in a brief war two years earlier and has since been helped by Pakistan to amass at least three – possibly eight – first-generation fission warheads for its fighter-bombers. It is spoiling for a fight, demanding cuts in OPEC production to drive up the oil price. It sends units of heavy armour towards the border of Kuwait. At the same time, Iran has formed an alliance with North Korea. North Korea has itself produced enough plutonium for at least five – possibly ten – fission bombs and has built its own Nodong 1 missiles which can carry them as far as Japan. Following the death of its long-time leader, Kim Il-Sung, the country divides into two factions: one which wants early unification with South Korea, another which wants to use North Korea's nuclear weapons to defeat the South and their American allies once and for all.

Most of this scenario is credible. Reality was bubbling accurately around the war-game even as it was being played. The day before, *The New York Times* reported that the Pentagon was considering how best to reinforce South Korea against a possible North Korean attack. On the day of the game itself, 2 December 1993, the *Washington Post* claimed that the latest US intelligence concluded that it was possible North Korea had acquired a bomb already. Later that day, the Reuters news agency carried a denial from Tehran that it was helping North Korea develop its long-range missile, the Nodong 1 (though it was widely suspected that this was a case of 'no smoke without fire', especially given another element in the Reuters report). It confirmed that in June of that year the commander of Iran's Revolutionary Guards had visited the North Korean capital, Pyongyang, and, in talks with military leaders, had urged 'closer ties'.

The ten war-game players, chaired by Sam Gardiner, the Pentagon consultant and seminar host, were given one hour to formulate a strategy. Among the questions confronting them were: should the United States reinforce the Gulf and South Korea simultaneously? If only one region was reinforced, would that exacerbate the situation in the other? Would either country actually use its nuclear weapons? Should the United States ignore that possibility? Or try to forestall it by loudly hinting that the American response would be a nuclear one? Or would the very mention of the nuclear question only add to the value of the weapons themselves? Should the US seize the initiative and try to destroy the nuclear weapons of both countries?

This was uncharted territory. The United States and its allies have never before had to confront a nuclear-armed regional power. Iraq had failed to achieve nuclear status before the Gulf War; nuclear weapons were never an issue in Somalia or Bosnia; in the proxy wars fought with the Soviet Union, both sides had been desperate to keep nuclear weapons well away. Suddenly though it has dawned on western military planners that the fact that nuclear weapons may fall into the hands of countries like Iran and North Korea presents a revolutionary challenge to their thinking.

The comments and questions came thick and fast.

Peter Zimmermann, a former National Security Council official and current USAF consultant, wondered if there were any options which would work quickly enough for 'neither we nor our allies to lose cities'.

Colonel Jamie Gough, of the National War College, warned that moving an American division into either region within range of a nuclear weapon could 'lose this war very quickly'. One 'nicely delivered nuclear device and all of a sudden you've got ten thousand American casualties and that may be the end of the war. We'd either have to retaliate massively or sue for peace.'

'Don't panic,' cautioned Rod McDaniel, a former presidential adviser on security issues. 'These are two weak states who happen to have nuclear weapons and act recklessly but they have no allies.'

'But what about our objectives?' Sam Gardiner wanted to hear specific proposals. Should the US think of a pre-emptive strike, even with its own nuclear weapons?

Daniel Goure, a former senior Pentagon official, saw no reason to rule out nuclear force.

Martin van Heuren, a former director of European intelligence for the CIA, objected. We want to play down the value of nuclear weapons, he said, to show 'that nuclear weapons are not very useful'.

'I disagree with that,' Goure answered back sharply. The rogue states in question had already taken the opposite lesson: that nuclear weapons are useful. There was no point 'denying yourself' the nuclear option.

John Rothrock, a member of Sam Gardiner's strategic seminar group, looked worried. 'The situation is characterised by the word "leverage" – and we don't have a lot,' he said. The traditional notions of deterrence would not work in this crisis; we need a different mind-set.

In saying this, Rothrock had voiced a long-standing fear of the former American Defence Secretary, Les Aspin, that the old Cold War nuclear strategies were no longer relevant. Aspin had warned that 'whole areas of study . . . universities and think-tanks and congressional committees' had devised a doctrine to deal with the Soviet nuclear threat which was now 'inadequate' for coping with the new nuclear powers. The United States, according to Aspin, had used the nuclear threat to counterbalance the larger conventional forces of the Soviet Union. Nuclear weapons, in that case, had served as an equaliser. Now though, he warned, 'nuclear weapons are still an equaliser . . . and the United States is now on the other side of the equation'. The truth was that even small nations, if armed with the Bomb, would be able to threaten America. Which is why he concluded that if nuclear weapons could be banned, 'we would'.

In the future world of the war-game in 1999, a ban on nuclear weapons has not materialised (nor is it likely to). Sam Gardiner is trying to gain a consensus on the most immediate nuclear threat, the one from North Korea. In the scenario, the US commander in the region has specifically requested permission to attack North Korea's nuclear facilities.

Colonel Gough protested: 'Do we just say that because they have nuclear weapons we ought to attack them? We're really getting into something we've never really faced.'

Martin van Heuren concurred: 'You show you're there . . . but you wait for things to settle. Military action will very likely bring a major North Korean entry into South Korea and we will have triggered a scenario we wanted to avoid in the first place.'

'I would argue the opposite,' interrupted Rod McDaniel. Even a few nuclear weapons in North Korean hands were 'a threat to world peace'.

Patricia Barwinczak, a consultant to the USAF on proliferation policy, took an even harder line. 'You have to deal with them in the currency with which they are ready to play.'

The hour ends. No agreement is reached. The buck is passed to the President.

The clock advances several days and both crises have escalated. North Korea's forces are poised to strike south at any minute, Iran's have already begun attacking Kuwaiti and American units. The CIA reports that Iran and North Korea have secretly agreed that mini-submarines, carried aboard civilian cargo ships, should deliver nuclear bombs to American ports.

The plan is evidently under way: one of the ships is intercepted in the Suez Canal and, as expected, is found to be holding a mini-submarine in which there is a crude nuclear device (of the same design as the one dropped on Hiroshima). Another cargo ship is spotted twelve miles off the Florida coast. It is boarded by US Special Forces. But a radio message confirming the presence of a nuclear weapon is abruptly terminated. The device has exploded with a force of 18 kilotons (Hiroshima suffered 15 kilotons). Two American vessels have been sunk. A radioactive cloud is now drifting towards the town of Jacksonville.

A curious silence fell on the players.

Colonel Gough, who announced the news, declared: 'Nothing could be more serious and we are the victims.'

'OK, so what do we do?' Sam Gardiner asked, grimacing heavily and glancing around the table.

Daniel Goure: 'I would argue this constitutes a state of war.'

Colonel Gough: 'We've gone to war for a lot less than this.' He urged an immediate conventional strike against all strategic targets in Iran. 'There is no question Iran is responsible. They have to fall in my opinion.'

Martin van Heuren disagreed. Iran might not be to blame for the bomb's explosion. 'It is not clear to me why it went off or who made it go off or whether it was meant to go off . . .'

Rod McDaniel too suggested that Iran might not have meant the nuclear device to detonate, rather to use the weapon to blackmail the United States only to find that 'this has got out of control'.

Several different players proposed a diplomatic 'pause' to allow Iran to climb down and, above all, to own up to the existence and locations of any further nuclear devices. A twelve-hour delay was suggested.

Peter Zimmermann said bombers should be launched towards Iran during that pause to add to the pressure.

That idea alarmed Sam Gardiner. 'Can we assure the President that if we undertake that campaign we won't see another nuclear weapon launched against us?'

Meanwhile intelligence arrives indicating that North Korea is going to attack within twelve hours. This inspired a vigorous argument over the best response.

Martin van Heuren urged: 'Wait and see, do not assume the worst.'

Rod McDaniel, usually cautious, called out: 'At the end of the day North Korea has got to be disarmed.'

Colonel Gough agreed. North Korea had to be treated in the same way as Iran. Both had nuclear weapons, both were rogue states. 'What's the difference?'

But the immediate priority facing the players is to draft a response to the detonation off Florida. Jacksonville is now in a state of panic. Chance television coverage of the mushroom cloud adds to the public's fears. The President must be offered a strategy. The players all agree that Iran must be bombed in retaliation; that much was straightforward. But they cannot agree on whether the bombing should be with conventional weapons or with nuclear ones.

Their argument reflects the difficulty confronting military planners in the post-Cold War world of suddenly having no rule-book. The old one, informally drawn up with the former Soviet Union, has vanished. The circumstances in which nuclear weapons may be used against the Warsaw Pact were relatively clear: they would be launched if conventional defence failed. But in the situation as experienced in the war-game, the facts are sparse and the arguments for and against a nuclear response are more obscure. The British Defence Secretary, Malcolm Rifkind, had identified the same problem in a speech a month before, in November 1993. There would be 'more room for uncertainty' over the scale and nature of aggression which would justify nuclear retaliation, he said. He asked rhetorically whether the use of chemical or biological weapons by an enemy would justify a British nuclear attack; or if there was a difference between British cities being attacked and British forces overseas.

Sam Gardiner: 'Do we use nuclear weapons? I hear a lot of talk but we've got to come to a decision.' He asked each player, one by one.

Sam Watson, a former National Security Council official, went first. He said there should be a nuclear response. There should be the twelve-hour pause to find any other Iranian devices and then 'we must go after the Iranian leadership with a nuclear weapon or two'.

Patricia Barwinczak agreed. It was important to show that what happened at Jacksonville would not be tolerated. 'I'd say hit the leadership with one nuke.'

John Rothrock also favoured the use of a nuclear weapon against Iran but only after Iranian leaders were given twelve hours to make amends.

Peter Zimmermann was more forthright. 'We go with a nuke because nothing else gives us the high probability of success.'

So far four out of the ten players had voted for nuclear retaliation. But the rest did not see the issue as sufficiently clear-cut. They urged caution, seeing risks in using nuclear weapons: it might provoke a further nuclear attack by Iran and, in the long-term, might accelerate nuclear proliferation. The group was now becoming divided. Just as Malcolm Rifkind had warned, the justification for nuclear use was no longer so obvious.

The fifth to vote, Colonel Gough, was the first to oppose using nuclear weapons. 'We're good enough to do it conventionally, we're great enough not to have to use them.'

Daniel Goure followed suit: 'A nuke-for-a-nuke is not the policy you want.' Conventional weapons should be used first.

Martin van Heuren: 'No nuke.' He repeated his view that since nuclear weapons could not 'be removed from the face of the earth', the United States should try to devalue their usefulness.

Audrey Williams, an adviser to the Defence Nuclear Agency on proliferation policy, said simply: 'No.'

Rod McDaniel offered another variation: 'The message should be "maybe", but what we actually do should be "No".'

Which left five voices against nuclear use, four in favour. Sam Gardiner, who did not cast a vote, suggested that the President should be told of the group's divided opinion. The exercise ended uncomfortably. It had raised some disturbingly realistic dilemmas for the country which invented the nuclear bomb. Two small nuclear powers had successfully challenged the United States and the nation's top security advisers had failed to agree on how to respond. Proliferation was shown to be more than an abstract fear and to be changing the way the United States viewed the world and the role of its forces in it.

The scenario of the double war with North Korea and Iran is only the latest in a series run by the RAND corporation for senior and middle-ranking officers and for officials from the Pentagon, the CIA, Congress and Los Alamos and the other laboratories (several hundred people in all have taken part). Other scenarios have involved Moscow losing control of its nuclear weapons and triggering a nuclear civil war; the impact of Iran becoming a nuclear power on allied attempts to repeat Operation Desert Storm and keep open the Persian Gulf oil-route; a nuclear attack by North

Korea on South Korea; and a nuclear war between India and Pakistan. Long regarded as unrealistic, each of these scenarios is now seen as perfectly plausible – and horrifying. 'These are issues which make people's heads hurt and stomachs ache,' according to one of the authors, Peter Wilson. In the dying days of the Cold War, when the games had first been dreamed up by Wilson and a RAND colleague, Roger Molander, the very idea of gaming anything other than an American–Soviet nuclear war had been dismissed. 'There was the view that if you don't have ten thousand of the weapons, you don't count,' Wilson says. 'Now, there's the revelation that even a handful of nuclear weapons could have a strategic effect.'

It is ironic that what Wilson calls this 'rediscovery of the true significance of nuclear weapons' should have come at RAND. RAND (standing for 'Research and Development') was established after the Second World War to advise the US Air Force on how to use its new nuclear bombs and went on to acquire a reputation for extreme Cold War hawkishness – its analysts were described as 'the Wizards of Armageddon' for dreaming up complex theories on missile throw-weight, strategic vulnerability and nuclear war-fighting. RAND has since broadened its outlook and has conducted research on a huge variety of topics for the US Army and the Office of the Defence Secretary as well. Now, fifty years into the nuclear age, it has come to focus once again on the weapons which led to its foundation.

Wilson and Molander, who have both served in a variety of senior positions in government (Wilson in the CIA and the State Department, Molander on the National Security Council), have reached some gloomy conclusions. The American armed forces, they believe, have yet to come to terms with proliferation. Even the Pentagon's recent review of itself, known as the 'Bottom-Up Review', which decided that the United States ought to be able to fight two regional conflicts simultaneously, took no account of the possibility that those wars might involve nuclear weapons. 'It was far too optimistic,' according to Wilson. The best of America's forces, if sent, for example, to the Gulf, could be wiped out by a single, crude nuclear device. The likelihood, in Molander's view, was that a nuclear-armed regional power could say: 'I'll make sure the US never comes back to the Middle East again – because that's probably what would happen.' A fear of extremely high casualties could effectively close the least stable parts of the world to American forces. Washington's entire military strategy for overseas operations could be made redundant.

In a similar series of war-games, called 'America's Wars: 1995–2015', run specifically for middle-ranking officers at the National War College and other educational institutes for the military, Sam Gardiner has watched how the average American commander reacts to the enemy's use of nuclear weapons. At the very least, it forced a major change of tactics; at worst, the experience encouraged extreme timidity. In one set of games rerunning Operation Desert Storm with its battle for Kuwait, he assumed that Iraq was armed with nuclear missiles which had a range of 1,000 kilometres. Twelve different teams of officers played the American side and ten of them realised that the Gulf, which was within missile range, was denied to them; they were forced to deliver ground forces to the region via the Red Sea, a safe distance away. One lesson, learned even before the mock-war had started, was that the leisurely build-up of forces through the Gulf ports which made Operation Desert Storm possible could never have happened if Iraq had had the Bomb.

A second insight was that the United States could itself easily provoke a small nuclear power into using its forces. Teams of American officers playing North Koreans or Iranians, with modest nuclear arsenals of perhaps fifteen weapons, found that if air attacks destroyed half of them, there was a strong need to use the rest before they were lost too.

A third insight from the war-games mirrored that of the RAND exercise in December 1993: it is extremely difficult to decide how to respond to a nuclear attack. In the Gulf War scenario, the nuclear-armed Iraqis killed over 1,000 US Marines with two of their missiles. Yet despite the horror of the attack, a staggering eight out of ten American teams chose not to respond with nuclear weapons themselves. The problem they found was that 'nuking Baghdad', though initially appealing, would kill tens of thousands of innocent civilians and almost certainly fail to hit Saddam Hussein. Other targets of greater military or strategic importance outside the capital also risked the same cataclysmic loss of civilian life. Striking targets in the north or south would decimate the Kurdish or Shiite populations. The same restraint was apparent in games dealing with Korea. Even though on one occasion, Gardiner noticed that a Marines colonel was 'close to tears' after his men were hit with a North Korean nuclear weapon, most American teams refrained from a nuclear response. Aside from concerns about finding suitable targets, there were worries about the reactions of allies: would the members of a coalition withdraw if the Americans went nuclear?

That becomes an especially complicated calculation if an enemy attacks not with a nuclear weapon but one with similarly destructive power: with a chemical or biological warhead. Weapons which carry toxic gas or lethal germs have come to be considered 'weapons of mass destruction' as much as nuclear ones. (Though chemical weapons have been dubbed 'poor man's nukes', it is biological weapons with their potential for spreading instantly fatal diseases on a massive scale which deserve that description.) In the Gulf War, the United States hinted to Iraq that any use of its chemical arsenal would be met with an appropriate response, the implication being that the use of a weapon of mass destruction would be met by another of the same category (and since the United States has forsworn chemical and biological weapons, that only left its nuclear weapons). It was a formula repeated in the Pentagon's 1994 Report to the President and Congress. 'The role of US nuclear forces in deterring or responding to such non-nuclear threats must be considered,' it said, stirring up an immediate political controversy over its implications. Some argued that the United States had to retain a credible option against the threat of chemical or biological attack; others that investing nuclear weapons with this degree of usefulness would only encourage yet more countries to seek the Bomb.

Sam Gardiner is not totally pessimistic about this, but he believes the military need to think fast about developing new strategies (such as organising themselves so they fight at longer range and present a less inviting target for a nuclear strike). Peter Wilson claims to have innate confidence too. 'I'm still hopeful that human progress is sufficient to walk away from this.' But he has weighed up the different possibilities for the future and is frightened by almost all of them. 'Nukes won't magically go away. This technology can never be disinvented. The best we can do is maybe control it or manage it without massive loss of life . . . We ain't gonna die of boredom.'

*   *   *

51

Diplomatic efforts to control nuclear proliferation continue. There are agreements to control the export of relevant components and equipment, and plans for these to be tightened. Many officials still talk of 'non-proliferation' as an achievable goal, that nuclear weapons can somehow be stopped from spreading beyond the original five nuclear powers. Others though have coined a new term, 'counter-proliferation', which implies that the weapons have already spread and now need to be tackled – either by seeking them out or by building an impenetrable shield to fend them off.

3

AN IMPENETRABLE SHIELD

*Forty years ago we made choice for mutual assured destruction
and deterrence. Today we make choice for mutual assured protection. This is the future for mankind for the next century.*
Yevgeni Velikhov, Chief Scientific Adviser to the Russian
President, BBC interview, 17 September 1992

Professor Nikita Moiseev has watched thousands of nuclear wars
explode across his computer screen. A kindly figure in his late sixties
with a shock of unkempt grey hair, he has a defeated expression. His
career has involved long hours in a badly lit office in the Institute of
Cybernetics in south Moscow. Hunched over clumsy Soviet equipment, he discovered disturbing truths about the effects of nuclear
weapons and now conveys a sense of having witnessed catastrophes
of a scale and savagery that most mortals could never comprehend.
His pale-blue eyes are tired, his demeanour melancholic. He has
seen too much simulated nuclear war and now fears that, with
nuclear missiles falling into maverick hands, real nuclear wars could
easily follow. He shares the passionate concern of his late colleague,
Andrei Sakharov, that, as a scientist contributing to nuclear weapons
expertise, he is morally obliged to warn the world of the dangers of
his work and to act to head them off.

In urgent tones in an interview at his dacha, Moiseev conjured
up an image of a race against time. The democratic nations – he
included Russia – had a pressing need to build themselves a new
Great Wall to fend off the nuclear barbarians beyond. 'The only
future for civilised mankind,' he said, 'is to build defences; we must
build a shield together.' It was not merely a practical necessity to
head off the threat of nuclear blackmail by the likes of Saddam
Hussein, he said; having created nuclear weapons, we now faced a

moral imperative to guard against them. He spoke with vigour, even anger, as if I, too, should help in this task.

It was a warm summer evening and we were talking in Moiseev's garden, admiring his vegetable plots and a noisy chicken-run. The dacha was one of a cluster of cottages built for leading scientists, an academicians' weekend colony, some forty miles south-west of Moscow; it was one of the few privileges to have survived the economic turmoil following the collapse of the Soviet Union. Moiseev ushered me towards a Wendy House in the corner of his garden. The matronly figure of his wife appeared with a shy smile to say proudly that he, Nikita, had built it himself for their grandchildren. Moiseev ran his hand over the decorative carving above a little window, a melodramatic gesture which prepared the ground for his next point. 'We are all at risk, but not only us: the next generations, our children, their children. We have to do something for them. We must.'

As his wife called us in to tea, Moiseev repeated his call for a common shield to be built; it was the only answer. All the time he stared at me intently as if to check that I had understood the gravity of his message.

Professor Moiseev has reason to be fearful. Now semi-retired, his job had been to simulate the Domesday implications of Mutual Assured Destruction, to bring mathematical understanding to the unpredictable reality of atomic Armageddon. It was his task to calculate the effect of hundreds of Soviet nuclear explosions over Washington and London. He studied the likely interplay of the mushroom clouds – what nuclear planners call the 'fratricide' of one nuclear blast spoiling the effect of another. He tried to assess variations in the explosive yields of the warheads and in their numbers and patterns of attack. He devised a computer model of the impact of nuclear war on the atmosphere and the weather, the first detailed theoretical work on how the dust generated by atomic explosions would darken the skies and create the effect known as 'nuclear winter'. Most important of all though, he had to estimate the impact of a western nuclear attack on his own home city, Moscow.

This last task was given the greatest priority. Under an unusually secret contract with the Soviet Ministry of Defence, Moiseev and his team had to evaluate how the Kremlin might avoid destruction. According to the Cold War theory of nuclear deterrence, the Soviet Union's principal defence against a NATO strike was to retaliate –

to annihilate the key western capitals in return. But that balance of terror left both superpower adversaries armed only with swords: if one struck, the other would respond in kind and both would die. The wish to escape from that inevitable trap has been an enduring one in both countries. It is a vision that sees the construction of an impenetrable shield; only in the Soviet Union though has that ever been realised. Moiseev was ordered to calculate whether the shield developed for Moscow would ever work.

The attempts by the United States to develop an 'umbrella' defence against missiles are better known. President Reagan's dream of a 'Star Wars' space shield, launched as the Strategic Defence Initiative in 1983, was the latest in a long line of projects to crumble in the face of exorbitant costs and an underestimation of the scientific challenges involved. As early as the 1950s, Pentagon planners first suggested fielding anti-missile missiles. For a brief period in the 1970s, the concept was realised when missile interceptors were deployed under the Safeguard system, a project quickly abandoned as futile. More recently, a highly localised defence was offered by American Patriot missiles in Saudi Arabia and Israel to protect against Iraqi Scuds; evidence shows that these were of greater psychological than military value (of which more in the next chapter). Yet it was Soviet scientists and engineers who became the first to build space-age fortifications. With a defence system known to military insiders as the 'nuclear crown', they turned Moscow into the only city in the world to have any protection at all against ballistic missiles.

It meant constructing an elaborate 'layered' defence: early warning satellites up in space, interceptor rockets based at ground level and, as a last resort, bunkers deep underground. The satellites, equipped with infra-red sensors, were positioned over the United States to detect the sudden blast of heat as American missiles left their silos or submarines. Huge space-tracking ships, thinly disguised as freighters, were positioned to watch for the moment in orbit when the missiles jettisoned their warheads towards earth. Radar systems as far away as Ukraine, Latvia and Siberia were designed to track the exact approach of the warheads themselves and calculate their trajectories. More accurate radars at three sites around Moscow would estimate the best points at which to mount a defence; a fourth radar, at Pushkino, just north of the capital, was to track the final approach of the warheads. And then, from a ring of a dozen bases hidden in the birch forests surrounding Moscow, giant interceptors were meant to rise towards the edge of the atmosphere, or even just beyond it. There, their own nuclear warheads were supposed to explode, creating the cosmic equivalent of a medieval fire-trench. The incoming weapons would be caught in an intense storm of gamma rays and neutrons, their radioactive ingredients distorted, their electronic components rendered useless. A shock wave would knock them off course. Inactive and ineffective, the warheads were supposed to fall into the countryside around Moscow. In theory, the Kremlin was to be saved.

This Anti-Ballistic Missile (ABM) system was not without its problems and uncertainties. One of the greatest constraints, submitted to voluntarily, was a diplomatic one. In one of the few agreements reached during the Cold War, the United States and the Soviet Union had tried to contain the scope of the arms race. While the competition between them raged unchecked in most areas of weaponry, the ABM Treaty of 1972 set deliberate limits on the scale of defences each side was allowed to deploy. The treaty stipulated that a maximum of 100 defensive interceptors could be fielded to guard either the capital or another site, such as a key missile base. It also ruled that early warning radars were only to be built on each nation's periphery, not further inland where they could more easily provide guidance information for the interceptors. With the recent easing of the nuclear stand-off between Moscow and Washington, such a treaty – compelling both countries to remain largely unguarded – might now seem to make little sense. At that time though, it was accepted as logical. Each side had to feel confident that, if it was attacked, its own retaliatory strike would succeed; too large and effective a defence system on one side would jeopardise that balance.

Both countries generally supported the spirit of the ABM Treaty, if not the letter, for much of its existence. The United States decided against fielding an anti-ballistic missile system around Washington, as the treaty would have allowed, partly because such a large proportion of the American population would have been beyond its reach, further north or on the west coast. It also soon gave up an ABM system built earlier, near Grand Forks in North Dakota, which had been intended to protect the region in which most American ICBMs are based; the system was seen as too costly, unlikely to work and was anyway never popular politically. The Kremlin though took a different view. It chose to try to defend Moscow to the maximum extent allowed by the treaty – and sometimes beyond it. Its secretive developments around the Soviet capital provoked frequent accusations from Washington that the treaty was being violated. Indeed Mikhail Gorbachev was forced to admit, after years of denials, that one large radar, built near Krasnoyarsk in Siberia, was in breach of the agreement.

On top of the legal constraints imposed by the treaty, there were practical difficulties with using nuclear weapons to 'catch' others as they fell towards Moscow. Test-firings of the interceptors, with their warheads detonating at the edge of space, had revealed a host of potentially damaging side-effects. The sudden burst of neutrons and gamma rays, it was discovered, caused a 'black-out' of all radar systems within a certain range on the ground below, affecting the defending forces more than those of the attacker. This would only last between several fractions of a second and a few seconds but might well be enough, in a conflict, to deny Soviet operators their best source of intelligence on other aspects of whatever attack was under way. At the same time, it was found that the nuclear explosion in space caused a second problem, known as 'red-out'. This was the loss of communications caused by the weapon's Electromagnetic Pulse (EMP), a massive surge of power blanketing the electromagnetic spectrum, putting radios out of action for minutes or even hours. Since the interceptors' warheads would of necessity have to be detonated over Soviet territory, it would be the Soviet side that would suffer most markedly from both effects.

That did nothing to allay western fears. The Moscow ABM system attracted obsessive attention from western intelligence during the lengthy period of its construction from the late 1960s. Information about each new enhancement to the radars and guidance computers and about every test-firing of the missiles was studied in minute detail by MI6 and the CIA. Monthly reports of Soviet progress in the project were circulated in Whitehall and Washington; several successive British prime ministers asked to be kept informed on a regular basis. British nuclear scientists made their own attempt to 'model' the Moscow system, piecing together each nugget of intelligence into what one source called a 'jigsaw' of understanding about it. As soon as the existence of new interceptors was confirmed by electronic eavesdropping on the test-firings, NATO codenames were provided for the weapons. SH-02 Galosh, a missile designed to perform its interceptions 'exo-atmospherically', just beyond the atmosphere, was spotted as the first in service. ('Galosh' turned out to be an unintended but appropriate pun; a very similar word in Russian slang is used to describe another form of protection -- a condom.) During the 1980s, it was gradually replaced by the SH-04 Gorgon, a missile with a similar range and task. More recently still, the SH-08 Gazelle, an extremely fast missile, was introduced to intercept NATO warheads 'endo-atmospherically', within the atmosphere, in case the outer layer of defences was to fail.

'Gorgon', though known about for years, remained unseen in the West until November 1992, when sources in the Russian Ministry of Defence provided me with video pictures of this missile for a BBC documentary. When the cassette arrived from Moscow, I asked one of the country's leading missile experts, Duncan Lennox, editor of *Jane's Strategic Weapons*, the most authoritative of the military reference books, to help corroborate my information about the weapon. A reserved man, with infinite respect for detail, he was convinced that this footage of a large white missile, blasting off at a slight angle, was indeed a 'Gorgon'. 'You've got something here,' Lennox said, allowing himself to admit a little excitement at this discovery. He was not alone: a still photograph from the footage ended up on the front cover of *Jane's Defence Weekly*, the most prominent of the military periodicals.

Much of the interest in Gorgon, and its counterparts, stemmed from a long-standing fear in London that the Moscow ABM system might be able to resist a British nuclear attack. As with other second-tier nuclear powers like France and China, Britain's nuclear force has always been relatively small compared to that of America or Russia. The ABM system was seen to pose a fundamental challenge to Britain's ultimate means of defending itself (which was to threaten Moscow) since the 100 Soviet interceptors would certainly outnumber the maximum of 32 Polaris warheads which the Royal Navy could deploy. The result was that the government of the day, Harold Wilson's, felt obliged to act to improve Britain's Polaris missiles. To enable them to evade the Moscow defences, a highly secret project known as 'Chevaline' was commissioned at an eventual cost of over £1 billion (see next chapter). It was assumed, among other things, that once the Soviet interceptors had detonated, the loss of radar through black-out would not last long enough for Britain to launch further warheads undetected; and that the Soviet Union anyway would be able to make use of alternative radar systems positioned away from Moscow. At that stage in the Cold War, the worst-case scenario was assumed, that the Moscow shield would hold. The Chevaline system, by trying to hide Britain's genuine warheads amongst a confusing clutter of decoys, would attempt to defeat it.

The ABM system was evidently a cornerstone of Soviet military thinking. The concept of safeguarding the capital seems to have struck a deep chord with each generation in the Kremlin. Nikita Krushchev boasted that the system was so accurate it would be able to 'swat a fly' in space; under the reforming Mikhail Gorbachev, it was equipped with a new generation of missiles. Even under Boris Yeltsin, the system, which is estimated to have cost some £10 billion,[1] has been maintained, if less effectively and at a lower level of finance. Major-General Gennadi Ivanov, a specialist adviser on nuclear issues to the Defence Minister, Pavel Grachev, in a rare interview on the subject, told me Moscow was 'the pride of our country' and that the defence system was therefore designed to be 'highly effective, reliable, even invincible'. History had shown how vulnerable Moscow could be, he said. Napoleon's cavalry and Hitler's tank armies had indeed come very close to success. Only the stretching of their supply-lines and the viciousness of the Russian winter had seen them off. But it was evident to recent Soviet leaders that neither of those factors would impede nuclear warheads falling from space towards Red Square at up to 10,000 m.p.h. A defence of unprecedented sophistication – and secrecy – was required.

Finding out more about Moscow's 'nuclear crown' became the central task in my research for a programme for the BBC *Assignment* series. One of the few sources of publicly available information about the Moscow defence system was the Pentagon's annual assessment of its adversary, *Soviet Military Power*. This publication, designed to scare Congress and public opinion into supporting new American weapons projects, brimmed with fuzzy photographs and artists' impressions of mysterious and apparently potent Soviet military hardware. The series died with the Cold War in 1991. But the last edition, the title of which was hurriedly changed to *Soviet Military Forces in Transition*, contains several pages of detail about Moscow's defences. One map of the Moscow area marks the locations of some of the key radar sites and silos; another depicts the routes of three special underground railways connecting the

Kremlin with the deep emergency bunkers in the city's outskirts. There is even a photograph, labelled as having been taken from a Moscow State University building (presumably from its roof), showing the huge air-vents allegedly used in the construction of one of the most modern bunkers, in a district in south-west Moscow known as Ramenki. This installation, the booklet says, is 200–300 metres deep and is large enough to house 10,000 people. With 'highly effective life-support systems', it can continue operating 'for many months following a nuclear attack'.

We went to investigate. It was 1992 and, although the *coup* attempt the year before had forced the military to be more open, the defence of the capital was still a highly sensitive issue. One Russian friend had even warned me it might be dangerous to probe too hard. It was difficult though to try to film at Ramenki without looking immediately suspicious. We approached the site indirectly, through a muddy, dishevelled sprawl of workshops and garages. In the precise area marked by the Pentagon map stood a line of unfinished skyscrapers. Well-maintained barbed wire and floodlights ringed the site. A few figures were undertaking some desultory work inside. At the base of the tower-blocks we could see what looked at first sight like large windows; through a zoom lens they turned out to be air-vents. A mechanic emerged from one of the workshops to watch us and we asked him what the place was called. After some hesitation, he replied. 'It has no name, no address, just a Post Office number,' he said. 'All I know is, not to ask about it.'

We drove round to another side of this huge, unexplained site. Within minutes of parking and starting to film, a severe-looking official in civilian clothes came out to challenge us. He barked out some angry questions and noted down the registration number of our car – a highly unusual move in what was then a generally more open Russia. We thought it best to leave. When I later described this scene to a western intelligence official, he told me: 'you were on the button'. A Russian official shook his head in disbelief at the very idea of us filming there: 'Ramenki, very secret, very secret'. According to one western source, the construction of the skyscrapers was meant to provide cover for the more important excavations and building work underground. The Pentagon was right: this was one of the components of Moscow's shield.

Hardly surprisingly, all formal requests for access to this or any other part of the Moscow defence system were rejected out of hand.

An informal approach would be the only way, preferably handled by Russians; fortunately there was no shortage of people to fulfil that role. Since the opening up of Russian society under Gorbachev, a coterie of well-connected television professionals has grown up, specialising in getting cameras into secret military facilities. Usually operating alone, these merchants of *glasnost* never explain whether it is the strength of their contacts or gifts of vodka or dollar bribes that secure them access. It is probably a combination of all three. Their wares – video-cassettes – are then hawked around the Moscow offices of western television companies. Business is good, if highly competitive.

One of the most prominent figures in this market was Sergei Moskvitch (he has since emigrated). With lank blond hair, damaged teeth, a worn face and the stench of chain-smoking, few who meet him can believe he is only in his mid-thirties. He has a demanding, insistent manner and his visits to the news bureaux were often dreaded. He pushed for high prices, dragged out negotiations for hours or even over several days and never seemed to let up. Yet his pictures were usually first-rate. He enjoyed good relations with several key military officials and the results were self-evident: he produced a number of scoops. Sergei was the first to film the highly advanced mobile SS25 missile; the inside of the Blackjack, the latest Soviet bomber; and the warheads inside a nuclear storage site. The BBC, NHK of Japan, ARD of Germany and the American network NBC have all benefited from his work.

Quite how the son of an exiled dissident, born in Siberia, established such a role for himself was never clear, especially since his criticism of the old regime and of the ineffectiveness of the present government was outspoken. Yet despite his political reputation, the military seemed happy to deal with him. In particular, Sergei cultivated two colonels. Their task was to extract the necessary permissions, stamps and signatures for each of his projects; I chose not to ask what they were receiving in return. In the course of several long meetings with Sergei, in Moscow, Paris and London, he promised that, with the help of these two officers, he could gain access to the defence system. It would be difficult, he said, but not impossible. In our conversations, he emerged as a highly likeable, soulful, if trying man and we managed to strike a deal. For a fee comparable to the normal rate for the hire of a film crew in Russia, and with payment only on the basis of results, he agreed to take the project on. Wherever possible, he would take me along as well, though we both knew from experience that the presence of a western correspondent on his filming trips would more than likely jeopardise permission for visits to the most secret facilities.

In June 1992, we made our first foray, to one of the bases forming the outer ring of interceptor sites around Moscow. The Pentagon map had marked a missile site north-west of the capital and, after an hour's drive crammed in a Lada (Sergei insisted my Japanese hire car would be too obvious), we were amid the rolling fields surrounding the scruffy market town of Klin. Little barns and cottages dotted the landscape; the occasional tractor broke the quiet. A high-technology defence of Moscow could hardly have seemed less appropriate in this impoverished countryside. There were no signs of military activity at all. Only on one side-road did we find a notice that gave anything away: in peeling paint, it warned of government property ahead. We ignored it and, a mile further on, pulled into an untended paddock. Sergei pointed to a line of trees. Peeking above it, like the head of a giraffe in the African bush, was a radar scanner, aiming north.

We moved closer. Through an unguarded gate, secured only with a rusting padlock, we could see a watch-tower – unmanned – and dozens of white missile canisters. Later we worked out that these held what the Russians call S-300s, known in the West as SA-10s, equivalent to American Patriot missiles. These have conventional warheads and are designed to destroy incoming bombers or missiles, forming one of the 'layers' of Moscow's defence. Some of the missiles were mounted on launchers, most were lying in stacks. With no one watching over them, they would have been easy pickings for a determined gang of arms dealers. The others in our team had had the same thought. 'How much dollar?' one of them whispered to me, grinning. We crept along the perimeter fence, beating back clouds of mosquitoes, and saw a series of camouflaged bunkers. A few lorries were parked haphazardly. Again, there was no sign of any personnel. We filmed as much as we dared and left, puzzled at the lack of activity.

It emerged later that the unit manning the base was desperately short of men. The break-up of the Soviet Union had stripped it of all its central Asian and Baltic recruits. According to one officer at the base, Captain Constantin Bubilyev, who agreed to be interviewed a few weeks after our visit, some units were operating with only

8–12 per cent of their normal staff. 'It is very painful,' he admitted. Yet he claimed the system was still functioning. 'Moscow needs to be defended and will remain defended – that is our duty, we try to think less about politics.' The base at Klin, he said, was one of fifteen around Moscow, connected to a central command; tests had shown it to be effective. His pride was undimmed. 'A lot of sweat and tears have gone into producing this technology . . . it is very good, it has to be.'

But, off the record, Captain Bubilyev's colleagues were less brave. There were complaints about shortages of food, spare parts and even wages. Financial pressure had left the base's garrison town more isolated than ever. One woman lieutenant moaned about the lack of public transport. 'To go to visit friends even in Klin is difficult because the last bus back leaves at 7.40 p.m. – so there's nothing you can do.' A captain pointed out that price rises and general economic collapse had meant that the officers were reduced to carrying out basic maintenance work themselves on their communal quarters. One of their number had to be delegated to this duty every day; 'this seems funny to people outside,' the captain added, embarrassed at this predicament. A more fundamental problem was uncertainty about their future. 'In these complicated and troubled times,' another captain said, 'there is a lot that we don't understand.' His concerns were to be echoed in other parts of the Moscow defence system.

Sergei and his colonels successfully negotiated their way into a stretch of the military Metro system and into a secret underground road running from the Ministry of Defence to the south-western outskirts. Their pictures provided the first independent western proof that such networks existed and were still working. The tunnels seemed to fit a historical pattern. A Russian author, Vladimir Gonik, who has written about what he calls 'subterranean Moscow', claims some tunnels date from the time of Ivan the Terrible and that the networks are as 'extensive and varied' as the street pattern on the surface. Sergei's video did not support that assertion, but it did illustrate the durability of Moscow's obsession with shielding itself against its enemies.

However, the fact that the tunnels continue to be maintained – and regarded as important – meant that Sergei's intrusions did not pass unpunished. Within hours of returning from filming the rail tunnel, which ran towards the bunker at Ramenki, he noticed two men in a grey Lada parked opposite the entrance to his apartment block. The car had official licence plates. Inside, when he tried to call a colleague to warn him of possible trouble, he realised his phone was playing up, producing strange clicks and only working badly. The colleague, when Sergei managed to contact him, had also noticed a security man in plain clothes loitering outside his own apartment building. Nothing happened that night, though both men were nervous; the experience was an alarming throw-back to earlier times. But the next evening, when Sergei returned from another day's filming, he found his apartment had been broken into. His expensive western television, video-cassette-recorder and stereo music system had been left untouched; nothing was stolen; only his notes relating to this project showed any sign of disturbance. Sergei took the raid to be a warning not to investigate the Moscow shield too thoroughly.

Undaunted, Sergei and his colonels chose to continue with the project. They even managed to play off two rival military departments, each unsure of its relative strength in the internal power struggles of Yeltsin's early days, to get themselves into a large underground command centre, some forty miles west of Moscow, at Rusa. The video pictures of their visit there show a bleak military compound in which, tucked discreetly amid some shrubs, stands a small, unmarked green doorway. The cameraman kept recording as he was led into it, and down. A guard is seen wrestling with heavy wheel-handles, of the sort found on ships, on no fewer than four steel doors, each one-foot-thick, each of which has to be opened in succession. The task of entering this nerve-centre of Moscow's war planning lasts well over two minutes.

The staff, totalling about 300, call the bunker their 'submarine'. Equipped with banks of communications consoles, huge racks of oxygen bottles and a large map of the former Soviet Union – on which each city and major bunker was marked with a little light – it is designed to serve as a crisis management centre. It has enough beds for 700 in wartime. A duty officer is poised at all times over a red telephone reserved for the exclusive use of the defence minister. The equipment, though appearing rather clumsy in comparison with western electronics, looks unusually advanced by the standards of most Russian military installations. Yet even here, the commanding officer, who chose to remain anonymous, reported severe shortcomings. His staff numbers had dwindled dramatically during the course of the year, as conscripts finished their service and new ones failed to materialise. Worse, for the first ten months of 1992, no wages had been delivered. By November of that year, pay-packets had started to arrive but by then any sense of privilege from belonging to an élite corps safeguarding the capital had evaporated. The shield was looking dented.

That became clearer still during a visit to the space-tracking centre at Galitsino. This is the Russian military's equivalent of NASA Mission Control at Houston, where information about all space activity above or near Russia is monitored. It is where intelligence about a NATO missile attack would be analysed and the first decisions taken about mounting a defence. Rows of officers face an electronic map, the size of a large cinema screen, which charts the flights of missiles and satellites; a large globe marks the locations of the intelligence-gathering ships; banks of ancient-looking telephones await orders. There was a competent air about the place but even here self-doubt was evident; it was at this stage in the project that we encountered the first admissions of failure in the arms race, the first signs that the Moscow shield might not be all it was meant to be. A colonel, who preferred not to give his name, declared, unprompted, that 'we lag behind' the West. 'They could strangle us because we are simply not on their level technologically.'

We were to find an even greater sense of defeat in the Russian government, notably from President Yeltsin's adviser on the future of the arms industries. A short, dapper figure in a western suit and new tie, Mikhail Maley is dwarfed by his huge office in the old Central Committee building. He acts as an ambassador for Russian science and, to my surprise, became embarrassed when I asked about the Moscow ABM system; here, at the highest level, was profound scepticism about whether the system would work. Yes, he said, it was 'quite powerful' but 'it is impossible to prove the absolute reliability of machinery'. Even if the system was 99 per cent reliable, he said, and 100 missiles were launched against Moscow, then one weapon would get through, and just 'one megaton warhead would square my account with life'. In Maley's view, the system would never have saved ordinary people, possibly only the defence minister and the Communist Party Central Committee. 'When the military built this system, they were deceiving the population.'

From a career military scientist who himself had had a hand in Moscow's preparations for nuclear war, this was potent criticism; Maley evidently rejected the entire concept of a 'nuclear crown' that would only shield the leadership, and may well even fail in that task. His past experience must have exacerbated that sentiment. One of Maley's more esoteric assignments had been to help design a personalised nuclear shelter for the late Soviet leader Leonid Brezhnev. His particular role, he told me, had been to devise a machine which, in the event of a nuclear war, would lessen the risk of Brezhnev becoming contaminated by radioactive fall-out. It was a bizarre scheme, to say the least: it involved a rapid change of the then leader's blood, the machine intravenously removing his existing supply and replacing it with fresh blood, all at high speed, to help ensure his survival in the atomic aftermath. Maley noticed my fascination with this revelation – I was scribbling notes as fast as I could – and he quickly clammed up. 'A few things will always be secret,' he said, though by then he had made it abundantly clear that he regarded the invention as an absurd, if clever, example of misguided Russian science.

Maley's hesitation over this particular disclosure reflects a general uncertainty in the Russian military research establishment about the value – or cost – of greater openness with the West. Pride demands continued secrecy; pragmatism calls for an acceptance of western superiority in key areas and a willingness to co-operate. We saw that dilemma for ourselves at Star City, the space training centre, outside Moscow. Although much of this vast complex is increasingly open to western visitors – the British cosmonaut Helen Sharman is among those to have trained here – one compound at the heart of the site remains screened off. It is a military research centre, devoted to developing techniques for fighting space war. It was here that much of the theoretical work on Moscow's 'nuclear crown' was undertaken. By good fortune, Sergei knew one of the leading computer scientists in the compound and, after several hours' delay (during which I was asked to keep quiet and 'look Russian'), we found ourselves being waved through the security gates.

We entered a campus of dilapidated concrete buildings. The presence of the military was all too obvious: officers of all ranks could be seen at computer terminals or working with laboratory equipment. One, a captain, was assigned to accompany us; he seemed bemused rather than concerned by my presence. He led us up an unswept staircase and into a dark corridor – like so many Russian institutions, even this one lacked light bulbs. The smell of untended lavatories was pervasive. In a doorway, the captain punched in the access code on a numerical lock. 'You are a lucky man,' he said, with Sergei translating, 'you are the first journalist in here.'

It was disappointing, initially. Four rows of grey computer banks hummed loudly in the centre of the room; terminals of a distinctly out-of-date appearance stood against the walls. Military and civilian technicians were fiddling with a rat's nest of wires inside a console. But then, to one side, I saw the point of all this equipment. A captain, in full uniform, was gazing intently at three television screens which jointly displayed a staggeringly clear 3-D view of the Russian space shuttle, Buran, in orbit. Using a joystick and a battery of controls, he was simulating the view from another shuttle manoeuvring nearby. It was far more realistic than any video-game and of a better quality than any of the latest simulation systems I have seen touted at western military exhibitions. The image of the spacecraft spread effortlessly over the three screens; the shadows were sharp and adjusted instantaneously; the beauty of the colours was bewitching. Since the three screens were meant to represent the three cockpit windows in Buran, the simulator was designed to give cosmonauts near-real experience of working – and fighting – in space. According to several Russian sources, this simulation system and its earlier generations proved crucial in the design of the Moscow defences. Now, its future was unclear.

Although the simulator was impressive, it was notable that a large roomful of computer equipment was required to power it. The racks of Russian-made processors seemed oversized and ungainly compared to the systems found even in most western businesses. I had also noticed that, in an adjoining room, pride of place on the manager's desk was given to a new computer bearing what seemed to be an American label. I did not get a chance to note the name. As soon as the staff saw where I had wandered, I was firmly ushered away. When I asked how they had managed to get round the tough restrictions on western computer exports to obtain this machine, I was offered a mumbled reply and no clear explanation. The superiority of western electronics poses a painful choice for Russian military scientists. If they open their projects to international scrutiny, they will earn themselves access to the latest equipment on the world market with obvious benefits to their progress; but if they choose to preserve the secrecy of their work and their pride in it, they will deny themselves the assistance of the most advanced microchips and, possibly more important, the chance of outside funding.

The scientist in charge of the computer room, Sergei Atamanov, a squat, nervous man, was torn between the two options. On the one hand, he was happy to announce that the details of his simulation software would remain not only highly classified but also world-leading; on the other, he gave me a business card, in English and Russian, which included his fax and electronic-mail numbers, and talked about the need for new sources of finance and technology. When pressed, the latter approach seemed preferable even though it was evidently humiliating as well. In the rush to justify himself, Atamanov frequently broke into German if he felt his Russian was not being translated quickly enough. 'It would be very interesting for our side,' he said, 'to receive access to American microtechnology.' But he felt the need to couch this appeal in the terms of a partnership which would have social rather than military benefits. 'The results of such co-operation could . . . raise the standard of living of our people.' The truth, which Atamanov was unable to confront, is that Russian science risks being left behind technologically; worse, without a dramatic injection of western capital, it risks collapsing altogether.

Sergei and his crew finished filming and we set off back to Moscow. He had kept his side of the bargain; he had produced pictures of most of the key components of the Moscow defence system. Yet what we had found was not the gleaming, confident safeguard of Russian sovereignty which we had expected. Instead, the people involved in the Moscow 'crown' were in the grip of a profound crisis over finance and technology, and many realised it was not without irony: to keep alive the shield over the Kremlin, they would need to co-operate with the very powers whose weapons had led to the shield's construction in the first place.

Within months of the demise of the Soviet Union at the end of 1991, every corner of society was feeling the pinch of the fracturing command economy. The so-called military-industrial complex was especially vulnerable. Under the old regime, it had accounted for nearly two-thirds of the country's entire industrial output and had commanded a share of the national budget too large to be properly accounted for. It is estimated that at one stage some seven million people were employed in this sector of the economy, working at over 5,000 separate institutes and factories. With the cold blast of market forces, however, huge cuts had to be made in the orders which had kept this system alive. According to the Russian Committee for the Defence Industries, government spending on new weapons fell by 68 per cent between 1991 and 1992 while its spending on military research was cut by about half over the same period. The US Defence Intelligence Agency cites several specific examples: in 1990, the old Soviet Union produced seventy attack helicopters while in 1992 Russia made only 5; in 1990, 1,300 tanks were manufactured compared to 675 two years later; and over the same period, artillery production fell from 1,900 units to 450.[2] By 1994, when the Russian Ministry of Defence submitted a request for a budget worth 28.3 trillion roubles (about $18 billion), it was told it would receive only one-fifth of that amount.[3]

Even space research, the most prestigious sector of the military-industrial complex, has suffered. A report by the Western European Union notes that the Russian Space Agency's budget for 1992 was nearly one-third lower than requested and that its 1993 budget had been frozen in spite of inflation of around 20 per cent per month.[4] The Russian Space Agency itself claims matters are even worse. Its deputy chief, Vadim Zlotnikov, said that by mid-1993, the agency had received less than a quarter of the funding it required for the year; the cosmodromes were in a 'pitiable state' and space-flights may not be possible without fresh finance.[5]

The impact of this decline has been devastating. In 1992, there was widespread publicity surrounding rioting at the Baikonur cosmodrome, where workers went on the rampage for food and wages. In a second riot in June 1993, several buildings including barracks, a hospital and a library were burned. In a protest letter to the Russian and Kazakh Presidents, the staff of Baikonur claimed that they had endured the winter with very little heating, that many of their apartments had been looted and that crime rates were soaring. 'It is painful to see the town . . . decaying, which not so long ago was the pride and treasure of our country,' the residents wrote. 'The town has become a refuge for vagabonds, criminals and those on the run . . .'[6] A report on Radio Moscow claimed that standards at the launch-site itself were suffering too with the widespread theft of copper wiring and roofing material. It was even suggested that a communications satellite, known as Gorizont, which crashed into the Pacific soon after its launch in June 1993, failed because its launcher had run out of fuel – the suspicion, according to the report, being that 'someone must have stolen some of it'. Later that year, one hour before the launch of a joint Russian–French space mission, the electrical power supply failed; just after the launch 'the whole town was blacked out'.[7]

More surprising was a report on Russian television on 5 July 1993 about a protest at a city known as Arzamas-16, the once-secret site 250 miles east of Moscow where the first Soviet nuclear weapons were developed by Andrei Sakharov and others. This was a place at which Stalin ordered that no expense should be spared; it was his vehicle for challenging America's nuclear monopoly and it had to succeed. Like most scientific and engineering centres, living standards had long been markedly higher there than in the rest of the country; one Russian acquaintance remembers his uncle, who worked at Arzamas-16, arriving to stay with bags of fruit and cheeses which were never normally available. Now, according to the television bulletin, circumstances at what was the pinnacle of the military research establishment have been reversed. An unnamed official was seen addressing a turbulent crowd of scientists and laboratory workers. He did not mince his words:

'The Russian federal nuclear centre is on the verge of bankruptcy and collapse. Its extremely grave financial and economic situation has led to the point where wages have not been paid for over two months now.'

The television commentary explained that a decree by President Yeltsin authorising the delivery of wages to the city was only valid for the year in which it was issued, 1992. By April 1993, the pay-packets stopped coming. 'To call things by their proper name,' the commentator said, 'the people at this unique scientific centre with world-famous names like Sakharov ... were left to the mercy of fate, abandoned by the central authorities with virtually no means of subsistence.' The scientists have been reduced to living off their personal savings and their kitchen gardens, and many have left to work in private business, the report said.

A similar protest had been held in the same week at another of the secret nuclear cities, Chelyabinsk-70, in the Urals. The Atomic Energy Ministry admitted it was paying its top researchers slightly less than most workers on the Moscow Metro. A government promise several months earlier to double salaries at all scientific institutes had not materialised. 'People are nervous,' said a union leader.[8]

Responses to this sudden decline of the old order are varied. One strand of opinion – of growing significance – wants to fight back and rebuild a formidable Russia. The strong showing of the ultra-nationalist movement in Russia's parliamentary elections in December 1993 is one indication of this; much of the support came from people within the armed forces and the military industries, apparently tired of Yeltsin's supposed surrender of superpower status. In answer, the Russian government has since tried to talk up the prospects of new initiatives in military research and weapon purchases. According to Andrei Kokoshin, the Deputy Defence Minister responsible for long-term weapons projects, tests on a new fighter-bomber, the 1-42, and on an advanced battle tank had been completed during 1993 – despite crippling shortages of money – and work had resumed on a nuclear-powered battleship with the inspiring name of *Peter the Great*. Future projects would include new aircraft technology, high-precision weapons, radio-electronic warfare systems and means of increasing the reliability of Russia's nuclear forces, the minister said, in a move calculated to show that Russian prowess was not dead.[9]

But if nationalist pressure signals the start of a renewed arms race, another reaction to the plight of the military-industrial complex is just as feared in the West. It is that many of the most capable scientists will be tempted by offers to work for Iran, Iraq or other countries. In 1993, the Russian media indeed reported an incident in which the police arrested some thirty nuclear scientists on board an aircraft about to take off for North Korea. A study for NATO,[10] in which dozens of military scientists were interviewed, found at least two prominent aerospace engineers who admitted having received offers of employment in 'Asia' (they would not say where). One had been researching future high-speed jet engines known as scramjets but was now 'idle, disillusioned . . . and becoming ever more angry'; only his 'closeness to his country' led him to turn down the offers to leave. The other scientist, in his thirties, had been studying the next generation of vectored-thrust fighter-planes until he and his colleagues realised they could earn literally twenty times more by using the test aircraft to haul air cargo, 'anything from Snickers candybars into northern Siberia to fresh mutton from Kazakhstan to Moscow'. He too had rejected offers to do research in 'Asia'. But these may be the exceptions; others may already have left, though there has been no confirmation that any have emigrated so far. In an effort to encourage Russia's scientists to stay put, the United States, the European Union and Japan together pledged

$67 million to keep them occupied on non-military projects. The risk of a brain-drain remains high though.

But the most common reaction of Russia's beleaguered military scientists is to strive for ever closer co-operation with the West. 'We should combine our brains and your money,' as one scientific manager put it to me. That is the policy of the Yeltsin government, while committed to encouraging market reforms and free trade with the West, and there is considerable support for it in the scientific establishment. The NATO study found that 'much fewer xenophobic inhibitions appear among these scientists than . . . in other segments of society' and that they are ahead of others in 'their interest in true co-operation with the . . . western world'. But putting that into effect is proving to be easier said than done.

Many scientists, unfamiliar with the practicalities of western business protocol, have found themselves eagerly, and sometimes clumsily, learning the ropes. One tactic to find western commercial partners has been for the Russian defence industries to stage a series of exhibitions in western Europe in which they display a range of declassified technologies which they believe may have a future as civilian products. In June 1993, this show of intriguing inventions and ideas came to the National Exhibition Centre near Birmingham. The makers of the world-famous Kalashnikov assault-rifle, the terrorists' favourite, were offering a new line in hunting guns; an artillery-shell manufacturer had designed a collapsing fishing-rod, which concertinaed into the length of a truncheon; and a specialist in alloy materials for aircraft had brought along nails made of bullet-proof glass, as tough as metal but not as prone to rust.

Even the people whose products were still aimed at the West – in the form of nuclear weapons – were here, suggesting a new approach. Vladimir Barantsev, the chief designer of the St Petersburg Marine Engineering Bureau, was promoting the conversion of his enormous missile-carrying nuclear submarines into underwater cargo liners. He pointed to the hundreds of miniature containers inside a beautifully made model submarine and emphasised how many days' sailing would be saved on journeys between Japan and Europe if the routes under the Arctic could be used instead of those through the Panama or Suez canals. A colleague from the Almaz shipyard in St Petersburg, the export manager Nikolai Shavrov, meanwhile handed out his company's brochure. Adorned with a photograph of the yard's principal product, the world's largest armoured hover-craft, the brochure states clumsily: 'Shipyard also produce room furniture and souvenirs.' An accompanying photograph shows a collection of spindly metal trolleys.

Nikolay Babaev, chief scientific secretary of Minatom, the Russian Atomic Energy Ministry, which provides the radioactive material for Moscow's nuclear warheads, was showing off a toy glider, made of a specially developed lightweight plastic; a gawky figure, with an embarrassed giggle, he failed to prevent the plane veering wildly off course and crashing into the stall displaying underwater components. His colleague, Olga Morozova, the head of Minatom's marketing laboratory, was drawing our attention to a range of CDs, apparently far cheaper than western models, manufactured with the help of lasers originally designed for nuclear research.

As an occasion meant to encourage investment, it was amateur and, for some, humiliating. Visitors were greeted by a cloud of distinctly Russian tobacco smoke. And though the scientists were equipped with freshly printed business cards – bearing their fax and E-mail numbers, like Sergei Atamanov's at Star City – they only too readily admitted that contacting them would never be an easy task, given the unpredictability of the Russian telephones. The PA system used by the folk-singer, a plump woman meant to jolly everyone along, was so loud that nobody in the hall could continue their conversations once she had started. The industries' stands were like tatty fairground stalls with coloured lights and clumsily drawn pictures. And questions about prices and production costs – crucial for any would-be western investor – were met with vagueness, even flippancy.

Yet this search for new funding is seen as vital work, to keep alive Russian military science and to achieve a more political objective as well. Many Russian scientists see international business partnerships as a fundamental way of cementing Russia's place in the community of democratic nations. In part, this is to guarantee their country's position inside the capitalist camp as a hedge against the emergence of a new Communist or nationalist government. But the idea also has the merit of appealing to the political idealism apparent among many scientists. From their logical and sometimes politically naïve perspective, they argue that global problems need to be solved by global co-operation, even by a global government, notwithstanding the pressures of national domestic politics. According to this view,

73

nuclear proliferation is the most pressing example of a problem that can only be tackled with international co-operation. And to ensure that Russia remains well shielded, many see a shared defensive system with the West as the only answer.

The clearest statement of this argument comes in an internal Russian scientific working paper. 'Members of the world community,' it declares, 'cannot fully provide their own national security.' With the world at risk from ecological damage, climate change and nuclear war, the paper says, a new system of international security is required to observe the actions of individual nations, to 'foresee likely dangers' and 'to adopt necessary measures in time'. It is a blueprint for the United Nations to act as a benevolent Big Brother on a global scale. The paper grudgingly acknowledges current political realities – such as the evident lack of enthusiasm of nation-states to surrender their sovereign powers – by noting rather stiffly that 'all the necessary conditions' for this world-wide spy-in-the-sky 'have not yet taken shape'. Yet it says the time is right to propose this global system none the less. The document calls for the establishment of a network of shared satellites in which American, Russian and European intelligence gathered from space would be pooled for everyone's mutual benefit. The satellites would monitor the chopping down of forests, the construction of nuclear power plants, preparations for war and – above all – the deployment of nuclear weapons. Since any one of these acts could affect the entire planet, 'the world community must be kept informed' and any 'covering-up of such information' declared a crime against humanity. This is important, says the paper, 'from a moral point of view'.

Written early in 1992 by four military computer scientists, led by Nikita Moiseev, the document has served as one of the most influential testimonials in favour of adopting co-operation as the best policy with which to save Russian military science. It was circulated within the Russian Academy of Science, senior levels in the armed forces and President Yeltsin's inner circle of advisers. But its motives are not as purely 'moral' as the authors claim. The paper argues that with the space industry – the mainstay of Russian security – 'on the brink of catastrophe', and other key industries in a similar state, Russia is in danger of becoming 'a third-rate country without real levers of influence on the world'. The 'optimum means . . . of rescue' lie in a reorientation of the country towards international co-operation, a decision which the authors accept will be 'difficult'.

Carrying out this suggestion would require 'courage and decisiveness from our political leadership'.

In its nine pages of densely typed text, the document obscures a tangle of conflicting views, which only become clear in conversation with the authors. After long years employed in the business of preparing to fight and, if necessary, to obliterate the western democracies, Moiseev and his colleagues – Yevgeni Pavlovsky, V. N. Tsigichko and K. B. Cherevkov – now seem to feel a sense of shame about having worked in support of the Communist regime. Their call for a global defence system, harnessing the best of the Russian military advances, may be a way of appeasing that guilt. At the same time, they state that the proliferation of nuclear weapons and the ballistic missiles to carry them demands urgent attention, especially since many of the countries most eager to acquire these capabilities lie along Russia's southern borders; a co-operative international system would be likely to be more effective in combating that threat, given Russia's economic plight. In addition, the scientists know Russian pride and security are at risk if there are insufficient funds to continue research in space while American efforts in that direction show far less sign of restraint.

One of the authors, Yevgeni Pavlovsky, has seen firsthand the implications of the United States emerging as the only competitor in the space race. His conclusion, shared by his colleagues in their paper, is that America could easily end up enjoying a 'total monopoly' in space and that this 'supremacy', in malign hands, could lead to 'the establishment of a pan-American world'. Under the guidance of Nikita Moiseev, Pavlovsky had been commissioned by the then Soviet Ministry of Defence to devise a computer model of the latest American Star Wars plan. The general staff wanted to see how well the plan might work and what it might mean for their own strategies.

They asked Pavlovsky to simulate not the first, wild schemes touted by Ronald Reagan's advisers for laser battle-stations in space which were supposed effortlessly to vaporise thousands of ICBMs; nor the similarly improbable vision promoted by Edward Teller of a single X-ray laser, the size of a standard office desk, allegedly able to destroy the Soviet force of land-based ballistic missiles with sudden highly accurate death-rays. The Soviet generals instead wanted an urgent analysis of the latest scheme known as 'Brilliant Pebbles', revealed in the late 1980s. Under this plan, 1,000 tiny American rockets would orbit the earth, ready to pounce at extremely high speed on any enemy missiles seen taking off beneath them. The rockets were dubbed 'brilliant' because they were to be equipped with highly capable miniature computers to help them steer themselves towards their targets; 'pebbles' because they would carry no explosive, instead inflicting damage by 'hitting-to-kill', using the kinetic energy generated by great speed to destroy the enemy weapons as they climbed towards space on their way towards America. The idea, another favourite of Teller's, was never popular with the United States Congress and was frozen when Bill Clinton became President (it was always seen as a Republican Party favourite). Yet it was evidently given credence in Moscow and, even now, the project is regarded as shelved rather than dead.

Pavlovsky, thin, earnest, with an uncontrolled grey beard and a penchant for open-toed sandals even in wet weather, set to work simulating Brilliant Pebbles in his office in the Institute of Cybernetics, equipped with half a dozen computers and a handful of staff. Though important work, it was not well funded and it was no surprise, when I visited Pavlovsky in June 1992, to find that the corridors of the institute lacked light bulbs and that the entryphone at his office door was broken. The door itself was locked as a security measure and my interpreter had to shout to get a response. Inside, amid full ashtrays, several pin-ups and glossy western computer brochures buried in mounds of flimsy Russian paperwork, it was hard to imagine this as the scene of an assessment of one of the boldest high-technology schemes yet conceived. But, when the key terminal was switched on and the first lists of technical data appeared on the screen, it was evident that this project had been accorded special help.

As line after line of intense detail appeared about the Brilliant Pebbles – missile weight, engine weight, fuel-consumption rate, fuel weight, speed, height of orbit – I asked where all this information had come from. Was it all openly available? Not exactly, Pavlovsky replied. I pressed on: did the KGB help get some of it for you? He chuckled: them and others. Presumably he meant the GRU, the military intelligence organisation. There was certainly far more detail here than has ever been published in open American literature. But whatever the sources of the information, when integrated into Pavlovsky's computer model, the data produced results that convinced the scientists that the Brilliant Pebbles scheme could work.

'It gives completely new qualities and possibilities, vitally influencing the geo-political situation,' he said. He showed me what he meant, his fingers darting over his computer keyboard.

He called up a crude map of the northern hemisphere. Brilliant Pebbles, like stars, were hovering in orbit; lines radiating from each one marked the area of ground monitored by its sensors.

A tiny red rocket took off from the general area of Russia and rose into space on its way towards the United States.

'This is an examination of a realistic attack . . .' Pavlovsky began a running commentary, hitting keys to trigger each stage.

'As you can see we are flying.' The view on the screen was as if we were sitting atop the spacecraft holding a Brilliant Pebble. The rocket was launched to attempt an interception. A table to one side of the screen displayed the relevant information.

'You can see the expected time of the completion of the attack, the current time, the current distance, the approach, the speed of approach . . . how much fuel there is on board. The blue background is the earth.

'We are approaching, there are only five seconds left, four, three, two, one second left and – a successful impact is taking place.'

Nothing much happened, except that the Russian rocket vanished. But the point was made: Pavlovsky believed the Brilliant Pebbles scheme could work and that, if it was ever built and deployed, it could put Russia at a major disadvantage.

As he and his co-authors concluded in their document, the uncontrolled deployment of this system could allow America to obtain 'sole possession of space' and that this would cause 'justifiable concern and opposition' in Russia and other countries as well. For advocates of the American Strategic Defence Initiative, who have long claimed that it was SDI that broke the Soviet back, this conclusion could be used to help justify their case. It would also explain the Russians' enthusiasm for developing a combined security system: that the safest option is to promote a network of reconnaissance satellites and Brilliant Pebbles under strict international – not just American – control. Whatever other motive there may be for Russian involvement as a contributing partner, such a step would help ensure that America did not take advantage of Russia's current weakness.

Pavlovsky explained how the two countries could co-operate and what Moscow had to offer. First, Russian rockets, widely accepted as reliable and relatively cheap, could be used to launch the weapons and sensors needed for the co-operative defence scheme. The cost of launching all the necessary equipment with the American Shuttle would be exorbitant, probably prohibitive. Second, sharing information from both countries' early warning satellites would expand their coverage of the globe to their mutual advantage. Third, there would be circumstances when both sides may well be better defended under a mutual system. A Russian reconnaissance satellite may be better placed than an American one to detect an attack on Europe. Or an attack on Russia may be more effectively intercepted by an American Brilliant Pebble than by any other system. With another flurry of keystrokes, Pavlovsky showed me how.

His screen displayed a map of Russia's southern flank. A small red rocket, similar to the one in the last scenario, took off from the area of Iraq and flew north for Moscow. A Brilliant Pebble, poised in orbit over the Mediterranean, had the missile in its sights, flew off and destroyed it. Russia was saved. 'You see, we can work together, you must believe us.'

President Yeltsin certainly believed them. Soon after his rise to power, following the *coup* attempt in August 1991, he was briefed by his chief scientific adviser, Academician Yevgeni Velikhov, and his senior military adviser, Colonel-General Dmitri Volkogonov, on the results of this and other work. His conclusion was that co-operation in missile defence should be a cornerstone of his new relationship with the United States. He was convinced that this would represent a revolution in the nuclear strategy which had set the two countries against each other for the previous half-century. Quite what swayed Yeltsin is not known, whether it was the argument that western funding was essential to save Russian science or that the American Brilliant Pebbles plan would leave Russia hopelessly vulnerable or that the country's best defence against rogue nuclear missiles would be a co-operative one. Or, as Velikhov put it to me in an interview, that the 'main objective is to really change . . . our behaviour as adversaries to the behaviour of allies'. (Velikhov, long an ardent critic of the American Strategic Defence Initiative, was now so eager to achieve a deep level of co-operation that he took to wearing an SDI tie.) Perhaps each or all of these factors was seen to have merit.

Either way, Boris Yeltsin wanted to pursue the plan with vigour; and his counterpart at that time, George Bush, was willing as well. The idea was first discussed in outline terms by the two leaders at Camp David in January 1992 – within one month of the demise of the Soviet Union – and firm agreement came on 17 June 1992 at the Russian–American summit in Washington. Though that day was dominated by the signing of the START-2 treaty, imposing deep cuts in both countries' strategic nuclear arsenals, the two leaders also signed a joint statement announcing a commitment to work together on a 'Global Protection System' to counter the threat of nuclear proliferation. It would be 'tangible expression of the new relationship'. The statement promised expert work would start 'without delay' on examining the potential for sharing early warning information, for co-operating on ballistic-missile defence technologies and for considering the legal basis of these developments. At a joint news conference later, President Bush summed up his view of the agreement: 'There's good science, good technology on both sides, and we're determined to work together on this global defence area.'

Even before the accord, scientists on the Russian side engaged in developing future missile defence technologies were already opening their doors, such was their enthusiasm. At the Kurchatov Institute in Moscow, which had been established in 1943 as 'Laboratory Number 2' to design the first Soviet nuclear bombs, a public relations official was appointed to look after foreign visitors to this normally secret installation; I was one of the first journalists to take advantage. We arrived at the institute's main gate, heavy snow gusting past a large, forbidding bust of Igor Kurchatov, 'father' of the Soviet atom bomb. Once past the security men guarding the compound, we were led through battered metal doors into one of the largest of the site's 300 buildings, the electronics department, and asked to don white overalls. It was hard to see the point: by now accustomed to the barely lit gloom of these establishments, I could tell that the garments were not especially clean. Yet our reception was warm. From within a group of nervously grinning scientists, a tall man with an honest expression and a flash of gold teeth emerged and introduced himself as one of the institute's senior scientists and leader of work on the global defence project. Nikolai Ponomarev-Stepnoi spoke articulately and passionately in favour of burying the Cold War by sharing each side's advances in the cause of co-operative defence. Russia had much to offer, he said.

In the course of a long day, picking our way through the slush that lay between the various laboratories, we were shown a sample of potentially useful technologies. In one grand but decrepit building reminiscent of a steam-engine museum, its cavernous red-brick halls filled with vast machines, a frighteningly clumsy array of electric cables surrounded a huge vacuum chamber. Inside the chamber, visible through a port-hole, was a pale-blue circle of light like a gas-ring on a cooker. This was an electric plasma motor for steering spacecraft, at least a decade ahead of its American equivalent and far more efficient than the more usual rocket-motors which are powered by fuel. But with string holding apart some of the cables, and covers that did not appear to fit properly over the equipment, it was hard to see how the research could survive much longer, without endangering those running it.

More elegant – though no less hazardous – was a minutely engineered device for focusing laser beams. In the optics department, an eager group of scientists huddled around a workbench preparing a demonstration. The problem with laser weapons, they said, is that the beam can easily be diffused in the atmosphere; unless it is accurately focused on to an area the size of a pinhead, it will not deliver sufficient energy to do any damage to the target. Their device, a bundle of tiny glass straws tapering to a sharp point, was meant to achieve that. They powered up a small laser and a red beam as thick as a pencil shone across the room; a piece of paper held in its path was left unscarred, the beam too diffuse to have any effect. One of the scientists then picked up the device, the size of an average torch, and lowered it into the beam. It glowed red. The light was passing through the straws – hundreds of them, tightly packed – each of which was guiding a part of the beam towards a central point; the tip of the bundle, now the focus of an extremely narrow shaft of laser light, had become unbearably bright. This time, paper held in the beam's path soon caught fire.

'Could you use this technique to shoot down incoming missiles?' I asked.

'Sure,' replied the project leader, 'if we get the money to work on it.' He was hopeful of securing funding from the Pentagon. It would be an ideal example of co-operation, he said: Russian technology to enable American lasers to defeat weapons that threatened both countries.

Wherever we went, the scientists' conversation followed a similar path: expressing confidence in their technologies and doubt over their ability to continue. It was understandable. Money was in desperately short supply and savings were having to be made in the most basic areas. Even in 'Building 109', the main experimental nuclear-reactor complex, I found that the lavatory reserved for the senior staff lacked toilet paper (old laboratory documents and copies of *Pravda* were offered instead) and the basin had no hot water, soap or towel. 'How could we afford them?' asked Yevgeni Ryzantev, the research director, with an air of despair. At least the digital Geiger counter positioned over the front door, to warn the rest of the institute of radiation leaks, was known to be working. But salaries were barely keeping up with inflation, he said. A rise from 800 roubles a month in October 1991 to 4,000 roubles a month in February 1992 was hardly enough to cope with the collapse in the currency's value against the dollar. 'We'd earn more driving taxis,' he said.

It was hoped that the agreement with the United States on a Global Protection System would provide new channels of funding. Besides becoming more open, the Kurchatov Institute changed its name to 'Russian Science Centre', offering a less overtly military image as an encouragement to western investment. A brochure was printed, playing down the institute's role in the nuclear arms race and emphasising its potential for helping create the new, collective defence system envisaged by Moscow and Washington.

The Bush–Yeltsin agreement was seen as a vital if modest beginning by Nikita Moiseev and his colleagues. It was not to be as rapid or as radical a process as they wanted, nor as wide-ranging, since there was no commitment to involve the United Nations, but it was a start none the less. As I left Moiseev's dacha, two days after the Washington summit, discussion of the summit's progress seemed to have cheered him up. He even managed a few jokes with the film crew and, when he saw my Mitsubishi hire car, he insisted on being allowed to drive it. It would be an experience of the western technology which Russia would be able to share as part of the newly agreed co-operation, he said. In the driver's seat, he was impressed by the number of controls, the level of gadgetry. He found first gear and, with a lurch, set off, evidently more used to the acceleration of his old Lada. He stalled at the end of the lane, while trying to turn round. The gear box crunched; the headlights, indicators and windscreen-wipers all came to life at different times as Moiseev fumbled for the right controls. When he returned the car to me, there were beads of sweat on his forehead and his customary, unhappy expression had returned. I could not help thinking that co-operation might not be as straightforward as the Russians imagined.

4

A SHARED SHIELD

In your face, from outer space.
General Chuck Horner, Commander-in-Chief of US Space
Command, on his plans for missile defence

On a free morning during his first visit to Moscow, Gregory Canavan
decided to stroll from his hotel to Red Square. It was summer and
Canavan, a tall, courteous American with a handsome, smiling face,
was curious to explore a city he had studied for much of his professional life but had never had the chance to see for himself. It was
1992 and the Bush–Yeltsin summit in June that year had inspired
new hope that a more stable relationship between the two nuclear
giants might ensue. Canavan took his time – looking into shops,
studying the Muscovites' faces and clothes, struggling with little
Russian to buy a soft drink – soaking up the details of a society
which until then he had only considered in the abstract. In a flea
market beside one of the railway stations, he was shocked to find
evidence of poverty, people 'trading meats and fruits and vegetables
to eat that you wouldn't hold in your hand'. But his most 'wrenching'
experience was to come.

Canavan reached Red Square and wandered across it, enjoying the
splendour of the onion-domes of St Basil's and the massive walls of
the Kremlin. He found himself drawn towards Lenin's Mausoleum
when, suddenly, he was struck by the significance of where he was
heading.

'A thought just sort of came to me out of nowhere: I mean, this is
DGZ-1 . . .'

DGZ-1 stands for 'Desired Ground Zero – One', the desired impact point of the first nuclear weapon to be launched in an American
strike. Canavan – former US Air Force target planner, protégé of

Edward Teller, leading light behind Brilliant Pebbles and senior figure at Los Alamos – was standing on the very spot he himself had once designated as the first to be destroyed in a nuclear war. The irony of his position did not escape him. Few military scientists have proved as influential as Canavan in the long-running debate on America's policies on nuclear weapons and missile defences: from the 1970s to the present.

'You'd always try to take out the mausoleum, see how well you could do it,' he told me later, grinning, with embarrassment rather than pride at the memory of his various schemes for obliterating Moscow. Canavan had at one stage been involved in designing the Pentagon's Single Integrated Operational Plan (SIOP), the top-secret list of targets to be hit in a nuclear war. The plan specifies the order in which the various targets are to be attacked and the types and explosive yields of the weapons to be used against them. To ensure that the key political and military installations in the Moscow area would be destroyed, and all normal forms of government brought to a halt, Canavan and his colleagues had decided to aim their warheads at the main road junctions in the city. 'We must have had hundreds set for those intersections,' he said. The skill of the war-plan lay in avoiding so-called fratricide, the problem of one blast negating the effect of another (Nikita Moiseev had analysed the same problem from Moscow's perspective). The key was timing, co-ordinating the arrival of the weapons to the nearest second, calculating how to wreak the greatest havoc in the shortest possible time to minimise the risk of the other side organising its retaliation. Lenin's Mausoleum, as the central symbol of the Soviet state, was apparently always assigned at least one warhead in every version of the SIOP – and Canavan was standing right by it.

The irony of Canavan's presence at DGZ-1 was all the greater because of the purpose of his visit to Moscow. He had arrived to take part in the first discussions about implementing the Bush–Yeltsin agreement on a Global Protection System, a shared anti-missile defence which was meant to make Moscow and Washington safe from attacks of the sort that he himself had contemplated while in the Pentagon. The agreement had established a series of joint working parties to examine different aspects of the plan and that meant bringing together experts whose lives until then had been devoted to the other side's defeat. For Canavan and his American colleagues, it would require a revolution in thinking to begin to regard Russia as a 'long-term ally like Britain and France . . . not just a collection of people we've treated as targets for the last seventy years'.

Among those that Canavan met were Yeltsin's scientific adviser, Yevgeni Velikhov, and the two computer modellers, Nikita Moiseev and Yevgeni Pavlovsky. He was well known to them as one of the architects of America's Star Wars plans. It was also public knowledge that Canavan had long been close to Edward Teller and that Teller respected the younger man's frankness and intelligence; it added to Canavan's reputation in Moscow. To some, if Teller was the father of Star Wars, then Canavan was one of its sons and the Russians accordingly expected him to play a prominent role in the discussions; he was indeed to do so, but not in the way his hosts might have hoped. It was soon to emerge that America's idea of a co-operative defence system – Canavan's in particular – was very different from Russia's. The concept of 'sharing' the early warning information and special technologies needed for a combined shield would not mean the same to both countries; Canavan would, in part, be responsible for that.

Canavan is 'pure hawk', according to one critic of America's nuclear weapons laboratories. His involvement in the nuclear debate and the parallel arguments over a possible shield against nuclear attack began in the US Air Force. He rose to the rank of colonel, after a career that had involved him in some of the pivotal nuclear planning decisions of the 1970s – whether to invest in new bombers, what type of nuclear missiles to design. Canavan then left the service and moved to Los Alamos. There he continued work of a similar kind, eventually securing a post with the deliberately vague title of 'Director of Advanced Concepts'. It was a free rein to explore new directions in weapons and strategy. Regarded as one of the most innovative military thinkers in the country – 'he's just very, very smart', according to one of his colleagues – he churns out papers and gives interviews on everything from Star Wars to the future of American military research to the difficulties of achieving accuracy in conventional warfare.

But his focus is on missile defence: 'If weapons of mass destruction fall into shithead hands, that threat could undermine us all.' He sees the future of this problem as being simultaneously 'horrible and wonderful'. Horrible, he says, if you need to find a solution overnight; wonderful if you can look a decade ahead and spend wisely now. The difficulty, he points out though, is that the latter course is unlikely to be adopted. The pressure of the democratic cycle forces decision-makers to take a short-term view; 'we didn't get the technologies we have now through luck, it took a long-term view some time back'. His innate optimism – one author describes him as having 'an all-American can-do kind of attitude' – is therefore tempered by pessimism about the foresight of his political masters.

Canavan is in constant demand, on the move from his home in Santa Fe near the Los Alamos laboratory to Washington, Europe and now Russia as well. His well-cut suit, regulation blue shirt with button-down collar and fashionably patterned tie give him the look of a senior executive; nothing betrays the horror of his particular trade. In the Los Alamos canteen – a bright, informal room with spectacular views over the New Mexico mountains – his dress sense marks him out among his colleagues, most of whom, in the casual atmosphere of this scientific eyrie, prefer to wear jeans and lumber-jack shirts. At the same time, he is unfailingly down-to-earth. As he guided me through the complexities of the various food counters – vegetarian, grill, New Mexican, salad – he chatted as amiably as one can about the Gulf War and the *coup* attempt in Moscow in August 1991, and never seemed to tire of questions that touched on classified areas and forced him to pick a guarded response.

One of Canavan's most notable achievements was to help change the course of America's Star Wars research – and make it of such compelling interest to the Russians. At the launch of his Strategic Defence Initiative on 23 March 1983, Ronald Reagan had conjured up a grand vision. He had called upon the scientists who invented nuclear weapons, 'to turn their great talents now to the cause of mankind and world peace, to give us the means of rendering these nuclear weapons impotent and obsolete'. This was to be achieved by research into a 'security shield that would destroy nuclear missiles before they reach their targets'. His dream summoned up images of futuristic technologies, death-rays hurtling across thousands of miles of space to defend America. Within days of his speech, the catchline 'Star Wars' had become lodged in the public mind.

Answering that call from the President became a Republican Party cause, something of a touchstone of loyalty to the United States and to the fight against Communism. Dissent was squashed. Even the first in-depth scientific investigation by the Pentagon, which produced twelve volumes of profound scepticism about the likelihood of a foolproof anti-missile screen ever working, was suppressed, and still remains classified. It became politically incorrect within the military research establishments to raise objections to the feasibility of this new crusade. One senior scientist, Roger Hagengruber of Sandia laboratory in Albuquerque, New Mexico, remembers being 'taken to task in a rather vicious way' by a congressman for displaying a view-graph which showed that even the most limited space defence system would require far more Shuttle flights than could ever be reasonably expected to be mounted. The congressman had implied that 'you should never show a view-graph like that, whether it's right or wrong, because to show it would create pessimism about SDI'.[1] Politics was riding roughshod over science and the effect, in the rush to meet the President's challenge, was that any positive ideas, however improbable, were seized upon. The weapons laboratories, suddenly awash with new funding, experienced a gold-rush hunt for almost any technologies that might conceivably be relevant.

'The clock was running,' says Canavan, 'and we just desperately worked on whatever we could, through Excimer lasers, X-ray lasers, chemical lasers in space, through particle beams.' In simulation form, in the sophisticated graphics offered to the television networks, these wonder-weapons effortlessly destroyed hordes of Soviet missiles. But in practice none showed any realistic promise. Some of the devices worked – but only in the laboratory. Most would be too heavy to deliver into space. And all of them, being large, would be conspicuous and therefore vulnerable to pre-emptive attack by the Soviet Union. Most seriously for a project dependent on high-profile patronage, none of these potential weapons had the slightest chance of being ready quickly enough to maintain political support in Congress (which was paying the bills).

'After the first few years of thrashing around,' says Canavan, 'people started really getting nervous and very worried. They knew that we couldn't just keep running a four-billion-dollar-a-year research programme indefinitely – that sooner or later Congress would find out and close us down. So a lot of pressure started developing for an early deployment of something, some kind of defences – chemical lasers, some kind of rockets, whatever.'

In their desperation, the most ardent Star War advocates – by now dubbed 'Star Warriors' – adopted two different tactics. One was to latch on to any technology, however simple, that might actually work. The other was to cheat. In one notorious test of a laser staged for the television cameras, a booster section of an old Titan missile was fixed to the New Mexico desert, zapped with a beam of light and destroyed. It looked like a triumphant example of science fiction becoming reality. But critics, led by John Pike of the Federation of American Scientists, later argued that the test was not as honest as it seemed. Pike, who studied a video-recording of the test in slow motion, pointed out that the rocket had been tied down with cables and that a heavy crossbar had been placed across its top. Although the laser did successfully blast a hole in the side of the rocket, it was not the cause of the rocket's demise. The shattered parts of the rocket, rather than hurtling outwards as might be expected in an explosion, in fact flew down towards the ground; the cables had been pulling down on the crossbar and, in turn, that was crushing the rocket. According to Pike, 'You're not seeing a booster being blown up by a laser, you're seeing an old rocket carcass being crushed by some cables and steel bars.'

Another trick involved faking an interception. A project known as the Homing Overlay Experiment was rigged to improve the results, not least because the Soviet Union was known to be monitoring it closely. Officials, who were desperate to prove that it was technically feasible to destroy an incoming ballistic missile, feared that a miss would prove politically damaging. Their solution was to pack explosives into the target missile and, with a proximity fuse, set them to detonate as the interceptor drew close: a near-miss could then have the appearance of a successful hit. The stratagem, however, was to no avail. In the first three tests, the interceptor not only missed the incoming missile but also failed even to get close enough to trigger the explosives. A fourth test in the series, scheduled for June 1984, was cancelled, but the details – and the Pentagon's confession – only emerged nine years later.

More serious was the hyping of the proposal for an X-ray laser weapon, given the enticing codename of Excalibur. This was to form the backbone of Star Wars. The idea was that in a moment of crisis, an American missile would rapidly carry into space what was in effect a nuclear bomb bristling with X-ray lasers. As Soviet missiles were launched towards America, the device would explode, sending finely focused, deadly X-ray beams towards the incoming weapons. Edward Teller claimed that a single X-ray laser could destroy tens of thousands of warheads. He talked of this 'amazing new device' and said he had 'more and more hope that it will actually work'.

The effect was that the Reagan administration continued to have faith in the X-ray project – for a few years at least – and even an ever-sceptical Congress continued to fund it until 1991.

Yet behind the scenes, there was a growing acknowledgement that the claims for the X-ray laser were wildly inflated. Doubts surfaced about whether it was possible to focus the beams accurately enough and even whether adequate measurements of the effects of the device could ever be made. Since the research was being conducted by the Lawrence Livermore laboratory, which had been established after the Second World War as a rival to Los Alamos, scientists at the older establishment lost no time in pouring scorn on their competitor's boasts. Some thought the X-ray weapon required so much testing that it might not be available for at least a century. One official working for the Department of Energy, which is responsible for nuclear weapons, observed that 'to get from the understanding of physics to a weapon is perhaps a much bigger job than Dr Teller thought'.[2] Eventually, the truth about what had been a highly secret project became known and political support for it waned. The result was that within three years of the launch of the Strategic Defence Initiative, the scheme's main advocates were bereft of a central solution to the President's call. The so-called 'exotic' weapons invoked in the original initiative were to remain distant dreams. But the political bandwagon was rolling and the White House was demanding a credible solution now.

The answer came over breakfast, in November 1986, and has been credited to Gregory Canavan. He, Teller and another Star Warrior, Lowell Wood, were meeting in the Hyatt Hotel in Cambridge, Massachusetts. Though Teller was at that stage still committed to the vision of the X-ray laser – in public at least – all three were aware that a more mundane scheme would have to be developed if the initiative was to survive. By then, Lawrence Livermore scientists had proposed deploying 'smart rocks' in space, rockets that would guide themselves towards the incoming missiles and use the force of their kinetic energy to defeat them. The idea had developed – and its name changed – into Brilliant Pebbles. But with the SDI programme still heavily committed to laser weapons, these less glamorous and more rudimentary devices had been shunned. Until now.

One of the main objections to Brilliant Pebbles had been that they would be too vulnerable to Soviet attack. They would have to orbit at relatively low altitude and could easily be shot down. At least that was the opinion of Teller – and without his support, this project would never attract the level of funding needed to develop it. That November morning though, he was swayed by Canavan. Canavan argued that Brilliant Pebbles would be intelligent enough to look after themselves, small enough to be hard to detect and cheap enough to deploy in huge numbers. The Soviet Union would never be able to find and destroy them all. In short, they would be survivable. That proved to be a key word.

'As soon as I said "survivable", Teller got interested,' Canavan recalls.[3] The breakfast led to a new flurry of highly secret research and a massive shift in policy. Brilliant Pebbles became the chosen weapon – though still in secret. Only later, in an article written jointly by Canavan and Teller, was the basis of Canavan's persuasive reasoning revealed.[4] Brilliant Pebbles could be helped to survive, the article says, with three techniques. Hardening – building the interceptors with tough skins and robust electronics – would resist some forms of attack. Manoeuvre would allow the interceptors to dodge an attack. And the rapid use of decoys would confuse any attacker and further improve the chances of the Brilliant Pebbles enduring unscathed and still able to perform. These three characteristics, combined in an interceptor costing an estimated $6 million, offer 'a reasonable chance of providing a significant defence', the article claimed. The Star Wars lobby was won over, and so was the White House.

In March 1988, less than eighteen months after Canavan's pitch at the breakfast table and on the fifth anniversary of the launch of Star Wars, Ronald Reagan announced what amounted to a revision to his grand plan. Brilliant Pebbles were to be the promise of safety from Soviet attack; lasers were quietly moved to a much lower position on the agenda. George Bush, when he became President in the following year, continued to support the concept. But he introduced one important change. SDI would be scaled back and – though this was never admitted officially – would no longer seek to achieve the improbable goal of providing America with a shield against an all-out Soviet missile attack; such a task was not only looking unattainable but also, with the advent of Mikhail Gorbachev, unnecessary as well. Instead, Brilliant Pebbles were to perform the more limited role of guarding against attacks by handfuls of rockets either launched accidentally or by maverick regimes with small numbers of nuclear missiles – a scheme known as Global

Protection Against Limited Strikes (GPALS – pronounced 'gee-pals'). One thousand of the interceptors, assisted by ever-vigilant satellites known as Brilliant Eyes, were to be sent into orbit, a space-age counter to nuclear proliferation.

The shift in policy was scrutinised closely by other countries, especially the Russians. As soon as the first details of this plan became available – by fair means or foul – the information found its way to Moscow and into the computers of the Institute of Cybernetics. There, Nikita Moiseev and his colleagues began the calculations that eventually led them to conclude that this latest version of Star Wars might actually work. Their sums showed that Brilliant Pebbles could provide a viable defence system and that Russia needed to co-operate with the plan – or be disadvantaged by it.

Yet President Bush needed to win Russian co-operation as well. The plan for Brilliant Pebbles depended on it. The Anti-Ballistic Missile (ABM) Treaty of 1972, signed by Washington and Moscow, had imposed strict limits on the size and type of missile defences allowed by each side. For example, one clause specified that only 100 ABM interceptors could be fielded in each country. But another clause in the treaty was to become far more significant: the rule prohibiting the deployment of any weapons in space. At the time of the accord, both countries saw merit in keeping the heavens free of arms; the consequences of a space war were unimaginably terrible. Now, however, Washington viewed the case differently. It wanted to persuade Moscow to relent on this particular clause; it argued that it should be allowed to send its Brilliant Pebbles into space.

The collapse of the Soviet Union provided a new opportunity for the United States to try to change the key part of the treaty. Washington argued that the end of the Cold War meant that both countries faced common threats – and that the tough provisions of the ABM Treaty were preventing them from building an effective defence against rogue states. When George Bush and Boris Yeltsin signed their agreement in June 1992 to share a Global Protection System, American motives were not entirely altruistic. In addition to the parts of the accord that dealt with pooling early warning information and technology, the United States side inserted a clause calling for relevant treaties to be examined and possibly revised too. It was Washington's attempt to alter or ditch the ABM Treaty. The result was that the agreement amounted to a trade-off of vague promises. In theory, both sides were to get what they most wanted:

satellite reconnaissance data, micro-electronics and a finger on the Star Wars trigger for the Russians; approval to deploy weapons in space for the Americans.

Both countries were to be disappointed: their objectives were too different. For the Russians in particular, the dream of sharing expertise for a common goal soon turned sour.

On a crisp autumn morning, before the desert sun had grown warm, I was ushered into a gleaming laboratory in the New Mexico Engineering Research Institute in Albuquerque. It was a building typical of America's greenbelt high-tech industries: skylights, huge plants and tinted glass. Except that the first voices we heard were Russian. In one corner of the laboratory, a figure in blue overalls was busy unwrapping a loaf of rye bread from a copy of *Pravda*; in another, two others were chatting in Russian beside the coffee machine. Other men were collecting their tools, donning hard hats adorned with the American and Russian flags, as they prepared to start another day's work. They were nuclear scientists from St Petersburg. Two dozen of them were here in all – in the middle of the state that was the birthplace of America's first secret atomic weapons. It was hard to believe the sight.

In late 1992, the Russians had brought with them a unique invention, a miniature nuclear reactor called Topaz 2. The device, the size of a small lorry, had been air-freighted from their institute and the scientists were now busy assembling it. Another reactor was to follow. The client was the US Air Force and the objective was to improve the reactor so that it could provide long-term power for Star Wars satellites in space. It was an extraordinary deal. In exchange for $13 million – a pittance compared to an American military budget then running at over $300 billion – the Pentagon was buying Russian know-how developed in the greatest secrecy over the previous twenty-three years. For the Americans, who had followed a different and less successful technological route in pursuit of mini-reactors, it was a bargain. 'We've done really, really well,' one SDI official told me privately, 'but we oughtn't to say that too loud.'

The chief American scientist, Frank Thome, a gentle figure whose shyness belies the determination that saw the deal through, was surprised by the degree of Russian ingenuity in Topaz. 'It's beautiful, very sophisticated.' One of his fears had been that the first close examination would reveal a host of safety problems; the accident at the Chernobyl nuclear power station had raised serious questions about Russian standards. But the Russians 'had done their homework on this' and the Americans could not fault their technology.

According to Thome, the deal saves America several billion dollars in original research. Yet he saw another benefit as well: one in which science has an overtly political role. The Topaz deal, by keeping Russian scientists employed and by injecting hard currency into the Russian economy, would ease the transition from the Communist system to capitalism. 'We're trying to help transition them through that,' he said. 'This programme will help keep a lid on this explosive situation', and prevent 'a return to the old ways'. Thome acknowledged that the deal might antagonise hardliners opposed to co-operation with the West. But he refused to be drawn when I suggested that, in some Russian eyes, the deal would represent not only a sell-out of precious secrets but also acquiescence in foreign intervention in Moscow's internal affairs. On camera, with the Russian scientists nearby, he preferred to be diplomatic and to avoid the question. It was clear that he and his American colleagues understood the project's sensitivity.

For the Russians, the sale represented a mixture of pragmatism and idealism. It was a vital source of hard currency finance and the start of what was meant to be a long-term relationship to bury the Cold War. The initiative for the deal had come from one of the senior figures of the Kurchatov Institute in Moscow, Nikolai Ponomarev-Stepnoi, an ardent supporter of plans to co-operate on a missile shield. It had taken him months to obtain permission to sell Topaz. He had had to endure open hostility from several officials who felt he was surrendering one of Russia's few technological advantages over America. Eventually, however, to his delight, a US Air Force transport plane was authorised to fly to St Petersburg to fetch the crates containing the components of the reactor. The scientists soon followed.

One of the team was Ponomarev-Stepnoi's own daughter, Masha, a specialist in computer-aided design. Her task was to convert the Russians' hand-drawn blueprints of Topaz into computer form. She loved the work and adored the chance to be in America; as with the rest of the team, she was paid an average American wage for her three months on the project, far more than her salary back in Russia. A lively woman in her early thirties, she spoke warmly about the prospects for a new partnership between the old adversaries. 'Before Topaz we were like enemies ... now we become friends and never fight each other again.' She was all too aware of the obstacles raised in an attempt to block the project. It had imposed a severe personal strain on her father and his colleagues. 'Many of them became ill,' she said, 'but it seems to me that when Topaz is here everything is all right.'

The Topaz deal proved successful. The scientists felt they were pioneers in a new era, and they grew close. Frank Thome's son once stayed with the family of one of his counterparts in Moscow; gifts and jokes were regularly exchanged. At a social event in a cowboy-style restaurant in Albuquerque, where the Country and Western music is loud and everyone is asked to wear an appropriate hat or scarf, the Russians gradually unwound. Their feet soon tapped to the beat, the hugs and handshakes with their American colleagues became more effusive. There was an air of sincerity about the constant references to barriers being broken down. For the Russians, perhaps more prone to display their emotions, it was the beginning of their rehabilitation in international science.

The deal was achieving technical results as well. The order for the first two reactors was followed in September 1993 by an agreement to buy four more. Again, the Americans secured a bargain, only paying another $15 million. Their hope was that experiments in Albuquerque, with the help of the Russians, would boost the electrical power output of the reactors from the currently achieved 6 kilowatts to 40 kilowatts. The reactors would eventually serve as power-plants on whatever spacecraft may be required by future versions of the Star Wars project.

Yet the transfer of technology – the promised sharing – was all one-way. The talk of 'partnership' on the Topaz deal was a diplomatic gloss on the truth: it was a straightforward buy-out. American spending power was acting like a vacuum-cleaner, sucking up Russian inventions. Little, if any, American know-how was going to Moscow. The Los Alamos laboratory did open the doors of its long-term weapons projects, such as the giant Neutral Particle Beam system, to visiting Russian scientists but nothing concrete was offered by way of partnership. There was certainly no equivalent to the Topaz deal. No Brilliant Pebbles were sent to Moscow.

And of the research into designing the overall structure of an American missile defence system, none of the fruits were offered as a contribution to a co-operative arrangement. The advances made in computing – the harnessing of the vast computer power required for the battle management of the project – at the SDI's National Test Facility at Colorado Springs remained as secret as ever. Indeed, on a visit to that establishment in October 1992, security appeared unrelentingly tight. Our escort could only get us access after entering a special security kiosk in which a computer verified his identity by simultaneously checking his weight and 'reading' his retina with a laser beam. The entire building has an inner wall of sheet steel to prevent electronic eavesdropping. In its main computer room, green ceiling lights flash to indicate the presence of foreigners. Even as visitors from Britain – America's closest NATO ally – we were watched extremely closely. It was hard to imagine the Russians ever being allowed in, let alone given a chance to carry home the results of the work.

According to Gregory Canavan, however, it was never America's intention that the sharing should be that intimate. Like many senior figures in the military, he seeks to preserve American security through power – and that means, above all, achieving domination in space. Sharing with Russia hardly helps that goal. One analyst has likened the American military view of space to the Royal Navy's erstwhile quest for domination of the high seas, a degree of control which, in Britain's case, allowed the formation of the Empire. Indeed, the chapel in the Pentagon building provides evidence of that claim. The chapel has three stained-glass windows. The first, of George Washington at prayer, is an image of military faith; the second shows four Second World War chaplains who died at sea while rescuing fellow crewmen and portrays valour. The third depicts an astronaut in a gleaming white spacesuit walking on the moon, an image of celestial conquest. Stencilled on the window beside the astronaut is the first line from Genesis: 'In the beginning God created Heaven and Earth'. With that mind-set, co-operation will never come naturally.

Canavan was to make that clear. In a view which was largely accepted by American negotiators, he proposed that the guiding principle for co-operation with Russia should be the ability to back out of any agreement. 'Everything has to be reversible,' he said. If relations with Moscow turned sour, America would want to withdraw from whatever arrangements had been made – without leaving the Russians with the benefit of having once been partners. Any technology offered to Moscow must be at least one generation out of date, perhaps a full decade behind the current models in service in the American inventory. That way, America could never be disadvantaged by the deal.

As for the sharing of early warning information, Canavan's plan envisaged maintaining a similar position of American superiority. Though the two countries would benefit from pooling the data from each other's satellites, the American contribution would be dominant. The Russians would get used to the quality of the information they were receiving and even become 'dependent' on it. Then, in the event of a hardline takeover in Moscow, the Pentagon could simply switch the system off, leaving the Russians bereft of early warning. It was a plan that Canavan was pleased with: 'It's kind of neat.'

Not for the Russians though. For them, the fundamental point of the Global Protection System was to achieve a genuinely co-operative early warning system. It was meant to be the first stage of the agreement. Mikhail Maley, one of Boris Yeltsin's advisers on this issue, told me that Russia wanted a network of forty-eight satellites – twenty-four Russian and twenty-four American. He proposed that the system should be organised in such a way that it would only work effectively if both countries' satellites were switched on. If either side tried to deny the other its fair share of the data, both would end up blinded. 'That's the way we see it.'

The two teams negotiating the details of the Global Protection System remained far apart, their approaches irreconcilably opposed. The leap of faith required to regard former 'targets' as allies seemed impossible to make; perhaps it was too hurried an attempt to reverse so many years of distrust. At a political level, the rhetoric about co-operation remained firm. On 2 September 1993, the American Vice-President, Al Gore, and the Russian Prime Minister, Viktor Chernomyrdin, signed an agreement to work jointly on space projects; and, on 20 March 1994, the American Defence Secretary William Perry visited the Baikonur cosmodrome and declared that, 'instead of holding a fist clutched at each other, we extend a hand of friendship and co-operation'. Yet the reality was very different. One project in 1994, a joint experiment to investigate the use of ultraviolet sensors on satellites to track ICBMs, was badly delayed by American bureaucrats unsure how much information should be released.[5] Another, for collaborative work on lasers with which to detect tiny objects in space, ran into the sand when Russian officials suddenly cancelled a long-planned visit by American experts meant to take place in February 1994. The Americans believed their counterparts had become sensitive to western 'carpet-baggers'. One of them, a Los Alamos scientist, James Munroe, said the Russians were proud and wanted to be treated as partners 'rather than discount merchants'.[6]

It was an honest assessment. Boris Yeltsin's spokesman, Vyacheslav Kostikov, concurred in March 1994, saying the 'romantic embrace' of East and West had been replaced by a more realistic approach. Yet neither side has wished to break off the process, despite Moscow's growing assertiveness and Washington's mounting unease about it; too much was – and still is – at stake. But the co-operation itself was never to have a chance of achieving concrete results.

That did not prevent other countries from watching the talks with unease. America's allies in NATO were worried about the implications of offering Russia such intimate help. For Britain and France in particular, with modest nuclear forces, the prospect of Moscow's defences being significantly improved with American assistance was alarming: their missiles might no longer be able to reach their targets in time of war. The very principle of deterrence – the ability to threaten devastating retaliation – was being challenged. The result was some unusually outspoken criticism from Paris and London. British officials, for example, questioned whether Washington had understood the significance of the deal for other countries. The armed forces minister, Archie Hamilton, warned that Britain's Trident warheads could be 'blocked out' by better Moscow defences. He also implied that the Royal Navy's missiles may have to be equipped with more warheads than planned if the American–Russian plan went too far.

Intense, private British lobbying to change Washington's mind followed the signing of the Bush–Yeltsin agreement in June 1992. The deal had struck a raw Whitehall nerve. The credibility of the British independent nuclear deterrent rested on the so-called Moscow criterion: the requirement that Britain's warheads must be able to penetrate the Moscow defences. It was therefore critically important to British war-planners that nothing be done to change that equation. Above all, it meant persuading the Americans that the limits imposed on Russian defence systems by the ABM Treaty must never be relaxed. No easy task, as London knew only too well.

The British government had fought against similar pressures when the SDI programme was launched in 1983. Despite the overtly warm relationship between Ronald Reagan and Margaret Thatcher, his

Star Wars dream was anathema to her. The plan would mean aban-doning the ABM Treaty, on which the viability of the British nuclear force depended. It would also prove destabilising to the current balance of power. The deployment of a hi-tech American missile shield would force the Soviet Union to improve its defences or to build many more missiles to overcome it. A new arms race would have been triggered – one in which smaller powers like Britain could never afford to keep up. Behind the smiles of a photo op-portunity at Camp David in December 1984 – 'Ronnie' driving 'Maggie' in his white golf-cart – Thatcher fought hard to contain the scope of the Star Wars project.

In part, she succeeded. In a joint communiqué which, at face value, appeared to offer British endorsement for SDI, the British team had secured agreement for the insertion of a crucial phrase. 'SDI-related deployments,' says the second of four points in this brief communiqué, 'would, in view of treaty obligations, have to be a mat-ter of negotiations.' That indirect reference to the ABM Treaty was what Britain needed to safeguard the principle of deterrence – and its own deterrent. In his account of the agreement, the veteran dip-lomatic correspondent John Dickie concluded that, 'While it enabled Mrs Thatcher to appear fully in support of SDI, the Camp David accord in effect confined Star Wars to the research laboratory.'[7]

Nearly a decade later, in the autumn of 1992, British officials managed to impose a similar degree of restraint on the planned American–Russian Global Protection System. It was agreed that the deal should not allow Moscow to improve its defences to the extent that they might undermine the British Trident force. 'They've given us the reassurances we need on this,' said Archie Hamilton. Although the precise terms of the promise were not disclosed, one element of the agreement concerned the number of interceptors and radars permissible under the ABM Treaty; US officials undertook, for Britain's sake, not to press for too generous a relaxation of the treaty's rules on the deployment of these systems.

In doing this, America was showing that its close relationship with Britain was more enduring than its new one with Russia. Faced with a choice between placating a customary ally and breaking ground with an old adversary, the United States felt obliged to choose the former. It was yet another factor impeding the plan to build a co-operative shield with Russia. Despite the enthusiasm of Russia's leading scientists for the scheme, and the eagerness of America's laboratories to acquire Russian technology, the old framework of Cold War political allegiances remained paramount. The idealism of Nikita Moiseev and other advocates of a global defence system was not reciprocated; and changed political circumstances in Moscow and Washington would do nothing to encourage it.

The arrival of Bill Clinton at the White House signalled the end, for the time being, of American plans to place Brilliant Pebbles or any other weapons in space. That meant that even if the talks on co-operation showed progress, there would be less of an SDI programme for the Russians to share. For a Democratic president, the smothering of the Star Wars plan, identified with Ronald Reagan's most hawkish years, was an obvious step to take. Les Aspin, Clinton's first Defence Secretary, announced on 13 May 1993, 'the end of the Star Wars era'.

Yet he did not mean exactly what he said. Although at first sight, Aspin killed SDI, in reality he reformed it and altered its focus. He changed the name of the Pentagon department responsible for the research from 'Strategic Defence Initiative Organisation' to 'Ballistic Missile Defence Organisation' (BMDO). To Democratic Party insiders, it was a symbolically important gesture, shedding a Republican legacy; but, in practice, the task of developing a shield against missile attack would continue, albeit with a more restricted aim. While Reagan had originally sought protection for the entire United States against an all-out Soviet missile strike, and while Bush had wanted a screen against accidental or limited attacks, the Clinton administration was more interested in what is called 'theatre' defence – the shielding of US troops deployed in a military 'theatre of operations' abroad. It was a less ambitious challenge than its predecessors, but judged to be just as pressing. The proliferation of missile technology – and of the nuclear warheads that might be carried by them – posed a threat not so much to American citizens living within the United States (still beyond the range of most rogue nations' missiles) but rather to American expeditionary forces such as those sent to the Gulf to confront Iraq. In an era of defence cuts, Theatre Missile Defence (TMD) has become one of the few areas of growth.

On a chilly afternoon in December 1990, a US Air Force officer drove me through the broad suburban streets of the Saudi capital, Riyadh, to the city's VIP airport. The Gulf War was to start in only a few weeks' time (though, like most of the rest of the world, neither of us knew that) and the airport's taxiways were choked with spy-planes, air-tankers, early warning aircraft and the executive jets of the commanders of the main coalition forces. These are what the military call 'high value assets' so the best defences were made available to protect them. It was assumed that the Iraqis would try two different forms of attack: terrorism and Scuds. Well-armed patrols guarding the perimeter fence were deployed to counter the former; Patriot air-defence missiles for the latter.

The Patriot battery, when we reached it at the end of a bumpy dirt track leading to the edge of the airport, had the air of a scrap-metal yard. The dust and dirt did not help. Nor the fact that the battery's young crewmen had been sent from the United States in mid-August and had hardly had a break for the past four months. Those I spoke to seemed bored, demoralised and disgusted to be posted to so dismal a location; this particular stretch of desert was sprinkled with rocks that looked like rubble and plants so scrappy they appeared to be on the point of dying. In the camp itself there were heaps of crates and boxes, miles of cables and pipes, battered khaki tents, trucks, jeeps, aerials. Rubbish blew in the winter breeze around what felt like a forgotten outpost – and what turned out to be part of the world's first working anti-missile shield.

In one area stood the radar, scanning the skies in the direction of the Iraqi border. Near it were the command vehicles, camouflaged in pale grey-yellow colours, dark and icy inside, air-conditioning fighting to keep the computers cool. The centrepiece, the Patriot missiles themselves, were mounted in a large box, the size of a commercial container, on the back of a lorry. The box was elevated steeply, the missiles ready to intercept the Scuds on the final approach to their targets. Although the Patriot had originally been designed to shoot down fighter-planes, its manufacturers, Raytheon, had hurriedly written new software to help it defeat incoming missiles as well; no one was sure this system would work.

Worse, despite an investment of $30 billion in the Star Wars project and similarly massive research in Russia, no one knew even if an anti-ballistic missile system was theoretically feasible. The only actively deployed ABM system, defending Moscow, had never been triggered into action. The attempt to erect a missile screen in the Gulf was therefore a venture into the unknown. Everyone involved lacked experience. The Patriot crews themselves had never been in combat and their commanders had never faced the pressure of co-ordinating a response when the flight-time of a Scud from Iraq could be less than eight minutes.

Conversely, the dangers of coming under missile attack have long been understood. Ballistic missiles had been used in no fewer than four campaigns before the Gulf War – all with conventional warheads, rather than the chemical or biological agents which, it was feared, Iraq might use. London was the first city to be targeted. On 8 September 1944, a German V-2 fell towards the capital, unheard and unchecked by the only defences available at that time – radar, barrage balloons, Spitfires and anti-aircraft guns. Another missile followed that night and within two months an average of four were raining down every day. Nearly 1,400 missiles were fired at London in all, 518 of them landing within the city limits. Launched from Holland, these crude predecessors to Iraq's Scuds powered themselves to a height of about sixty miles, curving above the Channel and then hurtling towards the ground at a speed of over 3,000 m.p.h. Depending on precisely how each one landed, it could, at worst, destroy an entire row of houses.

So high were the casualty rates – 2,511 killed, nearly 19,000 injured – that the wartime government initially tried to suppress all news of the attacks. Hitler's propaganda chief, Joseph Goebbels, had predicted that the V-2 attacks would cause panic. He was right. The unpalatable truth was that, short of accelerating the allied advance through continental Europe and capturing the launch-sites, there was literally nothing the British armed forces could do. One defence scheme was proposed – the world's first attempt at a missile shield – by the Commander-in-Chief of Anti-Aircraft Command, Lieutenant-General Sir Frederick Pile. He 'wanted to have a crack at the rockets' by predicting their point of fall and 'firing the London guns to burst shells in their path'.[8] But even the general admitted that, at best, his men could intercept only one-tenth of the missiles. It is not thought that the scheme, if ever tried, had any useful effect. Arguably, if the attacks had begun earlier and lasted longer, the determination of the British people to win the war may well have been undermined.

The next use of ballistic missiles came nearly thirty years later. In the latter stages of the 1973 Yom Kippur War, as the tide of the fighting turned in Israel's favour, Egypt fired up to three Scud missiles at Israeli forces in the Sinai desert. Though little was achieved by this, the Israeli armed forces, like the British in the Second World War, had no means of resisting the attack. Nor did those of Iran and Iraq during the 1980–8 war between them. Each was targeting the other's cities, with Scud missiles and derivatives of them. At one stage, the attacks are estimated to have claimed as many as forty people a day. One especially prolonged exchange in early 1988 – dubbed the War of the Cities – may have caused 1,000 casualties in Iraq and twice that number in Iran.

The effect was to cause panic. One million people fled from Tehran in March 1988, with another million leaving the following month, leading to speculation that the missiles were influential in Iran's decision to end the war a few months later. Several studies into this conflict have highlighted how attacks by missiles seem to have a greater impact than those by aircraft, even if the latter drop a greater weight of explosive. The missiles that fell on Tehran at that time are estimated to have carried a total of forty tons of high explosive, a relatively small amount compared with the tonnage dropped in a similar period on Vietnam, Germany and Japan. One analyst says the reaction of the Iranian people was less to do with the casualties suffered and more with 'strategic and psychological shock' at the 'ease and persistence with which Iraq struck Iran's cities'. The attacks were literally unstoppable.

Less well documented is the fourth missile campaign to take place since the Second World War. In 1989 and 1990, Soviet advisers helped the Afghan army fight the mujahedin with Scud missiles. Although nearly 2,000 of the missiles may have been fired in all, there is little evidence that they had much effect on the bands of guerrillas hiding in the hills. The likelihood is that ballistic missiles will cause far more physical and psychological damage when fired against defenceless cities. Indeed, one expert, Martin Navias, has argued that conventionally armed missiles should be called 'weapons of disruption', since they cause chaos and fear rather than massive destruction. Hence the importance of the Patriot batteries deployed in Saudi Arabia before the Gulf War: Iraqi Scuds posed a minor threat to the military campaign, a much larger one to the foundation of political and public support on which the entire allied operation depended. Much was resting on one weapon.

The night of 18 January 1991 saw the first use of Iraqi missiles in the Gulf War – and the first firing of Patriots in response. It was the birth of the missile defence age and the results seemed staggering. Up to eight Scuds were fired into Israel which, at that stage, had no Patriot defence missiles, and caused twenty-two injuries in Tel Aviv and Haifa. By contrast, a ninth Scud was recorded as having been fired at Dhahran, the key allied air base in Saudi Arabia, which did have the protection of Patriot. At 4.28 a.m., a single blip was detected on the Patriot radar system and an interceptor missile was fired in response. It accelerated up to 17,000 feet. Television pictures recorded at the time show the darkened skyline of Dhahran suddenly lit up by the Patriot's bright-yellow exhaust plume as the interceptor rose into the clouds and exploded, the bright flash apparently signalling the destruction of the incoming Scud. It was heralded as a triumph.

In the days that followed, the sirens warning of a Scud attack were frequently followed by the distinctive double boom of the Patriots launching and then exploding at high altitude. The sound was soon heard in Israel as well. In an effort to keep the Israelis out of the war, President Bush pressed them into accepting Patriot batteries to defend Tel Aviv and other cities; with American crews manning them, these units quickly saw action. The shield seemed to be holding. The allied commander, General Norman Schwarzkopf, later wrote of his 'delight' in the first attack in which Patriot 'knocked the Scud from the sky'. The British commander in the Gulf, General Sir Peter de la Billière, noted that 'as people saw the Patriot worked, confidence gradually returned'. Of the eighty-one Scuds fired in all during the course of the war, official figures said most had been engaged. The manufacturer of Patriot, Raytheon, saw its share price rise. One of the missiles was even given pride of place in the lobby of the main media hotel in Dhahran, 'We Love You' scrawled on its side. The phrase 'Scud-busters' appeared on T-shirts. American technology seemed to be working miracles.

Yet all was not as it seemed. The Scud supposedly fired at Dhahran on the first night turned out to be a false alarm, a confused radar reading which was probably the result of an electromagnetic emission from another allied radar system. The Patriot which raced to intercept it had blown up in empty airspace; another twenty-three are estimated to have done the same on later occasions. The US Army, responsible for the Patriots, claimed in the immediate aftermath of the war that the system had achieved a 96 per cent success rate. Two years later, under pressure from critics, that figure was revised downwards: the army's new claim was that 40 per cent of Scud attacks on Israel were successful, 70 per cent in Saudi Arabia. More recently analysts have pointed out that only 40 per cent of the US Army's claims for successful intercepts fall into the category of 'highest confidence'. The reality therefore is that a little over one-third of the Scuds fired in the Gulf War can be safely said to have been defeated by the Patriots. The shield had cracks, severe ones.

Two fundamental questions emerged from the Gulf War: had the Patriots made life safer for those on the ground, and was this the best way to organise a shield against Scud attack? The short answers are 'possibly but maybe not' and 'no'. Though the evidence is confused, since the Israeli and Saudi authorities censored or played down the extent of casualties and damage, it is arguable that in Israel at least, while Patriot offered valuable psychological comfort, it may well have caused more problems than it solved. One study shows that the average number of Israeli casualties caused per Scud attack actually rose from 4.3 to 6.6 when the Patriot units were deployed.[9] The number of homes damaged in the attacks increased as well: before Patriot arrived, 233 apartments on average were damaged by each Scud compared to 334 afterwards. There are several explanations for this. At least four Patriots, and perhaps as many as eleven, veered drastically off course and plunged into the ground, two of them exploding in residential areas of Tel Aviv. Additionally, even during a successful intercept, the Patriots themselves added to the volume of debris in the air. Since it was usual for two of the missiles to be fired at each reported Scud, each interception could increase the amount of potentially damaging shrapnel threefold.

Even so, some experts point to the fact that the V-2s in the Second World War had caused a far higher rate of casualties than the Scuds in the Gulf War; they claim that Israel and Saudi Arabia were therefore safer with Patriot than without it. Not only did the system bolster morale but also its successful interceptions – however few – at least slowed the fall of the Scuds and probably lessened their impact when they landed. It is a topic which has now become something of an academic football: one set of experts eager to debunk the boasts of the Pentagon and the manufacturers, another fighting to maintain the credibility of Patriot as the first step towards a missile defence system. Both sides in this battle, played in the pages of the international defence journals, agree on one thing: the running of the Gulf War shield could have been far better.

Warnings of Scud attacks were often slow and inaccurate. The first to detect the launches were the infra-red sensors carried by the Pentagon's five Defence Support Program (DSP) satellites, parked in geostationary orbit. These detected the intense heat of the exhaust as the missiles took off and the general direction in which they headed. The information was relayed via ground stations in the United States and Australia to NORAD, the American early warning centre buried inside Cheyenne Mountain in Colorado. The DSP satellites sometimes got it wrong and triggered false alarms. Those analysing the data at NORAD understandably erred on the side of caution and passed on warnings even if the evidence for them was not categoric. Such was the inconsistency of the satellites' sensors and their inability to plot an exact trajectory that there were immediate calls for improvements.

But there were problems too with the relaying of the DSP satellites' information. The Americans, though fighting in a coalition and seeking to defend their closest Middle East allies, Israel and Saudi Arabia, chose to guard their data jealously. According to General de la Billière, the British Ambassador in Riyadh often first heard of impending Scud attacks from his daughter in London who had seen reports on television, before hearing of them through official channels. Any delays mattered most to the Israelis, with the dense conurbation of Tel Aviv an easy target. For them, every minute of warning time was useful. The more time people had to rush indoors and don their gas-masks (for the long-expected chemical attacks) the more likely they were to survive. And since Israel lacked its own early warning satellites, it was entirely dependent on America's; this was the first test of a shared shield in action. Yet despite a maximum Scud flight-time of up to eight minutes, the Israelis were sometimes given as little as one minute's warning. It was only after the Gulf War that US officials revealed why. In a computer age and with war raging, the best communication the Americans chose to offer to link NORAD and Israel was, of all possible devices, a telephone. 'I guess we are kinda hesitant about this,' one senior official admitted later.

There were technical problems as well. The Scuds were attacked in the wrong place. Logic dictates that if a missile is intercepted early in its flight, it will crash down into the country that launched it; if the missile is only attacked in the final stage of its trajectory, it will fall on to the defending side and do its damage there. Worse, the Scuds fired by Iraq tended to break up during their descent, buffeted by the atmosphere. The warhead often became detached, as did other chunks of the missile. The result was that the Patriots' radar systems were confronted with a shower of incoming objects, swerving haphazardly and violently, any one of which could be the all-important warhead. The Patriots sometimes ended up chasing irrelevant components, missing the key one.

These weaknesses have been recognised and solutions have been sought ever since. Among the analysts commissioned to study the Gulf War failings and to recommend new approaches was Gregory Canavan, as prominent as ever in the quest for a missile shield. He led a technical investigation for the American Institute of Aeronautics and Astronautics and his report, still classified, was circulated in the Pentagon in June 1993.[10] He is blunt about its basic conclusion: 'People are just now beginning to acknowledge the fact that the Patriot didn't work very well.' His study focused on the likely successors to Patriot and assessed their potential for overcoming its drawbacks.

One system on offer is a more advanced Patriot. It carries what is called a multi-mode seeker, a bundle of electronic eyes able to hunt the incoming target and – in theory – distinguish between the different components of a fragmenting Scud. In practice though, like all new weaponry, the system requires careful development; in one test at the White Sands Missile Range in New Mexico on 26 October 1993, the multi-mode seeker failed to help the Patriot towards its target. It missed.

An alternative system, the ERINT (Extended Range Interceptor), was chosen by the US Army instead. Far smaller than Patriot, it operates in a different way. While the Patriot carries an explosive charge which is set to detonate when close enough to the target to destroy it, the Erint is a 'hit-to-kill' interceptor. Nearly 200 tiny rocket-thrusters in its nose provide highly accurate steering, technology which was validated in a test on 30 November 1993 in which an Erint successfully intercepted a dummy warhead. The test organisers had fitted the warhead with thirty-eight cylinders filled with water to simulate the canisters that could carry chemical weapons. They were anxious to see if the interception would destroy the canisters or merely scatter them over the ground below. According to one report, the entire warhead was shattered and only nine of the canisters were later found on the ground; of those, none contained any water.[11] An encouraging result.

More promising still is THAAD (yet another strange acronym, this time standing for Theatre High Altitude Area Defence). THAAD is designed to reach far higher altitudes than other systems to avoid the problem experienced in Israel of an interception simply creating a shower of dangerous debris. Its designers at the Lockheed Corporation believe THAAD will have the range to catch Scud-type missiles before they break up. Yet even this system suffers the same fundamental drawback of Patriot and Erint: that an interception during the descent of an incoming missile is still an inherently risky task; by that late stage, the advantage clearly lies with the attacker. In the opinion of the panel led by Canavan, none of these systems would be effective if future Saddam Husseins made a few obvious adaptations to their Scuds. It would be relatively simple, for example, to obscure the real warheads with decoys, or to set them to fall erratically, or to time the missiles to release their weapons loads (chemical canisters, biological bomblets, nuclear warheads) at higher than normal altitudes. THAAD and all the other successors to the Gulf War Patriots would be left impotent.

The study, by implication, was also critical of Israel's principal planned defence against missile attack: a project for an interceptor known as Arrow. Funded jointly with the United States, Arrow is in essence a longer range and more sophisticated kind of Patriot, designed to defeat an incoming missile as it falls towards its target. But, troubled by corruption scandals and a series of test failures, the project's managers have also been criticised for adopting this particular approach to missile defence. One Israeli analyst, Reuven Pedatzur, has observed that even if Arrow worked and successfully intercepted an attacking nuclear missile, three problems could ensue: the interception itself could trigger a nuclear explosion high in the atmosphere above Israel; or the collision could prevent the triggering of a nuclear detonation but leave the warhead free to crash on to the ground where it would scatter radioactive material; or the Arrow could damage the incoming missile but not the warhead, which would then fall and explode as planned anyway.[12] Interception, Pedatzur argues, can be as damaging as an uninterrupted missile.

These observations lead in one clear direction: that the earlier an interception is mounted the better. Ideally, the engagement should come when the Scud is in its 'boost phase', blasting off from its launcher, and still over the territory of the country that fired it. Boost-phase interception 'may be the best solution, it may be the only solution', one of Canavan's colleagues on his panel has been quoted as saying. This reflects a view long held within the American military – one that favoured Brilliant Pebbles since they were meant to pounce from space to attack a missile during its ascent rather than wait until the 'terminal' stage of the weapon's descent. As a result, the Pentagon's Ballistic Missile Defence Organisation has been examining a number of schemes; some of them, at first sight, seem far-fetched.

The 'Raptor-Talon' system is the most startling, not least because of its name, which is more appropriate to some mythical beast or dinosaur. (It is apparent that the project's title was twisted into an almost meaningless state to produce a robust and intriguing acronym: 'Raptor' stands for Responsive Aircraft Programme for Theatre Operations; 'Talon' for Theatre Application, Launch on Notice.) The project envisages squadrons of Raptors, giant pilotless gliders drifting 65,000 feet above hostile territory, controlled by radio signals and powered by solar cells and new-technology batteries which would allow flights to last for weeks or even months. In the shape of a single wing about 200 feet long, these aircraft would contain so few metal parts that they would be virtually invisible to radar. They would carry a 'sensor package' – infra-red and radar devices to watch for Scuds. And on their backs would be a batch of at least four tiny Talon missiles, mini-Brilliant Pebbles, poised to intercept the enemy missiles as soon as they take off.

The idea is attracting serious attention from the Pentagon; Israeli and British military officials have shown interest as well. With $1.5 million of US government funding already, and more promised, the designers, the American firm AeroVironment, have flown an early, small-scale version known as Pathfinder. Tests showed it could stay aloft for forty hours continuously, even allowing for the weight of four Talon missiles, estimated at 125 kilograms. One of the BMDO's senior officials involved in boost-phase projects, Lieutenant-Colonel Dale Tietz, claimed the system could be ready for use as early as mid-1996.[13] The BMDO is already devising battle-plans. The computers on board each Raptor aircraft will be able to communicate with each other, passing on data about a Scud sighting and calculating which of them is best placed to attempt an interception. A Talon missile, it is estimated, will need to be launched within twenty seconds of a Scud take-off to give it the necessary time to reach its target during the boost phase (which may last only eighty seconds). Given that demand for an extremely rapid response, Pentagon planners realise a commander on the ground may be unable to cope in time. One option – inevitably a highly controversial one – is for the Talons to be given automatic authority to launch themselves. Commanders would only have the ability to inhibit these robot Scud-busters rather than to provide the order for their firing.

Less exotic and possibly more likely is a US Air Force plan for its fighters to carry Talon-type missiles to perform much the same role. F15 fighters, which were involved in the hunt for Iraq's Scuds during the Gulf War, could be armed with a version of the Short Range Attack Missile (SRAM) or High Speed Radiation Missile (HARM). If Scud attacks appeared imminent, the planes could fly patrols over the suspected areas of the missile deployment and wait for the launches. As with the Talon, the SRAM or HARM would endeavour to hit a Scud as it climbed towards the edge of the atmosphere. As evidence of the importance of this role, the USAF planned to allocate over $450 million to it between 1993 and 1999.

Star Wars may have been declared dead but its successor, 'Theatre Missile Defence', has become big business. Even Britain and France, who opposed the original SDI plan, have gradually changed their views; their troops too were at risk from Iraqi Scuds in the Gulf War and their politicians have started to take note. The impetus behind the plan for a co-operative American–Russian shield has now been transferred to the goal of an American–European one instead. The uncertainty over the fate of President Yeltsin and his reform process, and the simultaneous rise of more overt Russian nationalism, has only confirmed that shift.

At his home in Maryland, in one of the newly created townships of Washington suburbia, Stanley Orman watched the Gulf War on television. He was horrified at 'the killing during dinner'. But it was the nightly battles between Iraqi Scuds and American Patriots which most gripped this retired British nuclear scientist, now resident in the United States and working as a consultant to the Pentagon's Ballistic Missile Defence Organisation. This first glimpse of a missile shield in action held special significance for Orman. More than anyone in the British defence establishment, he had been responsible for pushing through the Chevaline project, the system of decoys that would enable the Royal Navy's Polaris missiles to defeat the ABM system shielding Moscow. Now he was watching the Iraqis probe his own side's anti-missile system. He winced at its failings.

The sight left him convinced of the need for urgent improvement. 'We could have had a much better system; more importantly, we are still just as vulnerable.' Orman speaks plainly, with a tone of injured common sense. Just before the Gulf War started, he had devised his own plan for a co-operative defence system. He called it GODS, standing for Global Orbiting Defence System, and played on the acronym in the title of his book: *Faith in G.O.D.S.* Orman proposed setting up an international network of satellite sentries and interceptors to watch for and then defeat any Iraqi-style attacks. The plan was virtually identical to that suggested in Moscow by Nikita Moiseev and his colleagues at the Institute of Cybernetics. Yet coming from a man who had been a pivotal figure in the British nuclear establishment – at that stage still firmly committed to its policy of deterrence – Orman's advocacy of missile defence was potentially more influential. In taking up this particular cause, he became the first senior British military official to abandon the traditional Cold War approach.

As an institution, the Ministry of Defence had always opposed the concept of large-scale missile defences. It was thoroughly wedded to the opposite concept, deterrence, as the best means of safeguarding Britain's security. Even in the late 1980s, MoD officials argued that only the threat of devastating retaliation would prevent war and that the Americans were misled if they believed a foolproof screen could ever be built. They viewed the American plans with cynicism. All too often in the past, grand visions promoted by Washington had in reality become a sales pitch for American hardware. There was also the fear – unspeakable in public – that an American missile defence system could someday be turned on Britain's nuclear weapons, if there were ever circumstances in which London wanted to use them against Washington's will. (One possible scenario for this is a rerun of the Falklands War going so badly for Britain that the use of a nuclear weapon against Buenos Aires is considered; Washington, of course, would totally oppose nuclear war in its 'backyard'.)

Stanley Orman had shared that view for much of his career. Not at first, though. As a bright young scientist with degrees in physics and chemistry, he had taken a job at Aldermaston believing that weapons work was immoral and had asked to be assigned to non-nuclear areas of research. Yet he soon changed his view, convinced that Aldermaston was contributing to peace rather than undermining it. 'I don't believe the meek will inherit the earth,' he was to say later, explaining that he had begun to think that peace was better secured through strength, through deterrence. 'I believed I was doing more to prevent nuclear war than the people with banners,' he told me.

He rose rapidly through the scientific ranks, making his name with the Chevaline project (and with a fondness for brightly coloured bow-ties which he makes for himself). His task was to co-ordinate the myriad elements of what was to be a technological breakthrough while ensuring that the project would be able to achieve its goal: penetrating the Moscow defences. Since each component was being manufactured by different contractors in Britain and the United States, Orman was 'constantly on the road', enduring an 'incredibly arduous' time. But throughout the six years in which he was responsible for Chevaline, the motivation remained the same. Britain's warheads had to be able to outwit the Soviet shield if deterrence was to remain a viable policy.

Chevaline was accepted into service in 1982 and, as a reward, Orman was posted to Washington as a minister for defence equipment at the British Embassy. It was there that he heard Ronald Reagan announce his Star Wars initiative, signalling a move away from a belief in deterrence with its threat of mutual annihilation towards a more stable era of missile defences. Orman was intrigued. At first he thought the President 'either hadn't understood the briefings or he's been badly briefed – I knew what he was talking about wasn't on'. Nevertheless, in Orman's view, it was in Britain's interest to support the project, if only to grab a share of the research work and to learn more about the future techniques the Soviet Union might use to modify its defence system. He sent a diplomatic cable to that effect but it fell on deaf ears.

Later, as deputy director of Aldermaston, he led a study into SDI. It concluded that the scheme had no chance of working for at least fifteen to twenty years but that Britain could learn from joining the research. Orman was 'out on a limb' for wanting Britain to be involved. When the government eventually decided to support the research aspects of the initiative (Mrs Thatcher, at her 1984 meeting with Ronald Reagan, having first made sure it was unlikely ever to be deployed), Orman was given the post of director-general of the participation office which would liaise with Washington. He found himself fighting the rest of the Ministry of Defence. According to Orman, ministry officials managed to block him from ever seeing Mrs Thatcher one-to-one (even though she had requested such a meeting). It became unbearably frustrating. Orman decided to retire early, in 1990. He began writing a book on SDI.

'I started to think about things.' With the proliferation of nuclear missiles, he thought, deterrence would be unlikely to have the same meaning. In the Cold War, both sides were 'nodding and winking at each other' while facing off, each understanding the elaborate rules of the nuclear game. New nuclear powers 'wouldn't understand the nuances', which meant there were greater risks that their weapons may actually be used. At the same time, since the size of the threat was smaller – with far fewer weapons than in an all-out Soviet attack – it became more feasible to erect a defence. No longer would the task involve defeating thousands of Soviet warheads; an attack by a handful of Libyan or Iranian weapons was far more likely. 'As I wrote, there was a sudden flash,' he told me. 'I looked at the defence spending of various countries and Iraq stood out: thirty per cent of its GNP was going on the military. It was buying Scuds for the Iran–Iraq War. Here was an unstable regime in a conflict and this is what happens: they lob Scuds at you. Therefore, we need a defence.' The man who had done so much to help keep alive Britain's policy of deterrence had been converted to a new belief.

'I'm a poacher turned gamekeeper,' he admits. 'I don't believe deterrence will always be effective.' In his book he warns of the importance of his recommendation. He writes that 'missiles are a menace that has to be countered now . . . active defence on a global scale . . . is required, if the democratic nations are to maintain their freedom and independence'. In an interview, he added: 'We mustn't delay.'

What he advocates is a series of cautious, politically palatable stages towards the construction of an anti-missile screen. First, he says, the western allies need to develop a compatible early warning and communication system. Initially, the framework for this would be American since the United States alone in NATO has a space-based early warning system. The Europeans though could contribute radar information from their ground-based systems. The British radar and listening post on Cyprus, for example, could provide a vital eye on the Middle East.

Next, individual countries would provide their own hardware. Each nation would buy or build and then run its own missiles, an easier step politically than attempting to manage an interceptor force collectively, which would raise the highly sensitive issue of sovereignty, of precisely who is in control of the weapons, and under-mine support for the scheme. Orman's idea is that a two-tier system should be developed for Europe. The United States would provide the more sophisticated, upper layer of defence with its future THAAD missiles. The lower layer would involve the European nations' own systems, either improved Patriot missiles or updated Hawks, a relatively old air defence missile already in service with some twenty countries. For the future, as governments and public opinion adjusted to the novelty of a co-operative missile defence, more exotic anti-missile weapons could be introduced, preferably into space.

Stanley Orman was ahead of his time. His ideas have gradually caught on. Policy-makers in the major European countries began to recognise that their long-enshrined doctrine of deterrence may well fail against countries with newly acquired long-range weapons that did not fear the threat of retaliation. In a speech in December 1993, the Defence Secretary, Malcolm Rifkind, gave the first hint of a shift in British thinking. Warning of technological progress in ballistic and cruise missiles, he said, 'The present threat, for example from Libya, to some of our allies could, over time, become a direct threat to the UK. This is not an idle thought, it is a real possibility.' Mr Rifkind went one stage further in February 1994, announcing a two-year study into a missile shield. He was not acting alone.

At the NATO summit in January 1994, alliance leaders cautiously endorsed the principle of working 'to protect against' missile attack. Although the details of NATO's internal studies have been kept secret, it is known that one plan envisages building up the alliance's existing air defence network, currently only capable of detecting and intercepting aircraft, along the lines Orman suggests. Another plan would involve Europe's navies. The US Navy has been proposing that NATO warships could be fitted with advanced versions of its Standard missile and deployed wherever a threat develops. Like Patriot and Hawk, the Standard missile was originally designed to shoot down aircraft but is now being modified to intercept missiles as well. Both plans are being studied seriously. European countries closest to the Middle East, especially Italy, regard the requirement as most pressing: in 1993, the then Italian Defence Minister, Salvo Ando, warned that fifteen nations in the region would have ballistic missiles by the year 2000 and that an anti-missile 'umbrella' was essential.

Yet at the same time there is one fundamental constraint on the whole process: the risk that the very idea of erecting a missile shield could antagonise the nations it is meant to defend against. The move would be tantamount to a declaration that the countries outside the shield are, by definition, threatening. It could force them to respond: either militarily, by acquiring weapons that could beat the shield, or diplomatically by forming alliances with other nations perceived to be threats to international peace. The United States faced this dilemma when it announced in January 1994 that it planned to protect South Korea with Patriot interceptors. For months before, North Korea, armed with its own Nodong missiles, had been issuing bellicose threats against the South. The announcement of the Patriot deployment provided further fuel: the move was an 'unpardonable, grave military challenge', Pyongyang declared. Washington was forced to take note, initially delaying the move. Eventually, in March that year, the Patriots were despatched to South Korea – but by boat, as slowly as possible, to buy more time.

The difficulty is that there are many ways in which an aggrieved nation, finding itself outside an American-led shield, could plan to outwit the defence. If the shield is configured to detect and intercept ballistic missiles falling from space, the country might decide to develop cruise missiles. Flying low and fast (and possibly coated with stealthy radar-absorbent paint) these missiles could slip in undetected. It is a realistic fear: Iran is reported to have bought the latest Soviet-designed cruise missile, codenamed Sunburst, which flies supersonically and could cross the Strait of Hormuz in as little as seventeen seconds. But a cheaper and simpler plan to evade a missile shield would be to smuggle a nuclear device to the target, disguised as ordinary cargo. One analyst, Matthew Bunn of the Arms Control Association in Washington, has talked of the ease with which a nuclear bomb could be 'delivered to New York harbour on board a shrimp-boat', making a Star Wars missile screen redundant. With a combination of surprise, ingenuity and countermeasures, the advantage could lie with the attacker – unless the shield is sufficiently sophisticated.

But the greatest problem is political. A decision must be taken on which countries to include in a co-operative defence scheme and which to exclude. It is a challenge that generates similar emotions to the membership of popular clubs: how do you justify accepting some applicants and how do you soothe the hurt feelings of those who have been rejected? With NATO currently in the grip of a debate over expanding its membership, it would be particularly invidious to establish a missile defence system which only protected existing alliance members. Countries eager to join the alliance but so far denied membership – Poland, Hungary, the Czech Republic, Slovakia, Bulgaria and Romania – would rightly complain that NATO was leaving them vulnerable.

The difficulty does not end there though. A decision could well be taken to extend the missile shield to these countries on the grounds that they are moving closer to NATO. The January 1994 summit approved a plan to allow the countries of central and eastern Europe to become 'partners for peace', a step towards eventual membership. But what of the countries left out? If the six nations who most want to join NATO are included within the shield, their neighbours may well feel isolated and threatened. Ukraine, Belarus and Russia, among others, would rightly sense that they have been judged too unstable or distant to merit membership of the club.

Yet, if a bolder decision was taken by NATO to include those three countries as well, together with all former republics of the Soviet Union, the shield would extend deep into central Asia. That would not pass unnoticed. Iran, Pakistan and India would question NATO's motives and no doubt raise objections. Similarly, if the United States wished to offer Japan missile protection (as it plans to do with THAAD or Raptor-Talon), other Far Eastern nations such as China, Taiwan and North Korea would feel further alienated and insecure. The sight of a missile shield positioned on their borders would hardly encourage them to co-operate with the West in other activities. It may even spur their efforts to acquire more sophisticated weapons. As Alexei Arbatov, a Russian military expert, put it, a co-operative shield including Russia, America and others could accelerate the 'very dangerous process of nuclear proliferation' against which the shield is meant to offer protection; 'you will create precisely the danger you initially wanted to avoid'.

In his book, Stanley Orman offers his co-operative scheme as a 'pathway to a more secure and saner world'. He notes though, with a hint of petulance and cynicism, that 'like all major decisions, the route we take will be up to the politicians, not the scientists and engineers who have created the possibility'. That is an understatement. Political judgement will of necessity determine whether a missile shield is ever built and whom it should protect; the technology required is probably available. The decision will revolve around two issues: cost and risk. The system must be judged to be affordable, taking into account other military priorities in an age of dwindling defence budgets. It will also have to be seen as contributing to a nation's sense of security. Governments will weigh up the risks of remaining vulnerable to missile attack against those of alienating the nations posing the threat: an appalling dilemma, but one that has to be confronted. There is no sign that the spread of missiles and nuclear technology is slowing, let alone being reversed. The vision of a shield is an enduring one, yet the reality of its implementation is as contentious and hazardous as ever.

In the meantime, logic offers another approach altogether: no longer preparing to be defensive with a shield but going on the offensive instead. Since the task of stopping enemy missiles is technically difficult and politically controversial, many argue that it would make better sense in a conflict to attack the enemy's missiles before they take off. At face value, such action would be cheaper and easier. It would, however, depend on one key, elusive factor: the ability to spot the missiles in the first place. The RAF tried – and failed – to destroy Hitler's V-2 launch-sites in the Second World War and nearly fifty years later the Gulf War allies faced similar problems tracking down Iraq's Scuds. General Schwarzkopf likened the task to 'looking for a needle in a haystack'. Many of the Scuds were mobile, hidden during the day and only vulnerable briefly when they prepared to launch at night. The gift of unfailing sight, ever regarded as an essential asset in warfare, has never been so eagerly sought.

5

UNFAILING SIGHT

*We need to give James Bond not just X-ray specs but a Geiger
counter as well to see what's going on now.*
> A former USAF officer speaking privately,
> Washington DC, December 1993

We were at the edge of Turkish airspace about to cross into Iraq. The
mountains below us were bright with snow, the valleys yellowy-grey
with bare rock. It was early March 1993, two years after the end
of the Gulf War, and the United States, Britain and France were
maintaining both a 'safe haven' and a closely watched 'no-fly-zone'
to protect the persecuted Kurds living in the north of Iraq. Tension
was high. Even after his defeat over Kuwait, Saddam Hussein had
continually flouted the will of the United Nations, most recently by
fielding surface-to-air missile (SAM) systems in the areas patrolled
by allied aircraft; air-strikes in January 1993 had forced him to withdraw or dismantle these units. But within weeks there was evidence
that new weaponry was being deployed. His forces were constantly
on the move, he seemed to be spoiling for another fight. Reconnaissance – the purpose of this mission – was being stepped up. Iraq,
at this stage, shared with North Korea and Bosnia the dubious
distinction of being one of the most closely observed, most spied-on
countries in the world. From space and from the air, by camera,
by radar and by radio, the search was on for clues about Saddam's
capabilities and intentions: the full weight of western surveillance
technology was being brought to bear.

'Cougar', the call-sign of the AWACS airborne radar plane
controlling the operation, had sent a message in a deep, calm
American voice that the route ahead was clear. The flight could
proceed into Iraq.

A 'package' of nearly a dozen different aircraft entered hostile territory. In front were two American 'Wild Weasel' F-4G Phantoms equipped with radar-seeking HARM missiles; if the Iraqis were to switch on their radar systems and 'lock on' to an allied plane as a prelude to an attack, the HARMs would be let loose, as they had been repeatedly during the Gulf War and in the previous few weeks, to pursue the radar beam back to its source and destroy it. High above us was a pair of American F-15C fighters, watching in case the Iraqi Air Force defied the UN Security Council's resolution banning it from flying north of the 36th parallel. In the centre of the formation were six Royal Air Force Jaguars, fitted with Sidewinder air-to-air missiles and, most significantly, with F126 high-resolution cameras. Bringing up the rear was an RAF tanker, a converted VC-10 passenger jet, on which I was travelling. 'We're just over the border now,' the tanker's commander, Flight-Lieutenant Dave Edwards, told me over the intercom headset.

In the forty minutes before crossing into Iraq, the Jaguars had drawn fresh fuel from the tanker, inching close to the VC-10's wing-tips and connecting with the thick hoses trailing behind them. This was to give the Jaguars extra endurance over Iraq, to allow them more time to overfly the main roads, railways and military bases and take photographs of the operations under way. From medium altitude, with the cameras taking one photograph every second, a pair of Jaguars can scan a swathe of territory about one and a half miles wide; from low altitude, the cameras speeded up to shoot twelve frames per second, they collect a narrower strip of data but in far greater detail. Though the technology involved is relatively old, using ordinary 'wet' film rather than electronic video sensors, the RAF operators swear by its ability to see what is meant to be hidden.

The technique of aerial photography is just one of many types of reconnaissance. The entire electromagnetic spectrum – from visible light to the heat rays of infra-red to radar to radio – is exploited in an effort to gather intelligence. Satellites and spy-planes are equipped with a variety of sensors with which to peer at an adversary: optical cameras such as those carried by the Jaguars and others of greater sophistication; infra-red cameras which detect the heat 'signature' of objects on the ground, even at night or if hidden by cloud; and radar systems which, by accurately reading the 'echo' of a radio beam, build up a picture of a target that may well be obscured to the human eye. Additionally, eavesdropping on the frequencies used by radio and telephone traffic yields information about future operations. Seismic movement detectors can pick up the vibrations of underground nuclear tests; sonar uses sound waves to 'see' underwater. None of these systems though, mostly introduced around the time of the Second World War and then developed at immense cost during the Cold War, ever provided a truly confident understanding of enemy power, certainly not of the Soviet Union. Nor does the current intelligence effort fare much better against the closed and unpredictable regimes posing the greatest threats now: no one knows precisely what weapons they possess. And the risks of trying to find out remain just as great. The shooting down of the American pilot Francis Gary Powers in his U-2 spy-plane over the Soviet Union on 1 May 1960 is not forgotten by the present generation of aircrew on intelligence-gathering missions.

The refuelling had gone smoothly and the Jaguars had sped away deep into Iraq. The tanker's task was then to circle inside Iraq, ready to offer a top-up on the leg home to Incirlik, the allied air base in Turkey. The atmosphere on board was alert but relaxed. One of the crew busied himself getting lunch ready with a microwave oven. Another pointed out one of Saddam Hussein's summer palaces, a medieval-looking castle perched amid mist on a savagely steep ridge. It was a barren sight and, from 15,000 feet up, it looked devoid of life.

Then an alarm went off.

'Whoo . . . whoo . . . whoo . . . whoo . . .' A piercing police-car warble cut through all other sound in the headphones.

Dave Edwards and his co-pilots immediately glanced up to the controls above the cockpit window. A tiny black screen had come to life. The letters 'CWE' flashed repeatedly – warning that a hostile radar had illuminated the plane. Conversation froze, faces hardened. The co-pilot reached up to punch a series of buttons, hurriedly interrogating a computer for information about the type, range and direction of the radar below. He then twisted round for a thick handbook, marked 'Secret', containing print-outs of the latest intelligence on the various Iraqi SAM radars. It was known that at least fifteen of the systems were currently deployed in the area. But which one? The large Soviet-made SA-2 or 3 or the mobile French-built Roland? The co-pilot flicked through the pages, then ran through the details with the rest of the crew (out of my earshot). The warbling of the alarm had stopped by now; it had lasted about four seconds. The crew's discussion continued, the pages of the intelligence guide tossed back and forth.

Then the alarm started up again, for another four seconds.

The crew reached a conclusion: the radar was that of a Soviet-built SA-6, a highly capable anti-aircraft weapon, but it was not a 'lock-on'. The Iraqis were using the SA-6's general search radar rather than its guidance radar which steers the missiles towards their prey. We had been 'lit up', not targeted, and were anyway beyond the radar's thirteen-mile range. Yet it was a reminder that all of the aircraft taking part in the reconnaissance mission, especially our VC-10 tanker, were unavoidably visible to the Iraqis: in our effort to see their activities, they were able to see us all too easily. Only the 'stealth' planes of the US Air Force – the F-117A fighter-bomber whose sharp angles scatter radar beams in all directions and the B-2 bomber whose smooth flying-wing shape allows it to slip through them – can claim to be invisible to radar.

The VC-10 pilot chose to shift his holding pattern slightly further north to be safe. The smiles returned and lunch followed.

We landed in the evening light and watched the Jaguars touch down behind us. Even as the whine of the engines of the first plane was dying away, a pair of technicians ran to the bomb-like camera pod beneath the fuselage, opened it up and prised out the large black film box inside. The more senior of the two, a corporal, grabbed the box and ran to a waiting minibus which drove him the one hundred yards to the Reconnaissance Intelligence Centre. In this huddle of Portakabins and small lorries, draped in camouflage netting, the film was processed, dried and splayed on light-tables within four and a half minutes of the Jaguars' landing. The photo-analysts pride themselves on speed. They pored over the shots, frame by frame, faces lit by ghostly white light from below, squinting through jeweller's eye-pieces and magnifying glasses for signs of change in the deployments photographed in the same locations on earlier occasions. The details of SAMs, artillery, tanks and infantry were logged; any notable observations were passed up the chain of command to Defence Intelligence in London.

The best pictures were those taken at low altitude. In fine-grained black-and-white, shot from the Jaguars hurtling along at around 400 m.p.h., Saddam's arsenal was bared. One photograph showed a unit of SA-2s deployed in a field, each white fin on the missiles and each soldier stunningly clear. Others captured views of weapons that were meant to remain hidden: a small part of the radar particular to an SA-6, just visible through a warehouse door carelessly left open; a bomb-damaged building, seemingly abandoned, but with just enough of its roof missing to allow a glimpse inside of a collection of missiles. Another photograph disclosed that a depot which had been storing SAMs was suddenly empty, meaning that the missiles were possibly now deployed in the field. The RAF's cameras also caught Iraq's preparations for operations: tanks leaving their protective revetments and forming up in columns, conscripts queuing for their food. Even from higher altitude, the Jaguars were capturing the sight of entire formations of Iraqi armour on the move: tiny black dots on a photograph translated by the analysts into hard military fact. Little escaped the allied gaze, and commanders felt justified in claiming that the very act of watching the Iraqis so intently was deterring them from further aggression. Sight was proving to be a weapon in its own right.

Yet the operation was expensive, arduous and dangerous, and only covered one relatively small area of Iraq. It tied up several hundred RAF personnel and hundreds more from America and France. Even after just eighteen months, the strain of long days spent over the light-tables was proving too much for many of the RAF's specialists, such was the volume of raw material; volunteer reservists had to be called in to relieve the burden. Many of the pilots had had to do three- or four-month-long stints of duty; the ground crew stayed for longer tours and had to endure accommodation in tents.

On top of that, a similar operation was established in July 1993 over Bosnia-Hercegovina. This time the Jaguars flew daily missions from a base at Gioia del Colle in Italy and the analysts painstakingly counted the tell-tale dots representing guns and mortars in the Balkan hills. The Royal Navy was drawn in as well. Its Sea Harrier jump-jets flying from an aircraft carrier in the Adriatic were equipped with reconnaissance cameras to perform the same role. The task attracted special significance when NATO issued an ultimatum to the Bosnian Serbs on 9 February 1994 to withdraw or hand over their heavy weapons around Sarajevo: reconnaissance pictures were a rare, independent source of verification that the Serbs were complying. But two problems quickly became apparent. First, on several occasions after the deadline, the Serbs fielded weapons which had been successfully hidden in dense forest or clusters of buildings. Second, the European weather was humbling the high technology:

cloud was obscuring the view. In one six-day period leading up to the ultimatum, thick cloud had meant that the photographs laid on the light-tables were dominated by unbroken tones of medium-grey and yielded little useful intelligence. On one occasion during this period, I saw an RAF analyst at Gioia del Colle winding through yards of dull film, muttering 'cloud, cloud, cloud, guess what? More cloud . . .' NATO's threat to use air-strikes if the ultimatum was ignored proved difficult – in some cases impossible – to carry out. Indeed, one air-strike requested by embattled French UN troops in March 1994 could not be carried out precisely because of the bad weather; attacks on Serb forces around the Muslim enclave of Gorazde were frequently limited for the same reason.

This did not mean that NATO air power was crippled entirely. American TR-1 spy-planes (successors to the U-2s) equipped with highly accurate Synthetic Aperture Radar systems were able to see through the cloud. But, according to several sources, the quality of these highly classified photographs is not ideal: the definition can be poor and can therefore lead to uncertainty about identifying the weapons observed. And even if the TR-1s and other systems had been able to offer a faultless view, the operation required a level of intensity which was unsustainable in the long-term. Nearly 200 NATO aircraft were committed to Bosnia and several dozen to Iraq at a time when western politicians were eager to find an honourable exit from both tasks. It means the advantage probably lies with the spied-on rather than with the spy.

This is even more the case since high-tempo, well-organised scrutiny can only be applied to very limited areas. While the West's focus was on Bosnia and on northern and southern Iraq (where another air operation monitored the persecution of the Shiite Marsh Arabs), there was no possibility that wider regions could be studied at this level of detail. In the case of Iraq, even with the aid of two key assets – American reconnaissance satellites and a series of UN-authorised inspections on the ground – no allied official dealing with Baghdad has ever expressed total confidence in his knowledge of its current military potential. Before the Gulf War, satellite pictures ('good enough to tell a man from a woman but not their faces,' according to one expert) had failed to detect the scale of Iraq's nuclear weapons programme; and, during the war, they were not thought to have pinpointed the locations of Saddam's mobile Scud missile units either (until the giveaway heat of a launch appeared).

The inspections by the UN Special Commission, set up after the conflict to find and destroy Iraq's missiles and its nuclear, chemical and biological weapons potential, discovered entire plants and bases which had remained unnoticed from space and from the air. Tip-offs from Iraqi defectors and the seizure of key documents detailing missile and nuclear facilities (after the notorious hold-up of the inspectors in a Baghdad car park in late 1991) did allow the UN inspectors to unravel much of Iraq's secret military potential. Yet even after finding – and then dismantling – the key facilities producing nuclear material and agents for nerve and germ weapons, the inspectors found themselves doubting the extent of their knowledge. 'You just can't shake off that feeling in the pit of your stomach that you don't know the whole story,' one British expert involved in the inspections told me. 'I really don't know if there's some huge secret underground plutonium plant still hidden somewhere.' The Duke of Wellington, over two hundred years earlier, would have understood the sentiment: he had said he spent half of his military career wondering 'what was on the other side of the hill'.

Of all the potent weapons which most need to be tracked, one of the most important happens also to be the hardest to find: mobile missiles. Yet this is not a new problem. In late 1944, the British government was desperate. Though the D-Day landings had succeeded and the tide of the war was going in the allies' favour, London was meanwhile being obliterated. With Germany's V-2 missiles proving unstoppable – 518 of them plunging into the capital without the slightest warning – the only answer was to despatch the RAF to the launch sites in Holland. Under Operation Crossbow, initiated to perform a similar task against the bases of the V-1 glide-bombs which had been launched earlier, RAF reconnaissance planes and bombers were diverted from other pressing missions to bring a halt to London's destruction. It was far from straightforward. The allies discovered that the V-2 launchers were not only mobile and camouflaged but also hidden amongst the civilian population of Holland: even if the targets were found, attacks had to be undertaken with a degree of restraint. And the operation exacted a high price. In one ten-week period alone in 1944, the RAF lost nearly 450 aircraft and around 2,900 aircrew while missile-hunting.[1] The effect of this was to encourage the allied powers to accelerate their push through continental Europe: if the missiles could not be destroyed by air, they would have to be captured on the ground. It was one of the factors leading to the decision to launch Operation Market Garden, the disastrous airborne landing at Arnhem in which the allies suffered 17,000 killed, wounded or missing.

Forty-seven years later it seemed little had changed, certainly that little had been learned. General Norman Schwarzkopf faced the same challenge: how to find strategically vital but mobile needles in a hostile haystack. 'The launchers turned out to be even more elusive than we'd expected,' he wrote later. His entire campaign was being threatened by Iraq's Scud attacks because if Israel felt forced to enter the war, it was likely that moderate Arab support for the operation would collapse. Schwarzkopf's British counterpart, General de la Billière, described how within three days of the start of the campaign the mobile Scuds had become 'the most immediate menace to the coalition'.

But Scud-hunting was no easier for the Gulf War allies than it had been for those of the Second World War. Although more than 4,000 US Air Force sorties (individual missions) were flown to find and kill the missiles – some 40 per cent of the strategic air effort, about three times more than had been planned – the Israeli Defence Minister, Moshe Arens, later claimed that 'not a single mobile missile launcher was found and destroyed from the air'. A US Army official, Major-General Jay Garner, supported that claim: 'They haven't killed one [mobile Scud] yet.' This was despite a promise from President Bush that the allies would launch the 'darndest search-and-destroy mission that's ever been undertaken'. Even that would not be enough. As one analyst put it in a letter to the pre-eminent American defence magazine, *Aviation Week & Space Technology*: 'In the missile age, if you can find the target, killing it is easy.'

Because the Scuds were fired from the same vehicles that carried them – Transporter-Erector-Launchers (TEL) in the military jargon – they could be prepared for use within twenty minutes and moved off in less than six. Even if a take-off was spotted by satellite or a surveillance aircraft, the launcher could have left the scene by the time a fighter-bomber arrived. During the day, the vehicles and their weapons remained hidden from view in civilian buildings or under bridges and, when they were deployed to their launch positions at night, they were barely distinguishable from ordinary articulated trucks; they looked especially similar to fuel tankers. To confuse things further, the Iraqis did their best to deceive the allies. 'With typical low cunning,' according to General de la Billière, dummy rockets were built and filled with fuel 'so that they exploded satisfactorily when hit by a bomb and caused the pilot of the attacking aircraft to chalk up another kill'. The effect was to create massive uncertainty in allied headquarters. Intelligence had originally estimated that Iraq had twenty mobile launchers; that figure was soon revised upwards. It turned out that the Iraqis had designed and built their own improvised launchers, which they were using in addition to the Soviet-built vehicles supplied with the missiles. Even after the war, when Iraq handed over a total of nineteen mobile launchers to the UN inspection teams, doubts remained about the true size of its stockpile.

The very latest technology at the coalition's disposal had been used. KH-11 photo-reconnaissance satellites scoured the likeliest areas for signs of the giveaway groupings of vehicles associated with a Scud unit. DSP satellites with infra-red sensors watched for the sudden burst of heat from a Scud launch. Two J-STARS aircraft (Joint Surveillance Target Attack Radar System) were put into action even before their development programme was complete. Using their sideways-looking radar, packed into a long, thin box fitted to the belly of an otherwise ordinary-looking recycled Boeing 707, these planes could 'see' some 400 miles into Iraq whatever the light or weather conditions. The radar systems were tuned to detect vehicle-sized metal objects and the results were startling. With a resolution of about three metres (meaning that anything smaller would be indistinct), pictures released after the war showed columns of Iraqi tanks standing stark against the desert background. Since allied intelligence knew the 'launch-boxes' or regions in which the Scuds were operating, one facing Israel, the other Saudi Arabia, the J-STARS teams were able to fine-tune their search.

Assisting them were newly equipped RAF Tornado GR1-A reconnaissance planes. These carried an infra-red system which employed three cameras, two looking sideways and one down, and recorded their images continuously on to videotape. The navigator on board, or analysts back at base later, could replay relevant parts of the tape to identify suspicious objects. In theory, the aircraft should have been able to transmit the images directly back to intelligence staff in 'real time' but that part of the system, which was rushed into service, was not yet ready. Even so, one of the aircrew remembered the satisfaction of getting 'a good picture of a Scud out in the open because they were very good at hiding them'. But although several Scuds were spotted by the Tornado GR1-As and by the American J-STARS planes, valuable minutes were lost analysing the information and organising an attack. No kills of mobile launchers were ever confirmed as a result.

The US Air Force tried to speed up its response time by maintaining patrols over the 'launch-boxes' with F-15E fighter-bombers. Intelligence gathered about the movements of the mobile Scud launchers was relayed to the pilots, who were then ordered to strike. A number of successful attacks against Scuds were reported at the time but it is unlikely that any proved genuine. The quickest response time was about fifty minutes. The reality was that, despite the boasts about high technology, the allies lacked an infallible means of seeing what the Iraqis were doing and acting on the information instantaneously. By the time any of the mobile Scuds had been spotted and the co-ordinates passed to bomber crews, 'the Iraqis had scrammed,' according to General Schwarzkopf.

Exercises since the Gulf War have tried to produce a quicker reaction. One test at the White Sands Missile Range in New Mexico in January 1993 showed that an F-15E pilot took thirty-two minutes to find a mobile launcher which had fired a short-range Lance missile. But the search required no fewer than three different types of spy-planes (one U-2R, one J-STARS, both with radar, and one RC-135 Cobra Bell with infra-red sensors) and one ground-based radar. Later tests tried to connect the various different sensors into a single integrated data network in an effort to cut the response time to ten minutes or less. The US Air Force admitted this was little better than an attempt to 'lash together' existing equipment into a system that could perform more effectively than the allies did in the Gulf.

Since even the high-technology systems were evidently failing against Iraq's Scuds, a more basic technique was employed as well: the deployment of forces on the ground to find and destroy what the airborne and space-based devices were failing to. British Special Forces soldiers were covertly inserted into the Scud operating areas from 20 January 1991, three days after the start of the war; American units were to follow. One SAS team was ferried into Iraq by helicopter only to stumble upon a Scud launch minutes later. 'The earth erupted with noise and there was a blinding light in the sky,' wrote one SAS corporal in a book about the war; 'it looked just like an Apollo moonshot, a big ball of exhaust flames.' But there was nothing the team could do: the launcher was too distant and there was no time to radio details of its position back to headquarters. On other occasions though, it is claimed, SAS teams were able to track down Scud launchers and either call in air-strikes or mount an attack themselves. General de la Billière, himself a former SAS commander, later said these operations so inhibited and suppressed the Scud units that 'no effective launches' were made at Israel after 26 January, nine days into the war.

Yet this was a curious claim. The Israeli authorities themselves recorded that a further fifteen Scuds were fired at Israel after 26 January and that as many as twenty-two civilians were injured: the Scud attacks may have been slowed but they were not stopped. The special forces teams, though undoubtedly brave, probably had less impact than their commanders would have wished. Although General Schwarzkopf later called the special forces 'our eyes' in Iraq, they did not provide the power of sight that he needed. Not that this was the fault of the special forces units themselves. Operating in territory which was unseasonably cold and unexpectedly thick with Iraqi forces, they were not blessed with the best technology to assist them. Not only did radios occasionally break down but what would have been the most useful technical aid – an infallible night-vision system – simply was not available. Despite the fact that Scud movements took place at night, the SAS's standard night-vision aid was an image-intensifier, a device which draws on all sources of ambient light – the stars, the moon, distant streetlamps – to produce a visible picture. The Night-Viewing Aid (NVA) issued to the SAS patrols, like others of the same type, involves relatively old technology and suffers from a fundamental weakness: it only works if there is some light, however little, available. On the blackest of nights, it will fail. In one account, a member of the SAS, writing under the pseudonym Andy McNab, records that on a particularly cloudy night during an attempted escape from Iraq, with two of the unit wounded, a colleague was 'having trouble with the NVA because there was no ambient light . . . slowing us down as much as the two injured men'.[2]

The failure of the allies' spacecraft, air forces and behind-the-lines soldiers to find all of Saddam's mobile Scuds, let alone destroy them, has emerged as one of the greatest concerns in the aftermath of the Gulf War: not least because of the signal it sends around the world. There is a realisation that nations trying to acquire missiles will have understood the lesson that mobility coupled with the ability to hide are key attributes for the weapons. It did not pass unnoticed in western military circles, for example, that an announcement from the Indian Ministry of Defence about a successful firing in 1993 of one of its latest missiles, the Prithvi, pointed up the fact that the 218-mile-range weapon 'used a land-based mobile launcher and mobile control'.[3] India is not alone in this. Peter Wilson, the war-game specialist at the RAND corporation, is among those who believe that while Iraq in effect fought the allies on their terms – allowing them to put into action NATO's long-rehearsed war-plans and offering largely static targets – a future enemy will do the opposite. 'He'll understand: do not present a target which allows us to use our capacity to inflict enormous violence.' In other words, do not keep still. Yet many senior western officers and military scientists believe this potential threat has gone unrecognised, despite the fact that a number of countries are not only trying to buy or build mobile missiles but also seeking to equip them with nuclear warheads.

There have been efforts to galvanise support for a crash programme of research into new techniques for hunting nuclear-armed Scuds – what the military call 'Critical Mobile Targets'. One Pentagon consultant and former US Air Force intelligence planning officer, John Rothrock, was asked to write a scenario for a future and far more dangerous Gulf War involving mobile missiles with nuclear warheads. He circulated his paper, 'Iraq Revisited in February 2007', in the highest levels of the armed forces and intelligence services and found it well received. One four-star general, writing privately, described the scenario not only as 'plausible' but also as 'very challenging to us as we are structured and equipped today' – a polite way of saying they could not cope if this work of fiction became reality.

Rothrock's scenario for 2007 envisages both Iraq and Iran possessing missiles with a far greater range than the Scud, perhaps as much as 3,000 miles, but with similar mobile launchers and deception techniques. Iraq hides its best missiles in specially built shelters where they would be hardest to attack – in the towns and villages of the Kurds in the north and of the Shiites in the south. Iran has stationed its missiles in the mountains, disguising their presence with clever use of shading to confuse satellites and spy-planes. Rothrock then introduces a cause for conflict. Saddam's successor crushes the fundamentalist Islamic opposition in Iraq. This provokes Iran to the brink of war. Iraq in return warns that if it is attacked by Iran it will be forced to fire missiles at the major capitals of Europe. The

Europeans are thrown into a state of panic. The United States has to decide whether to intervene and, if so, how. To make matters worse, the rainy season has just started, obscuring the key areas with dense cloud for weeks at a time.

As Rothrock observes, this scenario confronts the United States, as the only country capable of acting effectively, with a series of unanswerable questions. Although military intervention to head off a conflict has superficial appeal, it is fraught with uncertainty. There could be a bombing campaign either against Iran to prevent it attacking Iraq or against Iraq to prevent it attacking Europe or against both to attempt to neutralise both threats at once. The alternative is to do nothing in the hope that both sides be deterred from embarking on such a disastrous course. The difficulty is that almost any action would no doubt fail to be comprehensive since too little is known about the targets in either country to guarantee that every weapon would be destroyed. A pre-emptive strike with the intention of minimising the effects of war would almost certainly trigger an immediate response itself; and unless the pre-emptive strike destroyed all the weapons concerned, that response would be catastrophic. The humbling reality is that there can never be certain knowledge about how many weapons any country has or where they are or how ready they are for use. It is a 'tyranny of small numbers', as RAND analysts have called it. The Pentagon simply has no means of seeing the targets to identify and count all of them, let alone being sure of finding and destroying them all. Rothrock admitted to me that he found his own scenario 'really scary' because there was no solution on offer within the time-scale he himself had set.

As the US Air Force Chief of Staff, General Merrill McPeak had shared his concerns. 'We ought to be worrying about how . . . we can detect nuclear weapons,' he said in a magazine interview in December 1993. 'Can we devise, say, an airborne sniffer system of some kind that with great reliability could identify precisely the location of dormant nuclear weapons?' Such a system, he said, was 'not do-able' with current technology.[4] Other senior officers have warned of a similar problem in their attempts to find different kinds of weapons. Vice-Admiral Douglas Katz, commander of US naval forces central command, responsible for naval activity in the Gulf, disclosed that attempts to check whether Iran was buying new Chinese-made Silkworm anti-ship missiles were proving useless. He received intelligence that ships were arriving at the main Iranian naval base at Bandar

Abbas with Silkworms but was unable to check them. 'We see huge boxes on the ships, the ships are emptied but we do not know what is in them.'[5] General Joseph Hoar, overall commander of US forces in the Middle East, admitted an even greater weakness. Despite an intense search by reconnaissance satellites, spy-planes and warships, his forces failed to find a North Korean vessel, the *Dae Hung Ho*, suspected of carrying new versions of the Scud missile to Iran. 'We made every effort to locate that ship and we were unable to do it, clear and simple,' he later told Congress.[6]

Against a background of diminishing funding for military research, the key weapons manufacturers and laboratories are trying to address this problem. Grumman Aerospace, makers of the J-STARS radar-imaging plane, for example, claim to have significantly improved its performance since the Gulf War: the resolution of its radar pictures has been reduced to one metre, allowing its operators to distinguish individual types of vehicles or heavy weapons, not merely their presence. In another development, satellite photography is being enhanced to capture not just the sight, heat and radar signature of objects on the ground below but also the particular characteristics of the light they emit or reflect. Known as 'hyperspectrometry', the technique involves measuring the tiniest variations in the different wavelengths of light and building up a 'light signature'. The light reflected by satellites hundreds of miles high in orbit, for example, has been analysed minutely enough to be able to calculate the precise metallic composition of the spacecraft. Assuming the system could be made to work in reverse, a satellite or spy-plane could analyse the effluent from a suspected nuclear weapons or nerve gas factory in a hunt for clues about its true purpose.

Another technique is being pursued by Los Alamos, which formed a special office in 1992 to co-ordinate all its research into the war against proliferation. The laboratory's director, Sig Hecker, argues that only the nuclear weapons research centres like Los Alamos 'have the full sweep of technological capabilities' to understand and respond to this threat. Wisely sensing that the money is no longer available for designing new American nuclear weapons, Los Alamos has diverted resources to the most promising techniques for detecting the presence of the most potent weapons – nuclear, biological and chemical – or at least of the plants where they are manufactured. Foremost of these is a laser sensor known as LIDAR

(LIght Detection And Ranging) which looks for tell-tale particles of particular chemicals in the air – an atmospheric fingerprint. While hyperspectrometry seeks to measure light reflected from objects, Lidar transmits laser light in much the same way as radar or sonar systems use bursts of electrical or sound energy to force an 'echo' from the molecules suspended in the air. It sends out an ultraviolet laser beam which scans a sector of the atmosphere. The light has the effect of exciting molecules and illuminating them so that a sensor can 'see' them. Since the characteristics of different molecules are known in advance, the Lidar researchers can build up a 3-D picture of the atmosphere in an area of suspected weapons activity.

In the Gulf War, where Lidar was rushed into service in as few as seventeen days, the device was poised to detect and identify chemical or biological weapons should Iraq have used them. More recently, Los Alamos has sent teams with mobile Lidar units to Mexico City and Barcelona to help analyse those cities' pollution problems. By 'seeing' precisely which pollutants are in the atmosphere and where they came from, the authorities were able to track down the worst offenders. The Lidar missed nothing. In one part of Mexico City, residents had long complained that however clear their air was in the evening, by dawn it was always filled with a noxious mist. No one knew why, so the Lidar team went to investigate. During the night, at 2 a.m., the Lidar's laser light, invisible to the human eye, spotted a particular factory defying the city's anti-pollution laws by covertly releasing a large amount of waste gas. The evidence was conclusive. On another occasion, while a power station was being scanned for illegal emissions, the team detected an unusual plume of smoke which made them suspicious: the Lidar analysis showed it to be from a barbecue in an adjacent garden.

The military potential is huge. A summary of Los Alamos research highlights for 1992 describes how Lidar and other detection systems may be put to use. One scenario envisages one way in which Los Alamos scientists might spy on the nuclear genie which their own predecessors let out of the bottle:

'A van equipped with state-of-the-art sensors designed by Los Alamos is parked outside a suspect facility in a Middle Eastern desert. Inside the van technicians analyse the atmosphere around the facility. After a computer prints the measurement results, encrypted information is beamed by satellite to IAEA (International Atomic Energy Agency) headquarters in Vienna. The sensor van has detected chemicals used to process spent reactor fuel for recovery of plutonium. This is a red flag for a possible covert nuclear weapons programme. Ten minutes later, a message is sent by the same satellite link from the IAEA to the technicians in the van: "Go inside".'

The Los Alamos document claims 'these technologies are possible today' but acknowledges the political hurdles involved in putting them to use. The terms under which international inspectors can visit a suspect nuclear weapons site are strictly defined to minimise their intrusiveness and it is hardly likely that a 'Middle Eastern' or any other sovereign country would permit nuclear snooping from a hi-tech van. The same problem applies to the laboratory's hand-held monitoring devices which can detect gamma-ray emissions and neutrons. These are now in service with IAEA inspectors. The Soviet Union too had developed a system for detecting the neutrons associated with nuclear warheads. In the late 1980s, Moscow claimed that its device, if held near a nuclear weapons store for at least eighty seconds, was sufficiently sensitive to confirm the presence of warheads inside. The Soviet plan, demonstrated successfully at least once on a warship in the Black Sea, was to fit the device to a helicopter which could hover nearby. The problem – as with the Los Alamos hand-held detectors – is that only a voluntary check is possible: permission has to be given for them to be used.

To get round that, Los Alamos scientists have designed ways of fitting sensor devices to aircraft or even satellites. Scanning up to 100 kilometres either side of a plane, Lidar, for example, can sweep a large area of airspace. A future version is projected to have a range of about 400 kilometres. That would make it possible for the Space Shuttle to carry the device in a low earth orbit, analysing the air below for what Hecker calls the 'critical chemicals that signal nuclear weapons activity'. He evidently has faith in the system, singling out Lidar as the key technology in the fight against proliferation in his 1992 annual report to the laboratory's managers, the University of California. The goal, as he said in a BBC interview, is 'to find nukes from space'. But that capability may be years away. One Los Alamos document complains that 'money, time and staff' are in too short supply to develop the potential of the technology – a curious reflection of national priorities. Los Alamos was given all the funds and personnel required to design and build the first atomic bomb in the 1940s and is now restrained as it attempts to cope with that invention's aftermath in the 1990s.

It may be that in the absence of significantly increased funding, the hunt for nuclear weapons will be more effectively handled through analytical ingenuity than technological research. One former CIA photo-reconnaissance expert, Dennis Colomb, has devised a computer-assisted technique for tracking down nuclear warheads and material. In his experience, the problem is less to do with the quality of the photographs taken by spy satellites and more to do with their vast quantity and the sheer difficulty for trained analysts of finding time to study them all in detail. At least three American reconnaissance satellites orbit the earth twice daily shooting hundreds of detailed pictures. The result is that though everything of interest may be seen by the cameras, little may be spotted by the operators. So, using a modest desktop computer in his office in Atlanta, Georgia, Colomb showed me how his software mathematically records every known dimension of a particular object – anything from a face to a nuclear warhead to a canister of nuclear fuel. The computer, then confronted with hundreds or even thousands of satellite reconnaissance photographs, can scan each one already 'knowing' which shapes to look for. Colomb used the example of a secret Israeli intelligence photograph taken in 1980 of the Iraqi nuclear reactor at Osirak (shortly before Israel bombed it). In one corner, he had spotted a pair of tiny white squares, the giveaway shape of storage containers for nuclear fuel; their presence indicated that the reactor was close to being started. Once the containers' particular shape had been analysed by the computer, similar containers could be detected elsewhere, in the same photograph or in others.

Using a system of this type, intelligence analysts would be able to focus their attention only on the reconnaissance pictures highlighted by the computer. As the number of countries trying to acquire nuclear missiles grows, the demand for satellite scrutiny will multiply. In Colomb's view, computer assistance will be the only way to stay on top of a burgeoning problem. Huge regions of the world in which nuclear weapons programmes are suspected will have to be scanned: only a computer will have the speed to sort the wheat from the chaff.

This is not an approach which appeals to the self-effacing British academic who has created something of a one-man industry out of studying satellite pictures. Bhupendra Jasani of King's College, London spends his life quietly poring over black-and-white prints and teasing out their secrets. With photographs bought from American, French and even Russian commercial satellite companies, he has patiently taught himself how to pick out hidden patterns of military deployment from seemingly meaningless dots, lines and shades of dreary grey. He is also an optimist: rather than trying to find individual nuclear weapons which are almost certainly too small to spot, he has learned how armed forces the world over tend to store their ammunition: conventional weapons are kept in bunkers about fifty metres apart while nuclear weapons are kept about 150 metres apart, a distinction clearly observable from space. Nuclear weapons sites are also noticeably better guarded: the fences and perimeter roads for armed patrols stand out unmistakably. What Jasani lacks in computers and resources and access to classified photographs, he makes up for with common sense.

Mobile missiles, for example, do not need to pose an insurmountable problem, he suggests. Units of Scud or other missiles cannot remain deployed in the field for ever: their crews need breaks back at base to rest. At some point, therefore, the missile units have to gather at a central point. That is when you try to count them. Camouflage can usually be detected, Jasani says, and even if you cannot see through it, you know that it is only used to try to hide something valuable. Even when the mobile missiles are deployed in the field, there is only a limited number of areas to which they can be taken. 'These things aren't small – they need large roads for turning the damn things.' If they leave the roads and head into obscure parts of the desert, he says, you can soon see the tracks. And if they try to hide in specially built tunnels (a speciality of the North Koreans, who are even reported to have dug an underground runway from which their fighters would emerge airborne), there will still need to be access roads to reach them and 'we'll know there's something funny' about roads leading apparently nowhere in the mountains. Those will be visible, as will the spoil from the construction of the tunnels themselves. To Jasani's eye, little is hidden.

The problem though is the speed of the analysis. In the scenario devised by John Rothrock in which Iran and Iraq are on the point of starting a nuclear war, the difficulty is gaining accurate knowledge about each side's weapons at that particular time. The military ideally need a 'real-time' view of developments. Intelligence a few minutes old can be useless (as in the case of the Scuds); hours old and it can be disastrous, as with the bombing of the bunker at Amiriya in Baghdad on 13 February 1991. The attack was supposed to have destroyed an important command centre; the US military had detected intense radio activity from the site and had seen military vehicles and personnel outside it. Their observations were no doubt accurate – at the moment the intelligence was gathered. In the intervening hours though, before the raid by Stealth F-117A fighter-bombers, the role of the bunker had changed. It was being used as a bomb shelter for women and children when the planes struck; around 400 died. It was the most controversial allied attack of the campaign and, once again, a failure of sight was to blame – it had not been in real-time.

Though there will always be limits on the extent to which an enemy can be seen – such as the nature of his activity in a deep bunker – scientific progress is offering transformed powers of vision in many significant areas. Already 'night vision' has made its mark in conflicts as diverse as Vietnam, Northern Ireland and the Gulf War. The ability to see in the dark has made twenty-four-hour operations possible. But the potential benefits have been restricted so far by the cost and weight of the most effective devices and by the technical weaknesses of the cheapest and lightest. Science is now on the brink of another breakthrough in this field.

One of them carries his laboratory files and books in a wicker basket, balanced African-style on his head. Another is always seen running between buildings. A third wears Wellington boots indoors. A good many fit the scientist stereotype by wearing open-toed sandals and socks, whatever the weather. This is the Defence Research Agency's night-vision hothouse at Malvern. A modest town in Worcestershire, Malvern is dominated in equal measure by the spectacular hills of the same name and by 1,500 of the cleverest scientists and engineers in Britain. The collective genius has produced a world lead in achieving what the human eye fails to: the ability to see in the dark and through cloud. The complex of laboratories has been granted no fewer than thirteen Queen's Awards for Excellence. From the development of the first effective radar systems to the invention of the liquid crystal displays used in almost every calculator, electronic toy and computer to the vision system known as TOGS which gave the British Army's Challenger tanks a crucial advantage in the Gulf War, Malvern has acquired a world-wide reputation. Eccentricity, ruffled hair and gawky movements in worn tweed jackets are an accepted part of the landscape.

The first scientists in Malvern were specialists in radar; theirs was the first major initiative to help the armed forces to 'see' more than human sight allowed. They were moved in a great hurry from their original site on the English south coast in 1942. The government had suddenly become nervous about their security. A raid by British commandos in which key components of a German radar had been seized had convinced ministers that Britain's radar research might be vulnerable to the same kind of raid. Malvern Boys' College was chosen to house this vital work: it was isolated and too obscure to be attacked by German bombers. It produced ground-breaking results, justifying the claim of A. P. Rowe, the laboratory's director at the time, that 'this war will be won on the playing-fields of Malvern'. The development of radar systems to detect aircraft and the dreaded German U-boat earned Rowe the Medal of Merit from the then American President, Harry Truman. At least one British minister had described radar as the greatest single contribution to victory.

The dull, single-storey buildings which housed that effort are still in use, their cream paint peeling, the corridors badly lit, the small workshops and offices crammed with equipment. The scientists' pride in ingenuity, though battered by budget cuts and resentment at new efficiency measures, seems to have survived as well.

'Military systems are critically dependent,' declares the laboratory's pet slogan, 'on the performance and quality of electronic components.' Viv Roper, the scientist in charge of electronics research, puts it more bluntly: 'A high-tech edge wins wars.' Like this, he says. He hands over a plastic box which holds a tiny gold disc about a quarter of an inch across. In the centre of the disc is a minute black spot, the size of a full stop. The spot is made of a Malvern-invented substance called Cadmium Mercury Telluride, which is sensitive enough to distinguish the heat of a human body from the heat given off by the background. Its invention in 1958 was a breakthrough – offering the ability to see almost as accurately by heat as by light. According to Roper, 'It was the end of the search for the Holy Grail.' Thirty-three years later, in February 1991, the crews of the seventy-ton battle tanks of the British 1st Armoured Division peered into the Iraqi night with the aid of tiny dots of Cadmium Mercury Telluride at the heart of their vision systems. 'I don't suppose many of the soldiers realised,' adds Roper ruefully.

Ironically, the military had rejected the idea of what is called 'Thermal Imaging' – seeing by heat – when it was first proposed. Little practical use, the generals declared. Though Cadmium Mercury Telluride was proved to be capable of detecting heat emitted on a wavelength of ten microns – the precise infra-red wavelength which humans emit – the project was cancelled. In April 1958, the review of the Royal Radar Establishment, as the laboratory was then called, reported that: 'This work has now ceased as there is no operational requirement for a detector sensitive to such wavelengths.' Malvern's own brochure on thermal imaging records, with satisfied hindsight, that 'behind every discovery there is a visionary or two, enthusiasts who . . . keep the research ticking over despite the sceptics'. The project, though officially dead, was kept alive in spite of the army's express disapproval. Accounting and oversight were lax enough to allow it.

Not so now though, says Viv Roper. The Ministry of Defence keeps far tighter control over the £700 million allocated to the Defence Research Agency each year. Work on the next generations of vision systems is funded under the DRA's Strategic Research programme. Proposals are submitted to a committee of Ministry scientific officials and their civilian advisers. About half are usually accepted. The unsuccessful projects founder; the successful are only given three years to prove themselves. It is the source of widespread bitterness. 'Did Edison have three years to make the electric light bulb?' asks Mike White, a leading figure in thermal imaging research. 'Did lasers only take three years to show promise?' A short article by White, littered with capital letters for emphasis, appeals against the short-term nature of the policy: 'We need Patience, Will and Investment to see that advances in Technology achieve their potential.'

The scientists of Malvern believe that given time and money they could help equip every foot-soldier, every rifle, every fighter, every artillery shell and even every truck with its own thermal imaging system. They see this as the next revolution in military operations – not just at night, but in daylight hours as well. Thermal imaging, by 'seeing' the difference in temperature between a warm tank hidden in cooler trees or a cool sniper lurking amid relatively cooler rocks, proves to be more useful than seeing by light. 'If I offered a commander the choice of binoculars or thermal imaging at midday,' says Rex Watton, one of the senior scientists involved, 'I bet he would choose the thermal imaging – it does what he wants by making the targets stand out.'

Watton is one of the scientists who pursued thermal imaging research through some lean, unrewarded times. Squat, hardly ever still and keen on severe hand gestures, he adopts an almost reverential tone when he describes the value of Malvern's work to the forces. 'They're completely stuck without these aids.' Watton has joined numerous army exercises to test new devices. 'I really enjoy seeing the soldiers get excited by what they can do.' What he enjoys, he confesses, is the ability to see without being seen, a khaki peeping Tom. 'You can stand back and no one knows you're there.'

The first night-vision systems had the opposite effect. Originally proposed in the 1920s as a device for spotting ships at sea, infra-red devices were deployed in the Second World War as a means of communication. The X-craft mini-submarines which led the attack on the German battleship *Tirpitz* in September 1943 used an infra-red system to rendezvous secretly with the mother submarine. After the war, research began into using the infra-red wavelengths as an aid to sight. The earliest systems though had the same fundamental weakness suffered by radar to this day: to work, they must transmit enough energy to produce a reflection. The first flash of infra-red from such an 'active' system would reveal its location. The goal therefore was to devise a 'passive' system which could 'read' the different temperatures of the objects in front of it without detection.

Scientists engaged in this quest first developed 'image-intensifiers' of the sort used by the SAS in the Gulf War. These have been adapted into rifle-sights, goggles and even monoculars to be worn on helmets. Some produce a curious Cyclops look: a pilot's eyes obscured by a single green lens mounted across the upper part of his face. Others position the lens over one eye only, leaving the other free to work normally (and the user looking like he has escaped from some bizarre ophthalmic experiment). The results were often poor. Major Bob Leonik, the US Special Forces commander who led the first attack against Iraq at the start of Operation Desert Storm, described using his night-vision system as like 'looking through a toilet-tube roll with a green shade on it'. Long before, the military had grasped the limitations of image-intensifiers: on the darkest of nights, the device had trouble producing an image clear enough to be of any value. 'The penny dropped,' recalls Rex Watton. 'The military suddenly saw that image-intensifiers only gave them a few more hours around dusk.' Thermal imaging, by contrast, was a 'twenty-four-hour-a-day technology'. The generals reversed the opinion declared in 1958.

The research into this next phase quickly divided. Two sects of scientists began pursuing different approaches, their beliefs held with near-religious zeal. One sect researches what is called 'Cooled Thermal Imaging', the other 'Uncooled Thermal Imaging'. Cooled systems are more accurate and are now standard equipment in the current generation of tanks. Uncooled systems are light enough to be hand-held and early models are in service with fire brigades as a means of finding bodies in rubble. The opposing teams inhabit different wings of 'A' building at Malvern. The jokes exchanged fail to disguise the competition between them.

As the name implies, a cooled thermal imaging system needs its Cadmium Mercury Telluride sensors to be kept at a constant low temperature. This allows them to distinguish the fine detail of the scene in view. The best of these systems, TOGS (Thermal Observation Gunnery Sight), is fitted to Challenger tanks. In November 1990, as allied forces were preparing for the Gulf War, I was one of a party of defence correspondents invited to see it working. On a starless night, we took it in turns to clamber inside the turret for a drive over the dunes. The sight was staggering. On a small pale-green screen, the contours of the land, the tents and vehicles of our hosts, the Royal Scots Dragoon Guards, and even individual people were all sharply visible. Only faces were indistinguishable. The crew claimed TOGS was so good they could tell the freshness of the camel dung.

After the war, the Commander of British Forces, then Lieutenant-General Sir Peter de la Billière, described TOGS as 'invaluable'. His memoirs record tank commanders being able to see 2,500 metres into the night, a far greater range than that available to the Iraqis. 'So sensitive were the sights,' he wrote, 'that the commanders' video-display units were constantly alive with small, moving blobs of light -- jerboas scurrying about the desert floor.' De la Billière concludes that the effectiveness of TOGS night-sights helped shorten the war.

Even when Operation Desert Storm was over, night-sights were to prove their value. The campaign had left the US Army in control of a ceasefire line which ran just south of the main towns of the Euphrates valley. The result was that when Saddam Hussein's forces crushed the Shiah rebellion just north of the ceasefire line, the men of the 2nd Armoured Cavalry Regiment and the other units in the area became unwilling witnesses. Their night-vision systems allowed them to watch Iraqi earth-moving equipment preparing mass graves, executions of suspected rebels and the movements of tanks as they razed homes to the ground. On a night-time visit to the ceasefire line in March 1991, I was allowed to look through the thermal imager in an Abrams MIAI tank. The picture was more yellow and murkier than that of TOGS but it was possible nevertheless to make out individual figures in a Shiah village one and a half miles away. The crew told me that earlier, soon after dusk had fallen, they had seen Iraqi soldiers arrive by lorry and beat a dozen village men standing in line. It was a frustrating time for American troops itching to continue their fight with the Iraqis. Yet their experience served as an example of how night-vision equipment can be used – for example, to gather evidence of human-rights abuses if not to help prevent them.

For the scientists trying to perfect the technology though, the Gulf campaign showed up the weaknesses of cooled thermal imaging. 'Cooling is a real pain,' according to one leading researcher. The cooling mechanism is 'one more thing to go wrong'. It adds so much weight the device has to be mounted on a vehicle. And the coolant itself requires supplies of compressed air. This means yet another product has to be delivered to units in the field, yet another ingredient in the logistical nightmare caused by modern weaponry. There is also the expense: a thermal-imaging device costs a minimum of £30,000.

Much better, says Rex Watton, who heads a rival team developing uncooled thermal imaging, to do away with cooling altogether. He has a vision of cheap, mass-produced night-vision devices. Look at the UN operation in Bosnia, he says. The aid convoys have to stop when darkness falls. If a convoy fails to reach its destination by dusk, guards have to be posted and a watch kept all night. 'Imagine if every truck had a thermal imager – you could keep going all the time.' He believes this development is inevitable – and not only for the military. 'By 2005, when you buy a car, it'll have a thermal imager as well.' It would make driving less dangerous.

Watton and a few colleagues have tried it. They fitted one of their uncooled thermal imagers to a car and drove into the nearby town of Worcester late one evening. In a badly lit street they encountered a party of young people staggering drunkenly on and off the pavement on their way from one pub to another. Even in the dark, the thermal imager helped the scientists to steer well clear. Watton was delighted: 'think how safe it could make things in the fog'. The pub-crawlers would not have realised either that they had been seen by a futuristic device or that the car that passed them carried inventors who think they will transform modern warfare.

Rex Watton's plan is to devise a way of mass-producing tiny thermal imagers so cheaply that any vehicle, soldier or weapon can have one. His ambition is to create a heat-detecting silicon chip. Some relatively simple uncooled thermal imagers are already available. 'You could go down to Woolworths here in Malvern and buy one for £29 – a burglar alarm.' That kind of device, often fitted to a garage, watches for the sudden arrival in its view of an object with a different temperature and switches on a light or bell. The same pyro-electric technology has been incorporated into the fire service heat-detecting camera. Television news coverage of disasters frequently shows a fireman peering into what looks like a fat tele-scope mounted on a pistol grip. Such has been the effectiveness of these devices at finding people trapped in wreckage – seeing them even through thick smoke – that the Royal Navy has bought 1,000 for its fire-fighting teams on board its warships. Smaller and more sophisticated versions are on trial with the army fitted as night-sights to rifles, probably with infantry units and the SAS. Watton refuses to be drawn. 'I'm not going to talk about that.'

However, Watton is prepared to show off. He stood in front of one of his thermal-imaging cameras and a television screen nearby showed a black-and-white image of him. It was not as distinct as a normal television picture but the heavy facial features were unmistakably Watton's. The sensors in the camera were detecting the tiny variations in the temperature of the different parts of his face. His neck, being relatively warm, was shown as white; his nose, being cooler, appeared black. It was impressively detailed. But it is not a flattering medium. A display-board has a heat-photograph of the Prince of Wales which cruelly emphasises the size of his nose. Watton shrugs it off. For him, existing technology is unimpressive. His mind is on the generations ahead.

The driving forces are weight and cost, he says. The limitation of present systems is that they depend on at least two stages. At the front are the sensors. These read the temperatures of the objects in view and produce electrical impulses: the warmer the temperature, the greater the electrical charge. The charge from each of the sensors is relayed back to a processor – a chip – which begins the task of producing a television image of what the sensors have seen.

Watton's vision is to combine both those stages on to a single chip. This involves delving into the netherworld of micro-engineering. The chip – the size of a fingernail – would be peppered with hundreds of tiny heat-sensing pimples. The pimples would 'sit' just above the surface of the chip and 'feed' it electrical charges. At the same time, they would have to be sufficiently isolated from the chip not to interfere with its performance by passing on unwanted heat as well. A tall order, on a scale where measurements are made in thousandths of a millimetre.

But Watton is undaunted. 'Here's one we've already made,' he announces. He flashes up a slide of what appears to be a table. In fact it is an extreme close-up of one of the heat-detecting pimples. He calls them bridges. The top of the bridge is 50 microns wide, each leg is one-fifth of a micron thick. (A human hair is 70 microns thick.) Sitting on each bridge is heat-sensitive silicon. Its electrical responses to temperature are relayed via the legs to the chip below. The fact that the heat-sensitive material is separated from the chip itself – by however minuscule a margin – means that none of the heat is passed on. It sounds too clever to be true.

Certainly, along the drab corridors towards another end of 'A' building, Watton's opponents in night-vision research, the supporters of cooled thermal imaging, greet his enthusiasm with polite cynicism. 'Rex Watton hasn't got it yet,' announced David Huckridge, a tall, intense Welshman. Huckridge has put his faith in miniaturising the cooling systems, reducing their weight and meanwhile enhancing the accuracy provided by a cooled thermal image. As to the potential for uncooled devices, he was dismissive: 'Rex Watton claims all these things but he hasn't done them yet.'

Watton though has faith in his idea. The attraction of the concept, he says, is that the manufacturing capability already exists. The world's electronics industry chose silicon as its preferred material (for its hardness and conductivity) and has invested billions of pounds in the techniques for engineering it. Etching out such tiny features as micro-bridges and micro-legs is within the scope of current producers. They already manage it with micro-circuits. There are problems but this is feasible. If we can get commercial firms involved, there can be mass production. Each unit will then be affordable. The military will benefit, they will love it. There is no other way, he concluded. It was a virtuoso performance.

It was hard not to be immediately convinced. Until now night vision has been an often inadequate privilege enjoyed by the pilots of certain aircraft, the crews of the best tanks and the élite of the army. Night-sights were in such short supply before the Gulf War that the Parachute Regiment, one of the few units to be equipped with them, had to surrender the devices to the Staffords, the infantrymen sent out to Saudi Arabia. Even then the vast majority of the personnel deployed in the British and other forces in that campaign had no ability to see at night. In prospect now is a lifting of the fog of war for everyone – the lowliest privates, supply-drivers, doctors, mechanics. A thermal chip on every military vehicle, issued with every uniform, is a possibility. And fitted to every guided weapon, there would be a much greater chance of accurately hitting the target. Night-time operations would be less likely to collapse in tragic confusion between friend and foe. Darkness would no longer be the cloak it can be even now.

Watton ended our interview suddenly. He was determined to return to his work. 'I expect we'll see a revolution in this in about ten years. Think about it: thermal imaging is the answer.'

In another corner of the Defence Research Agency empire, at its laboratory in Fort Halstead in Kent, another scientist is already thinking even further ahead. Nigel Haig, of the Novel Weapons Department, understands the advances Rex Watton and others are proposing and can see a problem: the gift of supernatural sight will lead to information overload. The soldier will need help to make use of the extraordinary power of vision granted him. Just as American satellite pictures have proved too numerous to be handled thoroughly, twenty-four-hour, all-weather sight will be difficult to handle as well. Haig's answer is for the next generation of vision aids not only to 'see' what the eye cannot but also to recognise different objects and 'react' in the same way as the human brain. Among scientists, this concept is viewed in terms of moving the initial computer processing of visual information 'up-front', designing the sensor itself to make the sort of initial judgements made by a human, rather than passing every scrap of data back to the operator, however useless it proves to be. As one put it, 'The question is not how much information can we give you but how little is enough?'

Nigel Haig talks of the idea as if it is obviously essential. He is an impatient man, one of the DRA's 'IM' or 'Individual Merit' scientists – a category for people too clever or too eccentric or too unruly to be promoted to managerial positions but too valuable to be denied the pay increases offered by promotion. The IMs have a reputation for irascible brilliance and Haig is no exception. His office is adorned with pictures of the vintage tractors he is fond of restoring. He paces up and down, his tie pulled loose and sweater rumpled, pleading to be understood. In his time he has designed gunsights, night-sights and various peep-hole devices for the intelligence services. Once, while helping improve the surveillance equipment on a particular operation, he realised how much better it would be to have a machine do the work instead of a soldier. The military had been tasked with maintaining a close watch on an enemy building and the only conceivable vantage-point was a nearby lake. The very idea that soldiers should have to stand in the water up to their necks was 'bloody ridiculous' in Haig's view. Automating surveillance seemed an obvious next step.

His account of his invention begins with his time as an air cadet. He was adept at recognising different aircraft but could never explain why a brief view of a particular combination of shapes and angles allowed him to make an identification. Later he began to study the relationship between the eye and the brain and, more generally, how the brain itself functions. The neural networks – the pathways connecting the different parts of the brain and organising the handling of data – offered a promising model for him to mimic. While most researchers in the field of automated recognition are turning to ever more powerful computers – single, large units or hundreds of smaller ones operating in parallel – Haig says he is using 'a natural design, evolved over millions of years'. Though his project, MIDAS (Multi-band Image Dissection and Analysis System), has an ungainly title it seeks to do little more than copy the working of the eyeball.

His system – like the eye – works on the basis of different stages of processing. Because the eye has about 125 million receptors but only one million neurones to forward information to the brain, the brain constantly has to make judgements about how best to focus the eyeball or adjust to changed lighting conditions. Objects in the centre of the field of view are treated to the most intense scrutiny – they are watched with the equivalent of a high-resolution camera; the periphery of the eyeball is geared to monitoring sudden movement. Haig's hope is to achieve the same mechanically. His process envisages a central area of observation with densely packed sensors to focus on objects of maximum interest and an outer area configured to spot dramatic changes in light.

Assuming it works, the technique could offer what would not only be a sharp eye but a wise one as well. The device could perform a 'silent watch' like a sentry during the night, allowing the soldiers in a unit to sleep while it scans the surroundings. The arrival of intruders would be detected, the sensor could swivel to face them and sound an alert if necessary. Haig even visualises the device standing dormant and then switching itself on when, for example, a door opens, and starting a video-recording. And by breaking up an image into a series of mathematically definable sections, its memory for particular faces or weapons could be highly accurate. The robot eye could even be told which people or types of guns or kinds of vehicles to watch for. Fitted to an aircraft, MIDAS could help pick out suspicious objects during a high-speed flight, alerting the pilot immediately and perhaps allowing him to return for a closer look. Haig is an optimist: he hopes to run a prototype in late 1995 and see the device in service sometime before 2010, if funding allows. His point seems to be that sight itself may not be the key to the success of future military operations: the objective must be to develop a means of rapidly understanding what is seen as well – and then using the information effectively.

As Lawrence Freedman, Professor of War Studies at King's College, London concluded after the failure of the allied Scud-hunt: the critical limitation may have been 'an accurate eye rather than an adequate punch'. In future conflicts, not only will the eye have to be accurate and intelligent, the punch will have to be unerring as well.

6

AN UNERRING AIM

. . . the ancient dream of building guided weapons . . . a substitute for magic.

Martin van Creveld, *Technology and War*, 1991

Dick Lawrence has devoted his professional life to the pursuit of accuracy. He has written a poem about it, he is known as the 'guidance guru' of the British defence research establishment. For the last thirty years his ambition has been to realise the long-held military goal of ensuring that weapons actually hit their targets; his particular speciality is to design missiles to be accurate enough to intercept enemy fighters and rockets. In a field of inflated claims by manufacturers and of impenetrable jargon, he is refreshingly candid. His south-London accent seems to emphasise his honesty in describing the challenge of the task: ''ow the 'ell do you 'it something that's manoeuvring extremely violently? It's blah-dy difficult.' His phrase 'bloody difficult' has stuck to him since it slipped out in front of a sombre assessment committee deciding on future funding. His track record though is one of problems solved and it has earned him the coveted 'Individual Merit' status within the Defence Research Agency.

It suits Dick Lawrence, a man obsessed with his work. 'It's all about precision, precision.' He waves a model MiG-29 fighter-plane and attacks it with the cheap blue biro that serves as one of his missiles. He gets excited by the scale of the problems, the 'mind-boggling' number of computer calculations required by the missile as it steers itself towards its evading target, g-forces so powerful they would kill a pilot, the astounding speeds involved as ballistic missiles fall towards their targets. 'You could have warheads coming in at four or five miles a second, swerving all over the place – think about trying to hit those.' My subject is the real world, he says. 'I'm just like a kid, I keep turning stones over and finding wriggly things underneath, it's brilliant.' And the demand for his work shows every sign of increasing; accuracy has become a military obsession.

The latest advances in highly accurate weapons – what the military call 'precision-guided munitions' – were first brought to public notice on the second day of the Gulf War. At a news briefing on 18 January 1991, the allied air commander, Lieutenant-General Chuck Horner, showed video clips taken from his fighter-bombers as they attacked targets with laser-guided bombs the previous night. 'Keep your eye on the entrance,' he said as a grey image of a Scud storage bunker loomed into view on a television screen. 'The pilot has released the bombs two miles away . . . lasing the target and you'll see two bombs fly into the door of the storage bunker. You'll be able to count each bomb – one, two.' The screen erupted with a flash of light. Another bomb was seen falling into the central air-conditioning shaft of the Iraqi air-defence headquarters; smoke billowed out of the sides of the building. It was a 'technology war', according to General Horner, and it amazed a world unfamiliar with the revolution in military development brought about by the Cold War. Of the 88,500 tons of bombs dropped in the Gulf War, only some 6,250 were precision guided – around 7 per cent – yet it was those 'smart' weapons which accounted for about half the Iraqi targets destroyed. It was a technical success rate which spawned the concept of 'surgical bombing', attacks so accurate they could achieve their ends with the minimum of harm to others.

The effect on the ground was extraordinary. On a visit to one of Iraq's largest airbases, at Tallil, immediately after the Gulf War, a camera team and I picked our way gingerly through the rubble, surprised at how many of the special aircraft shelters had been neatly pierced from above. Most had a single neat hole in the roof and a wrecked fighter-plane inside. Even aircraft which had been towed away and parked beside a road to evade the bombing had been picked off one by one. Much of the rest of the base, including the accommodation area, seemed to have been left untouched. The arch across the entrance to the base, bearing a huge portrait of Saddam Hussein, was left standing too (though that cannot have been deliberate).

But, as ever, not all of these weapons worked and not all of the claims for them were true. In a major study for the US Air Force on its performance in the Gulf War, Dr Elliot Cohen concluded that though there were 'glimmerings' of a revolution in military technology, some aspects of the war that had seemed dramatic at the time appeared less so later. Close study of the video clip of the attack on the Scud bunker, for example, shows that only one of the two bombs actually penetrated the door; in slow motion it was possible to see the first laser-guided bomb passing behind the bunker and exploding outside it. Later, on 13 February 1991, an RAF attack on a bridge at al-Fallujah went wrong when three of the bombs dropped failed to respond to the laser guidance. Two fell short and one veered towards the centre of the town and landed in the market-place killing as many as fifty people. There was no explanation for the failure; only an assumption that the laser-seeker unit, attached to the nose of each bomb, failed to detect the laser light being reflected towards it from the target. (The laser beam, aimed by the attacking aircraft, is reflected upwards off the target in the shape of an ice-cream cone. The bomb is meant to steer itself within the narrowing confines of the cone down to the particular point selected by the pilot.) More recently, in January 1993, in an air-strike launched against SAM sites in southern Iraq, only half of the targets attacked were destroyed. Clearly, a guarantee of accuracy is still wanting.

The oldest guided weapons, developed soon after the Second World War to attack aircraft, relied on a radar beam transmitted from a ground-based control unit on which they could 'ride' towards the target. More modern versions had what is called a 'semi-active' radar homing device fitted in the nose of the missile; the ground radar would track the target and the missile would chase the source of the radar energy reflected from it. The latest missiles carry their own 'active' radar transmitter with which to seek and find the target. Another approach for achieving an accurate aim – this time on the battlefield – is guidance by wire. Anti-tank missiles like the Milan, in service with the British Army, uncoil a fine cable behind them, allowing the operator to steer the weapon towards the target. Similar Soviet-designed missiles were used in the battles in central Bosnia in 1993; the streets of Gornji Vakuf could often be seen strewn with the thin control wires left by Muslim and Croat anti-tank weapons.

A more advanced technology involves guidance by television. One version of the air-launched Maverick missile, for example, has a tiny camera in its nose allowing the pilot to 'steer' the weapon to its target, the image suddenly vanishing when the weapon hits home. The American defence contractor Hughes is touting a similar weapon for use by soldiers. Its NLOS (Non-Line Of Sight) missile trails behind it several miles of fibre-optic cable down which a television image is transmitted to the operator and the operator's commands sent to the missile. One advertisement for the weapon, placed in the technical press, boasts of 'precision kill' and 'collateral damage avoidance' – meaning it should be able to spare civilians. The advertisement depicts several of the missiles in a Bosnian setting (arms manufacturers having previously favoured desert backdrops after the Gulf War) streaking carefully past a Serb Orthodox church and effortlessly steering towards Serb artillery positions.

The trend though is towards automatic guidance – for weapons computers to be given a description of the target and then left to find it themselves. The Tomahawk cruise missiles made famous in the Gulf War achieved this with the technique of 'terrain contour matching' in which an altimeter periodically compares its observation of the ground below with previously stored data of what should be seen at each stage along the route of the attack. In Operation Desert Storm, Tomahawks were seen following the line of particular streets on their way to targets in Baghdad. Much larger intercontinental ballistic missiles such as the American MX check the accuracy of their course by reference to the stars, comparing their view of the stars at a certain point with a pre-programmed view of them stored in their on-board computer.

In the pipeline though are even more esoteric systems of guidance to 'give us more punch on the battlefield', according to the former US Defence Secretary Les Aspin, using satellites, sound and more advanced forms of infra-red. The Sensor Fused Weapon (SFW), first delivered to the US Air Force in 1994, contains forty bomblets – known as 'skeets' – each of which has an infra-red sensor that scans about one acre of the ground below. If the sensor spots an armoured vehicle (recognising its heat signature) it detonates and sends a five-inch-long copper rod hurtling at 3,600 m.p.h. down to the target below. The result is that just one SFW could in theory destroy an entire formation of forty tanks spread over an area equivalent to six football pitches. Tests have apparently shown that the weapon does work and some 10,000 have been ordered already. More ingenious still is the BAT (Brilliant Anti Tank), a strange-looking missile with four wings and forward-pointing aerials, which first finds its targets by listening for them – its on-board computer is programmed with the acoustic signatures of different enemy vehicles. Once suitable targets have been found, the BAT swoops sideways to hover above them and then uses an infra-red sensor to identify the best point to attack. In the case of a tank, the BAT would 'know' that the top of the turret or the area where the turret joins the chassis are the most vulnerable; it would then strike. A future version may use radar instead of infra-red – to be able to identify vehicles even if they are stationary and therefore cool with their engines switched off. The US Army's plan is for swarms of BATs to be sent into battle on board large missiles.

More exotic still are weapons that hit their targets not with a projectile (prone to stray off course) but with a blast of energy. 'If you've got enough energy to fire off a missile, why not just focus that energy instead?' one American designer asked at the USAF's Phillips Laboratory at Albuquerque in New Mexico. 'It's one thing less to make you miss.' Lasers offer the most promising technology in this area and research in pursuit of the science-fiction dream of beam weapons has yielded some tangible results. Small laser weapons were deployed in the Falklands and the Persian Gulf on Royal Navy ships to dazzle the pilots of attacking aircraft (but were not thought to be effective enough to fend off aircrew equipped with a low-technology counter-measure: sunglasses). A more powerful laser weapon has been fitted to a USAF experimental plane. Mounted in a small turret, it has reportedly managed to fire enough energy at Sidewinder air-to-air missiles to knock them off course. But the cost and weight of the systems, together with the difficulty of achieving a fine focus and overcoming the atmosphere's tendency to degrade the strength of the laser beam, have limited their potential usefulness – not that that has halted work in this field.

The pressure for further research continues. With the proliferation of advanced weaponry, the case for trying to maintain technological superiority is a strong one and, of all decisive factors, greater accuracy is generally identified as one of the most important. Its benefit in air-to-air combat was clearly proved over Bosnia in February 1994 with the shooting down of four Bosnian Serb jets by American F-16 fighters. So confident were the American pilots in the efficacy of their fire-and-forget weapons that immediately after each firing they changed course to pursue the next target – without even waiting to see if the previous attack had been successful. In the end, five highly advanced

American missiles brought down four 1960s-technology ex-Yugoslav aircraft; it was no match. But NATO countries will not have been alone in noting the lessons.

The sale of the most advanced equipment from the former Soviet Union and from other countries means that future adversaries may well be armed with sophisticated weapons. Russia has already sold its latest MiG-29 fighters to Iran and its best interceptors, the Sukhoi-27, to China; further sales of these and yet more advanced and manoeuvrable aircraft look likely, together with the most modern air-to-air and air-to-ground weapons that accompany them. The effect is that precision guidance – 'smart' weaponry – has become a vogue topic with commanders the world over. Malaysia's Defence Minister, Najib Tun Razak, said, 'obviously we intend to enter this arena'. Equipping forces with 'high-precision weapons' was one of the priorities of the French 1993 Defence White Paper. The designers of the latest Russian bomber, the Sukhoi-34, claim it can navigate to 'within one metre' of a target, according to a glowing account in the Moscow newspaper *Izvestia*.

For Dick Lawrence and his immediate colleagues at the DRA, the implications in their field – air-to-air combat – are painfully clear. 'If you don't keep the pace of research going for the air-to-air precision, you get into a situation where you can't hit them,' he says. This could sound like the special pleading of a defence industry lobbyist. With some justification, critics accuse the military, and the scientists who support them, of resisting cuts because they cannot bear change. Lawrence though belongs to the school of thought which says that 'if we don't invent it, somebody else will'. And he has no personal axe to grind: 'If they boot me out of here, I'll get just as much satisfaction designing computer games.' So far he has not needed to think of another career.

A childhood in Dorking, Surrey during the Second World War put him under the flight-path of Hitler's V-1 doodlebug glide bombs as they flew towards London. Once as he stood watching them with his father and sister, they heard the engine of one of the missiles suddenly cut out, a sign that it would soon crash. His sister was stiff with terror. 'It went right over the roof of our house and landed up the road.' Though Lawrence was too young to be affected at the time, he says the trauma experienced by his sister has left an impression and, as a result, his greatest interest has always been in defensive weapons. He claims to have no moral concerns about his work. 'It's still a dangerous world.'

At first sight, at the end of one of the long corridors of linoleum and beige paint of the Defence Research Agency's Farnborough headquarters, Dick Lawrence's pale-blue shirt, grey trousers and sober Paisley tie mark him down as pure middle management. But he is keen to show otherwise; he resents the public image of scientists as humourless 'nerds'. As soon as he ushered me into Room 53, an office crammed with piles of books (on everything from brain research to Chaos Theory to astronomy), secret files and at least six different computers, his first act was to produce a small black-and-white photograph of himself, sporting white Elvis-style clothes and quiff, as a rhythm guitarist. It was taken in 1958 – 'we modelled ourselves on the Shadows, early Rock 'n' Roll'. Twenty-five years later, this was offered as proof of his humanity, his self-mockery. A short man, always looking for a laugh, he has the unpredictable air of the comedian Norman Wisdom: no one can be sure whether his next utterance will be profoundly serious or a joke. Even in his youth though, he was gripped by his work, by the enormous technical challenge of tracking a target and hitting it. He named his first band The Trakkers.

He was 'always potty about electronics', building amplifiers for his guitar which 'never worked'. He began as an engineering apprentice at the Defence Research Agency's laboratory at Malvern and soon found himself confronted by institutional snobbery. He applied to become a 'scientific officer' – the scientific equivalent of leaping from the non-commissioned ranks into the Officer Corps. But his application was refused because he had no degree. 'They liked Oxbridge or Imperial College, that kind of thing, not horrible, grotty little apprentices like me.' A stint in private industry and an M.Sc. from Birmingham University saw him back at Malvern in the post he had first applied for; his bosses ate humble pie. His work on the Blowpipe and Rapier missiles, now the mainstays of the British Army's air defences, together with pioneering research into using lasers to guide missiles, earned him unusually rapid promotion. 'I got Senior Scientific Officer in two years – they doubled my salary.' It was a high point in British military research. The armed forces were only beginning to shrink from imperial proportions and the scale of research had hardly reduced with the transition from the Second World War to the Cold War. 'We were at the cutting edge, there was money to burn and we were really pushing back the frontiers all the time.'

He loves to recall that heyday. Behind the shabby façades of the hastily erected wartime buildings, there was unrestrained excitement about the potential for technology. Lawrence and his colleagues threw themselves into it. Discovery was a joy. One evening, Lawrence aimed a laser at a nearby church steeple, intending to measure the beam's power. Instead he stumbled on the fact that the laser light being reflected back towards him was 'painting' a picture of the steeple in the dark. Even now the potential for using lasers to 'see' through dark or water is only beginning to be exploited. The young scientists also realised that the thin, invisible beam of another laser, based on infra-red, produced enormous heat on a tiny spot. Not quite the death-ray envisaged by the science fiction of the time, the beam could nevertheless ignite a piece of paper in an instant, as if by magic. The trick was performed to 'scare the secretaries'. Another laser required liquid nitrogen which had to be poured from a flask. It usually spilled on to their hands. 'It would freeze part of your hand solid, you couldn't move it in case it snapped off,' Lawrence remembers with delight. A generator built to produce an exceptionally high voltage would occasionally blow up, cooling-pipes burst, floors flooded. 'We were paid for having all this fun; well, not paid much, I suppose.'

His first experience of the politics of military science came with the troubled Sky Flash programme. Sky Flash was an ingenious British adaptation of the American Sparrow air-to-air missile. It involved fitting a new guidance system which was meant to improve the chances of the missile hitting the latest Soviet MiGs. By 1974 the project was in trouble. Repeated flight tests had failed, at enormous cost. Each test involved fixing Sky Flash beneath the wing of one aircraft while the scientists attempted to coax it into detecting another aircraft nearby. 'They were burning money.' Prestige was also at stake yet progress was non-existent. Dick Lawrence was monitoring the project on behalf of the Ministry of Defence, a role he resented. 'I was very unhappy being an official in a pin-striped suit turning up to all these meetings, at first I'd told them to get stuffed.' Against the will of his superiors, he began devising a mathematical model of how the Sky Flash should perform. It proved accurate. Pages of equations – 'I love them' – revealed a fault, that the missile was mistaking the radar signal of its target with the radar emanating from the aircraft carrying it. The project was brought back on track and Sky Flash is now successfully in service with the RAF.

Lawrence's role brought him a tap on the shoulder one day when he was hunched over his workbench. 'Just go away and think about guidance,' his supervisor told him, guidance for a secret new weapon. It was 1977 and the RAF needed a weapon that could attack the dense radar network guarding the Warsaw Pact. The Soviet forces had fielded the most intense anti-aircraft defence ever seen – thousands of guns and SAMs. All of them depended on radar to guide them. Therefore the next, logical step in this particular arms race was to find a way of seeking and destroying the hundreds of radar dishes. The RAF's preference for this role was an American missile, the HARM (High-speed Anti-Radiation Missile). Lawrence and his colleagues, backed by British industry, lobbied to build a British alternative.

There were various British options. One plan was for thousands of tiny model aircraft or drones to be fitted with homing devices and little warheads and aim themselves at the Warsaw Pact radars. That did not appeal to the RAF, Lawrence recalls with exasperation, 'because there was no room for Biggles with his white scarf'. Scientists like Lawrence pride themselves on showing disdain for military vanity. 'We have to persuade them that if they don't listen to us, they'll get shot down,' he said. Another plan, with more appeal, was for a missile, later called ALARM (Air-Launched Anti-Radiation Missile), which would be launched from a fighter. Once in flight, the missile would guide itself to an enemy radar. It was similar to the American HARM but had an important additional feature. The most obvious tactic for a Soviet anti-aircraft unit would be to switch off its radar when an attack began – to hide the target. To combat such a move, the ALARM would have the ability not only to 'loiter', swinging beneath a parachute, and wait for the radar to be switched on again but also to memorise the last recorded position of the radar and steer itself there automatically. The idea was accepted and a decade of expensive and painful development followed. Lawrence helped design the computer software that would give the missile its special memory. By the time the Gulf War began in January 1991, the ALARM was ready and by all accounts was successfully used against Iraqi radar.

By then Lawrence had moved on. ALARM was designed to attack stationary radar sites; far more challenging was the task of hitting fast-moving jets in supersonic dog-fights. By the late 1970s, the thinking about guidance had gone through several evolutions.

The earliest is known as 'Predictive Guidance'. The angle, speed and direction of an approaching aircraft is observed and its future position is predicted; a gun is then fired at that point. 'You have to try to work out where the thing's going to be when the bullet gets there,' according to Lawrence. The weakness is that the simplest evasive action by an enemy pilot will scupper the prediction. 'Pursuit Guidance' came next. This has been likened to a dog chasing a rabbit: a missile is aimed at an aircraft's present position and constantly alters its heading to close the gap as it tries to put itself on to a collision course. That often left a missile attempting to turn at a sharper angle than the aircraft – and failing – or ending up behind it without the speed needed to catch up.

Cleverer software was needed to allow a missile to sense the direction of the target and alter its path accordingly. Hence a third phase in the quest for perfect guidance: a solution called 'Proportional Navigation'. In essence, a missile's computer keeps updating its prediction of where the aircraft will be in a few seconds' time. The missile tries to establish the flight-path of the target and adjusts its course until its computer concludes that collision is inevitable. This is the system now adopted by all the latest anti-aircraft missiles in service in the West and elsewhere: the Sky Flash, Sidewinder and Sea Dart used in the Gulf War and the Advanced Medium Range Air-to-Air Missile, AMRAAM (used to shoot down one of the Bosnian Serb aircraft in February 1994), and its short-range stablemate, ASRAAM, developed later. Yet the system has a fundamental fault: it requires the target aircraft to settle on to a particular course long enough for the missile to hit it. As Lawrence explains, 'The proportional navigation guidance is running a hypothesis that the aircraft is not manoeuvring, so if it is manoeuvring, the aim-point will always be wrong.' A determined and able enemy pilot can make constant, violent manoeuvres to outwit the software. 'The missile has to keep adjusting, trying to emulate the movement of the target and it can't always do that.'

Further problems are the cost and weight of the system. Minutely engineered gyroscopes, lenses and processing equipment have to be shoe-horned into a tiny space – 'it's beautiful stuff, really'. In a Sky Flash missile costing about £150,000, some one-third of the expense will be on the guidance unit. In addition, to compensate for the potential inaccuracy, this generation of missile carries a large warhead and a fuse which senses when the target is close and detonates the explosive at the right moment. It avoids the need for a direct hit. However, not only does the weight of the components limit the number of weapons a warplane can carry but also the components themselves cannot guarantee accuracy. The quest continues.

Dick Lawrence had realised the limitations of 'Proportional Navigation' guidance as early as 1984. He was the British representative on a NATO study investigating building defences against Soviet ballistic missiles. The Ronald Reagan dream of a Star Wars space shield was at its height and, as Lawrence found, any American scientist who even suggested there might be difficulties was 'muffled and taken off to a padded cell'. It was a time of slick presentations. The American defence contractors and armed services were trying to improve their anti-aircraft missiles so that they could intercept enemy missiles, not just enemy fighters as originally designed to do. 'Guidance won't be a problem,' Lawrence remembers one executive declaring. 'I just kept my gob shut when I heard that.' The director of the NATO study had assumed that proportional navigation would be adequate for the task. But Lawrence's own computer model had shown that if an anti-aircraft missile such as Patriot used the principle of proportional navigation, it would fail. The pattern of flight of an incoming warhead would confuse the defending missile's software, he concluded.

Dick Lawrence ushered me to one of his older computers ('she's lovely, this one') and hit a series of keys to explain his point. Grid-squares soon covered the screen. In the bottom left-hand corner lay a pale-yellow line representing a friendly base and anti-aircraft missiles like Patriot defending it. From the right-hand corner came a red line, the high-speed streak of a Soviet SS-23. 'It's doing a helluva pace – look, here it is again.' The Soviet attack was so rapid I had missed it first time. A ballistic missile such as the SS-23 is fired into space and then falls back to earth at a breathtaking rate. An SS-23 re-enters the atmosphere travelling at a speed of about two kilometres a second (over 4,000 m.p.h.). That is only one of the problems for the guidance engineer. Another is that the friction of the atmosphere forces the weapon to slow down dramatically. This deceleration can reach 60g, equivalent to sixty times the normal force of gravity. 'To give you an idea of what that means, if you crash a car head-on into a wall at sixty m.p.h. you'll feel about fifteen to twenty g; with an emergency stop you'll feel just over one g.' His point was that even if a missile's path towards the ground may be detectable, its position on that path at any given time is far harder to predict.

Lawrence's solution was simple but novel. Instead of attempting to predict how far the incoming missile will have travelled along its flight-path towards the ground – 'you wouldn't have a chance' – he suggested plotting its likely course and firing the defending missile up in the opposite direction. 'You're bound to meet it somewhere along the way.' His computer models gave promising results, his intuition supported by hard mathematics. The screen showed a little yellow line – the defender – rising at a modest angle and then swinging up on to the predicted course of the SS-23 and hitting it. The results were passed on but were not readily accepted. 'I had to ram it down their throats, they thought they'd get away with the usual guidance.'

Lawrence never knew if his idea had been applied – until the Gulf War. With intense interest, he watched the television coverage of the Patriots trying to defend Tel Aviv from Iraq's Scuds. He saw the Patriots, usually in pairs, performing exactly what he had envisaged on his computer: launching at a fairly steep angle and then suddenly swerving upwards into a far steeper climb as they hurled themselves towards the Scuds. For Lawrence, that dramatic change of course was the giveaway. 'They were putting themselves on to the Scud's approach line,' he says with satisfaction. Their on-board computers were doing just what Lawrence had suggested seven years before. The intense hype about the success of Patriot during the Gulf War ignored a key fact. The system did as well as it did because of 'inverse trajectory shaping', an idea conceived and developed by a modest British boffin who bicycles into work and loses himself for hours at a time in the complexities of guidance mathematics. 'It's nice when they listen.'

Future systems already exist in the minds of Dick Lawrence and his colleagues. Most of the details of future systems remain secret. Only basic principles and aims can be revealed. 'We want to improve accuracy from getting within several metres of the target to getting within half a metre of a particular point on the target.' Rather than have a heavy, expensive missile like Sky Flash try to get close enough to an enemy warplane to cause perhaps only limited damage, the plan is to develop a tiny 'smart' missile which can throw itself directly at the most important part of the aircraft – the cockpit. Is that really achievable? I asked. Yes, came the answer, with none of the qualifications which usually accompanied

Dick Lawrence's claims. He switched on his newest computer. On a huge colour screen, four little boxes contained different views of a MiG-29 pulling a desperate turn to evade one of Lawrence's missiles. The images of the plane grew on the screen; the view was from the nose of the attacking missile, closing fast. Lower down, brightly coloured graph-lines squirmed as they recorded bearing, speed, acceleration and angle. The MiG-29 was now looming large in the four boxes, the missile upon it, the screen suddenly blank. Without a pause the whole process started again. Dozens of imaginary MiGs were pulverised in the time Dick Lawrence explained his work.

'I call it crystal-ball gazing, I want to predict the target's behaviour and get the computer to work out what'll happen – that's the way we're going now.' His idea is to develop programs that take account of all known intelligence about the performance and likely manoeuvres of particular planes and missiles. 'You might have learned from hard experience that in a certain situation such-and-such a move was always likely.' In this, he is trying to match the way humans think. A human brain, he says, constantly makes judgements about whatever object is in view by comparing it with relevant memories; the process assists decision-making. Central to this approach is the need to teach the computer to recognise a target from every possible angle – what the cockpit and engines look like from different positions – along the same lines as those proposed by Nigel Haig with his attempts to mimic the human eye. Lawrence calls this 'Dynamic Image-based Precision Guidance'. 'It's how animals and human beings look at things – we've got mathematical models of things in our memories and we use those to make the best use of information we're getting now.'

The next step is to teach the computer to guess the objective of the aircraft or missile. The scientists call this 'Goal-Oriented Tracking', judging the attacker's likely destination. If a naval task force is under attack, for example, a reasonable assumption is that the prime target is the flagship. That means the attacker has to reach that vessel from its present position. The defender cannot be sure of the attacker's course. But equipped with a hypothesis about its intention, he is more likely to be able to predict its route and therefore attempt an interception with a greater chance of success. 'You can launch half a dozen missiles each with different theories about the enemy's behaviour built in to them.' At least one of them should be right.

The final component of the plan is to equip the missile's computer with the mathematical models needed to detect the start of a manoeuvre and understand where it will lead – before the movement is complete. However swiftly an enemy pilot or warhead changes course, there is a brief delay between beginning a move and completing it. This so-called 'drift' may only last a fraction of a second. That briefest of times though may be all that is required. The missile's computer could assess the direction and angle of the aircraft or missile, compare it with previously stored information about various manoeuvres and make a confident prediction about where the aircraft will be when the move is finished. 'With that, even a small missile could be really accurate and totally lethal – it's the way we are going.'

The concept was only narrowly approved by Lawrence's superiors. The committee of advisers which hears requests for funding for long-term 'Strategic Research' took some convincing. 'This one professor was asking me what the value of all this was. So I told him: I said, "If you can stop a hundred-thousand-pound missile skimming in over the sea and sinking your flagship worth four hundred million pounds, then that's worth it." That shut him up.' The problem was probably more to do with persuading the committee of the value of this particular work rather than with understanding the need for ever greater accuracy in general. After centuries of warfare in which private soldiers commonly joked that the most dangerous combination on the battlefield was an officer and a map, the military now see the revolutionary benefits of precise guidance – not least to avoid hitting the wrong targets.

In an age of intense media scrutiny of military operations, the point of an accurate aim is not only to hit the enemy but also to minimise the risk to civilians. As one of Lawrence's colleagues put it: 'The world is very sensitive to accuracy – we are not allowed to miss these days.' So much so that the Pentagon is spending nearly $40 million modifying the computer software of its Tomahawk cruise missiles to minimise the risk of them going astray. The plan is that as a missile approaches its target – for example an individual building in a compound in a city such as Baghdad – it runs a series of checks to calculate the extent to which it has deviated from its course. If the margin of error is relatively small, the missile would steer itself towards a larger and easier alternative target such as the centre of the compound. But, if the extent of drift from the planned course is found to be large, the new software would automatically divert the missile well away from the target altogether – and towards the nearest uninhabited area, where it would crash harmlessly into the ground.

The event which triggered this research was a surprise attack on the Iraqi intelligence headquarters on 27 June 1993. The American government believed it had incontrovertible evidence that Iraq had been behind an assassination attempt against the former President, George Bush, during a visit to Kuwait and it decided to act. Twenty-three cruise missiles were fired – sixteen hit their individual targets, three drifted but still landed within the right collection of buildings, one vanished without trace and three missed altogether, crashing into a residential area of Baghdad. It was reported that at least eight civilians were killed and several others injured by the three stray missiles. In one account, Dr S. A. D. Ismail, writing an angry letter to *The Independent* newspaper, said his brother, a dentist, and his family were asleep when the Tomahawks fell.[1] They 'managed to get the screaming children to the basement, suffering some cuts from flying glass. They were left with shattered windows, a gaping hole in the roof of their house and children probably psychologically scarred for life. The other casualty was the family dog.' Dr Ismail protested that the 'immorality of attacking a target amidst residential areas without any warning to civilians must be clear to all'.

President Clinton seems to have heeded this kind of criticism by ordering the improvements to the cruise missiles. The attack had anyway attracted diplomatic hostility; the raid had not been specifically authorised by the United Nations and no allied approval had been sought in advance. It is evident that if the United States does want to retain the option of punitive strikes of this kind, the best way to minimise the reaction is to try to limit the impact on uninvolved civilians. The modified Tomahawks – planned to be available from late 1995 – will navigate with the very latest technology: guidance by satellite.

Midnight on 5 January 1980 marked the start of a new calendar and of a new era in warfare. It saw the launch of Global Positioning System time, GPS time, an alternative to the calendars of the major religions and profoundly important to people the world over. Hours and minutes made way for a 'Z-count', each 'Z' being the equivalent of one and a half seconds (deliberately chosen to avoid confusion with the normal second-by-second count used by the vast majority of electronic machines). Zs are the guide by which the most advanced armies, navies and air forces fought in the Gulf War and to which armed forces everywhere are now turning; they are also becoming the principal source of navigation for the major airlines and shipping fleets. The Z-count is transmitted from twenty-four American military satellites, orbiting in a constellation above the earth, broadcasting a continuous stream of data about the current state of GPS time and about their own positions. Down below, tens of thousands of receiver units – many hand-held by individual soldiers or fitted to missiles, others on warships and fighters, some on civil aircraft and freighters – tune in to the signals of at least four of the satellites and calculate their positions relative to the spacecraft. There has never been such an accurate navigational system: compasses, sextants, chronographs and gyroscopes have given way to GPS. For the first time in history, military units can be certain of their own locations and of the destinations of their weapons. No wonder at least one American general has called satellite navigation the 'most significant invention since the atomic bomb'.

Like nuclear weapons, GPS has had the effect of transforming military thinking. Navigation at sea, on land and in the air had previously been a process which was invariably inaccurate. The story is told of one British wartime pilot who, knowing the length of time he took to smoke a cigarette, calculated his position by the number of butts on the cockpit floor. Since the Second World War, various different systems of radio beacons have been the main source of navigational assistance. LORAN, the most modern of these networks, offers a 'fix' which is, on average, accurate to within 100 yards but coverage only extends to America, northern Europe and parts of the Mediterranean and Middle East. OMEGA, a system designed to provide global coverage, is less accurate, offering a navigational fix to within four miles. Even the first satellite navigation system, known as TRANSIT, fielded in the early 1970s, was only accurate to the nearest mile. Designed to help Polaris nuclear submarines plot their own positions (to be able accurately to programme their weapons), TRANSIT also suffered from the fact that it commonly took thirty minutes for the receiver to make the necessary navigational calculations. That waiting time of half an hour made the system unusable for fast-moving aircraft and risky for submarines attempting to remain hidden. This led to pressure for the development of a faster and more accurate system. The Global Positioning System was the answer and the military have fallen on it with a passion -- seemingly oblivious to dangers which would only become apparent later.

Sixteen of the GPS satellites were available in time for the Gulf War. Even before the operation began in the featureless desert, the British Gulf commander, General Sir Peter de la Billière, described the system as a 'potential war winner'. Christopher Bellamy, defence correspondent for *The Independent*, concluded that without GPS, the 'giant but at the same time intricate manoeuvres . . . would have been just impossible. In any other war, the units and formations would have got hopelessly lost, bumped into each other . . .' Instead, hurriedly equipped with almost 10,000 GPS receivers – some bought from mail-order catalogues by the soldiers themselves – the allied forces could be confident they would be in the right place at the right time. GPS provided what is known as a 'sixteen-metre Spherical Error Probable', which means that there is a 50 per cent chance that the receiver is within 16 metres of the location indicated in its display, a 95 per cent chance that it is within 30 metres and a 99.9 per cent chance that it is within 62 metres.

A classified Pentagon assessment of the performance of GPS in the Gulf War said the system would 'change the face of future warfare'.[2] While Second World War bomber crews had taken several months of training to become proficient at navigation (even by the standards of the time), US Navy Special Forces SEAL teams with GPS could be taught within a day, according to the report. Indeed, so accurate was the system that when one member of a SEAL unit accidentally dropped an expensive radio over the side of his dinghy one night off the Kuwaiti coast, a GPS position fix allowed the unit to return the next day and find the radio on the sea-bed. GPS was used to guide the Apache helicopter gunships deep into Iraq to fire the first shots of the war; it helped giant B-52 bombers and single-seater F-16 fighter-bombers find their targets. The US Air Force's Tactical Air Command, in a statement quoted in the Pentagon report, said the ground controllers whose task was to guide the aircraft to their targets 'would have been lost most of the time' without GPS. Ground forces lashed GPS receivers to the dashboards of their jeeps and soldiers from the US Army's 5th Special Forces Group, assigned to Arab forces in the coalition, remember being regularly asked to mark their locations with 'the magic compass'.

The report concludes that 'only a small sampling' of the potential for GPS was seen in the Gulf. 'Applications . . . in combat systems and tactics will be limited only by the imagination of engineers and tacticians.' It is a sentiment widely echoed. GPS provides such unprecedented accuracy that it is even forcing a redrawing of some maps; satellite navigation has shown that surveys made on the ground can be as much as 100 metres adrift. Its ease of use means GPS is already replacing most other forms of navigation – civil airlines in the United States are desperate to introduce it. Even transport planes delivering humanitarian aid to Sarajevo airport, where the normal system of ground-based radio beacons collapsed because of the war, relied on GPS to guide them; more remote areas of famine or disaster could be helped in the same way as well.

But it is in the guidance of weapons that many in the military believe GPS holds greatest promise, suddenly offering a new level of accuracy at relatively low cost. The receiver units are sufficiently small and light to be packed inside missiles such as the US Navy's SLAM (Stand-off Land Attack Missile). This new weapon, which was used in the Gulf War, approaches its target with the aid of GPS and then makes its closing attack under television guidance from a pilot. The Navy was delighted with its performance and, like the rest of the US armed forces, now 'wants to fit GPS to everything that moves', according to John Owen, a British Defence Research Agency scientist responsible for satellite navigation developments. From ballistic missiles to 'smart' artillery shells to the next generation of cruise missiles, GPS is seen as an essential mechanism for achieving accuracy. The manufacturers of the Joint Stand-Off Weapon (JSOW), planned for the US Air Force and US Navy, even claim their missile, guided by GPS, will be precise enough to act as a supply vehicle, delivering fresh loads of food or ammunition to troops on the front line, landing near them but not on them. 'It's a truck – load it up with whatever kind of freight you want,' said one official.

Yet GPS is a double-edged sword; the undoubted benefits come with huge risks. The first is that members of the armed forces may well become dependent on GPS and begin to abandon their skills in other forms of navigation. That is not a problem if GPS continues to operate. But there is no guarantee that during a war it will be able to: it is 'extremely vulnerable' to jamming, says John Owen. A potent enemy could damage the GPS constellation with anti-satellite weapons (in the 1980s both the United States and the Soviet Union developed techniques which made such an attack possible) or at least try to spoil their signals. The frequencies used by the GPS system to transmit the time and navigation data are known world-wide so a determined enemy could pump out a jamming signal which would make reception of the transmissions difficult or even impossible in particular areas. One scenario suggested by DRA scientists envisages an enemy, at an especially sensitive stage of a battle, choosing to fire special artillery shells, fitted with GPS jammers, into the front line to create confusion and force a retreat. Another possibility is for the approach route to a valuable target such as a bridge to be guarded with GPS jamming systems to reduce the accuracy of attacking war-planes or missiles. Curiously, despite the well-publicised use of GPS in the Gulf War, the Iraqis did not attempt to use any such tactics. That lapse on their part is unlikely to happen again – and there is a growing recognition that depending on GPS alone may be unwise.

Research is already under way into counter-measures to resist attempts to jam GPS signals. With the United States military paying an estimated $50 billion for the system and its maintenance, researchers are determined to protect it. In Britain, as soon as GPS became available, the DRA began developing so-called 'adaptive antennae' to evade the influence of jammers. If jamming is detected, the aerials which receive the GPS transmission respond by ignoring all signals from the particular direction of the jammer – while continuing to receive GPS signals from all other directions. John Owen, one of those involved in the project, is confident it will work; there are plans to fit it to the RAF's Hercules transport planes and Chinook heavy-lift helicopters, later to the next British combat plane, the Eurofighter 2000. Technological progress should see the cost of the device fall and make it affordable for a huge variety of army vehicles as well. But fitting the system to aircraft – a complex technical task – is bound to remain expensive, perhaps as much as £100,000 per unit, and may mean that most planes will not be equipped with it. The jamming of GPS will remain a worrying threat and therefore a continuing focus of research.

A second risk with GPS is that the signals from its satellites are available to all. Although GPS's arrival is compared in significance to the invention of the atomic bomb, the system has the curious characteristic for a hugely expensive military investment of being open to all – unlike nuclear weapons, the secrets of which remain closely guarded. When GPS was being planned, the US Congress decided to waive charges for users on the grounds that the collection of fees world-wide would be too expensive to administer. The result is that anyone is free to buy a GPS receiver and benefit from the system. The spring 1994 mail-order catalogue of the American military equipment firm US Cavalry, for example, offers a Trimble Scout GPS receiver for as little as $699.95 (roughly £400). The size of a large calculator, it is billed as the 'ultimate in locating convenience' and can be delivered in four to six weeks. There are no restrictions on who can buy the device nor on exporting it. In a future Gulf War, the Iraqis would be bound to be among those taking advantage. Certainly Senator James Exon, one of the most influential congressmen on defence issues, has said the Pentagon should 'assume that adversaries will be able to navigate precisely'.

The GPS designers had anticipated this problem but failed to prevent it. Their satellites transmit two radically different standards of data – one for the general civilian user and another, much more accurate, for the military. To achieve this, the navigation information is broadcast on two separate frequencies. The basic 'course acquisition' (CA) code provides the minimum data needed to allow a navigational fix to within 100 metres while the encrypted 'precise' (P) code offers the greater detail needed to achieve a fix to within sixteen metres. That was the plan. In practice, when the system began, the information provided by the basic CA code allowed users to ascertain their positions to within about twenty metres – only four metres less accurate than the service for the military. The designers realised the danger of this in the wake of the Gulf War and have since deliberately spoiled the quality of the CA code by randomly introducing encrypted signals to it. Yet even with this measure, the civilian system is accurate to about fifty metres.

The implications are clear. Even after the degrading of the signal, any military force can make use of what is still the best navigation system in the world. A future enemy can use it not only to manoeuvre his forces almost as well as those of the West but also to guide his weapons towards them. Just as the US military has plans to fit GPS receivers to the next generation of guided missiles, so too could a number of other countries. The spectre of a 'poor man's cruise missile' – an old weapon suddenly becoming extremely accurate through GPS – is one of the many nightmare scenarios now being contemplated. Iraq's Scud missiles were only accurate to within about one kilometre; guided by GPS they could be landed within fifty metres of their targets in Israel or Saudi Arabia by GPS. By using commercially available satellite photographs and maps, attacks on particular targets could be planned and the co-ordinates programmed into the weapon's guidance system. According to Pentagon sources quoted in the American press, the countries which have shown an interest in this so far include Iraq, Iran, North Korea, India, Pakistan, Indonesia, Egypt, Israel and Taiwan. Iran is said to buy its GPS receivers through a front company in Britain while China and Russia are believed to be co-operating on a joint project for a satellite-guided weapon to be offered for export.

Even terrorists could make use of GPS. A model aircraft fitted with a receiver and a small package of explosive could be set to fly towards a designated building – or even to a particular window. Scientists see this as perfectly feasible. The accuracy offered by the GPS system can be enhanced with a technique known as 'differential GPS' in which the information provided by the satellites is combined with an on-site survey or cross-checking with other navigational aids, such as the radio transmissions made from coastal stations for the benefit of the oil industry working at sea. Both options are open to a well-organised terrorist gang and could lead to an attack which is accurate to within one and a half metres. And against a surprise attack from a GPS-guided weapon, there is no useful defence.

One option is to encrypt all the GPS signals so that only authorised users can receive them. The code used in the military's 'precise' service is apparently so sophisticated that, according to one expert, by the time a supercomputer cracked it, if that were even possible, the code would have been changed. In theory, the more basic 'course acquisition' transmissions could be encrypted in this way as well. Another possibility is to increase the error built into the CA service so that it becomes militarily useless. The final option is one available to the US President: he has the authority to switch off the commercial broadcasts altogether, denying GPS to all but military users.

None of these offers a credible solution. The difficulty is that although it was the Pentagon which pushed for and paid for GPS, its general availability has whetted the appetites of several powerful civilian lobbies. As one American official said in February 1994, 'The reality is that within five years GPS will be an embedded component of our entire national transportation system.' The US airline industry in particular sees GPS as a mainstay of its future, perhaps even becoming its sole source of navigation. With some 5,000 airports in the United States lacking the equipment for all-weather landings, GPS could provide a cheap and simple answer. The US Coast Guard too is looking to GPS as its primary source of navigation: with it, said one official, 'we've taken the search out of search-and-rescue'. The result is that any threat to degrade the basic GPS signal or, worse, switch it off altogether produces howls of alarm. There is even growing pressure for the management of the system to be transferred from military to civilian hands – the subject of bitter controversy. It raises a fundamental question: in times of crisis or war, is it better for western commercial interests to continue benefiting from GPS or for an enemy to be denied it?

'No one has an answer to that,' according to John Owen. 'They've invented a system that's turned out to be too good and now the rest of the world wants it.' He himself admits to a change of view because of this. Having been a long-time advocate of GPS – arguing its case with the British armed forces as forcefully as he could – he says he now asks whether the forces believe they can avoid having to use it. He concedes that because of the relatively slow response of the British forces to the opportunities of GPS, compared to that of the Americans, they may – by accident – end up being less dependent on it and therefore less vulnerable to its risks.

As with the invention of nuclear weapons, the advantages of being first with satellite navigation are quickly lost. Nuclear weapons have been called 'equalisers' since they pose the same threat if they are held by a large country as by a small one; GPS by its very nature is an equaliser too. The whole world shares its benefits.

In the headquarters of McDonnell Douglas Helicopters at Mesa, Arizona in September 1993, a wall of smoke, haze, laser beams and coloured lights parted to reveal the company's latest gunship: the AH-64D Longbow Apache. As ugly as an insect and heavy with weapons, the helicopter looked much like the current version of the Apache which operated so ruthlessly in the Gulf War – except for the addition of what appears to be a large cake tin stuck above its main rotor. This is a highly sophisticated fire control radar which allows the helicopter to pop up from behind a hill or wood and, in a single scan, track as many as 256 targets at any one time before vanishing out of sight again. On-board displays and computers allow the two-man Apache crew to identify the targets, transmit the data about their locations to commanders and to other gunships, divide up the battlefield – and then attack: All within thirty seconds, McDonnell Douglas brochures say.

General Gordon Sullivan, Chief of Staff of the US Army, the keynote speaker at the unveiling ceremony, declared this to be the start of what he called 'information-age warfare'. With the brash immodesty so typical of weapons promotions, he said: 'We know where you are. We know where we are and we know where you are not. We're coming after you day and night until we win. And that's what this helicopter is all about. Teamwork. America's army. Information-age warfare.' Though the military have long grasped that accuracy is generally a function of the timely delivery of correct information about the enemy's location, only now does the technology offer that understanding to be put into effect. With GPS and powerful but miniaturised computers, helicopters like the Longbow Apache and almost any other vehicle can form part of a network in which data is transferred instantaneously to wherever it is needed. The US Army calls this the 'digital battlefield' because the data is to be distributed automatically: what appears on one commander's display should be visible on all others as well. Information, according to one army planner, is the 'life-blood of modern war', just as fuel was the life-blood of the first big manoeuvre battles of the Second World War and gunpowder that of the First World War. And the automatic passing of that information so that all units know where they are, where others are and where the enemy is would be a key mechanism for lifting 'the fog of war'.

One benefit of this digital information-sharing is that radio conversation can be minimised – a long-standing source of mistakes and inaccuracy. The Italian communications firm Larimart plays on this in an advertisement for its digital message system. It shows two frustrated radio operators hunched over their equipment, one calling out: 'Alpha, difficult, say again word after "contact", over . . .' The image is not unjustified. One US Army communications specialist said that 'fatigued soldiers incorrectly read and then transmit faulty target grid co-ordinates by transposing numbers'. It is a risk identified by the British Army as well, which reportedly devoted about four-fifths of all its radio traffic in the Gulf War to the issue of location. The British answer to this is a plan for its next generation of communications system, Bowman, due in service at the turn of the century, to provide automatic information about the unit's location each time a radio conversation begins. It would reduce the chances of interception and allow commanders, for the first time in history, to know precisely where their troops are at any one time.

The US Army is taking this one stage further. In its 'battle labs' – centres for exploring the implications of new technology and tactics – it has tested a system for 'seamless communications'. The Gulf War had shown that even if individual tanks and helicopters knew their own locations and those of the enemy, they usually had difficulty passing the information quickly enough either 'vertically' – up the command chain – or 'horizontally' – to fellow units better placed to mount an attack. In the hope of producing a common view of the battlefield, the US Army staged a simulated digital communications exercise at Fort Knox, Kentucky in March 1993. A scout helicopter spotted three enemy armoured personnel carriers and warned the nearest American forces, a troop of five M1A2 tanks. One of the tanks used its laser range-finder and GPS system to establish the exact location of the APCs and then transmitted the information – computer to computer – to his commander, who in turn passed it automatically to an artillery unit. The gunners, having been told precisely which co-ordinates to aim at, opened fire. Because it was an exercise, they were successful, hitting two of the APCs and forcing the third to withdraw. 'A big success,' announced an army research official. 'This is not some kind of George Lucas Hollywood fantasy – it is reality,' said General Sullivan. 'We have seen the face of future war and we are dealing with it.' He wants his first digitised division ready by 1998.

The move would be welcomed by America's allies. The Gulf War gave American soldiers and pilots a reputation for extreme inaccuracy on the battlefield – opening fire without checking the target first. On 26 February 1991, in the closing phase of the war, American A-10 jets mistakenly opened fire on two British Warrior infantry fighting vehicles, killing nine soldiers and injuring eleven from the Royal Regiment of Fusiliers. It was not the only incident of what the military curiously call 'friendly fire'. A staggering 77 per cent of all American combat vehicles damaged or destroyed during the war were hit by their own side. An automatic system by which all vehicles can be identified as friend or foe, have their locations confirmed and have that information distributed immediately to everyone involved would reduce if not eliminate the risk of fratricide. GPS and the digital transmission system might offer that.

Though the interest in the automatic exchange of data is partly driven by the dwindling defence budget – the forces will have to make better use of their existing weapons – the main motivation is the desire to 'maximise our potential for violence', as one Gulf War commander put it. It means improving accuracy so that each shot counts. Nowhere is the pressure for this greater than in the field of ground combat – tank warfare. If only one missile or shell is needed to hit an enemy, rather than multiple rounds fired inaccurately, victory is more quickly achieved, fewer soldiers on both sides are killed and civilians are less likely to be at risk because the war ends sooner. Advances in guidance have made that possible. A Second World War tank took on average seventeen shots to destroy another tank no more than 700 yards away. The Israelis, fighting the Yom Kippur War in 1973, reduced that average to two shots per kill from 1,800 yards. Some American M1A1 tanks in the Gulf War recorded one-shot kills as far away as 3,300 yards.[3]

At face value that last result should be the end of the story. But, as ever, the developments do not stop. The fear of countries like Iraq acquiring better weapons drives western armies to improve theirs. The best tanks fielded by Iraq in 1991 were Soviet-built T-72s with weak armour and out-of-date fire control systems. Far more sophisticated models are now on sale in the open market. The 20 November 1993 edition of the leading military news magazine, *Jane's Defence Weekly*, carried an advertisement by the Russian defence sales company, Oboronexport, offering its T-80U (a tank which was kept secret until the late 1980s). The tank is described as being armed with a 125mm-calibre main gun (slightly larger than that of the British Challenger tank) which can fire ordinary ammunition or laser-guided missiles; the tank is protected with 'reactive armour' (panels of explosive which fire outwards if hit, shearing away the impact of an incoming shell). For 'further details and business proposals', the advertisement says, ring Oboronexport's Moscow office on: (095) 231 0049. The latest technology can be obtained that simply.

The immediate western response in this particular corner of the arms race has been to plan to introduce bigger guns to obtain even greater power and accuracy: the faster a shell flies the less time it has to drift off course (a bullet fired two kilometres will drop at least two metres because of gravity). But current tank technology has reached its limits; that is acknowledged by tank designers in a number of different countries. A bigger gun and stronger armour add extra weight, possibly making the tank too heavy for the railway wagons usually used to transport armoured vehicles long distances. They also make the tank itself larger; and as its profile grows its vulnerability does too. It becomes an easier target for an adversary equipped with precision weapons.

'Everybody's racked their brains over this,' says David Hull of the DRA's Novel Weapons Division, 'and we know we mustn't limit ourselves to current technology – we've got to have vision to push for breakthroughs.' There is, it seems, only one way to achieve improved accuracy without adding weight: inventing a new kind of gun, one which is small, light but potent.

We were sitting in a drab office at the DRA's weapons laboratory at Fort Halstead in Kent. The room was overheated. The sight outside of silver birch trees in the grey winter light was reminiscent of Moscow. So was the security surrounding this establishment: no sign on the main road, no marking on my road atlas, high fences and cameras. Fort Halstead has been the home of future weapons design since the middle of the Second World War and it has always been one of the most closely guarded of the military research centres. The work here can be traced back through innumerable institutional reorganisations and name-changes to the fourteenth century when an Office of Ordnance was set up in the Tower of London to begin testing guns. Portraits of the long line of commanders and inventors associated with weapon design now hang in a corridor of Fort Halstead's main building. One is of a bearded figure, heavy with medals, labelled as 'General Sir Collingwood Dickson, Inspector of Gunpowder 1852–1854'. Now, 140 years later, his successor, the present Master General of Ordnance, is seeing if he can usher the army out of the age of gunpowder.

The army has commissioned the scientists of Fort Halstead to undertake 'a short, sharp look' at the possibility of developing a gun powered by electromagnetic force. In a programme costing some £10 million over three years, the aim is to see whether, at the flick of a switch, shells can be propelled at unprecedented speeds towards a target. The source of the energy would be electricity, channelled into a savagely sudden burst of reverse magnetism, repelling a metal dart out of the end of a barrel. Quite apart from the practical benefits to tank crews of no longer having to handle inflammable propellant charges inside the turret, an electromagnetic (EM) gun could fire unusually quickly and therefore accurately. Current chemical propellants – the modern equivalent of gunpowder – have been adapted and improved as intensely as possible and scientists have now reached the physical limit of the speeds achievable with them. While a bullet can be fired at about one kilometre per second and a standard tank round at about 1.5 kilometres per second, electromagnetic guns could increase that velocity to around 2.5 kilometres per second. 'If it comes off, it'll be a quantum leap forward,' according to David Haugh, head of the EM section.

The DRA is not the first to think of this. In the late nineteenth century, an inventor in Jersey proposed an electric gun but because he demanded a payment before demonstrating his new weapon, the army never pursued the suggestion. The French explored the concept in the 1920s, the Germans in the 1940s, the Australians in the 1970s and the Americans under the Star Wars project in the 1980s – none successfully. In 1982 Fort Halstead took up the challenge, assembling a series of small EM guns. One, known as Hyper I, has managed to fire a small projectile at 4.2 kilometres per second but with little control over its accuracy. It is hazardous work in uncharted scientific territory – something most scientists find amusing rather than unnerving. One was bruised when a projectile burst out of an EM gun sideways; another of the weapons caught fire; there are generally 'lots of sparks', according to Haugh. Even now, at the purpose-built EM gun laboratory at Kirkcudbright in Scotland – the first of its kind when it opened in 1993 – Haugh and his colleagues watch the firings from a control room forty metres behind the weapon. 'We're not stupid.' On one occasion, a hydraulic seal broke under the tremendous pressure – thirty tons per square inch, 'as much as an elephant standing on your finger,' according to Haugh – and sprayed the target area with twenty gallons of oil.

Yet the fact that the range has been built at all – and that the army wants to pay for the project from its dwindling budget – is evidence of the seriousness with which the EM gun is considered and with which the generals view its importance. Research into conventional propellants has even been cut back to pay for it. The plan, says Haugh, is to have the gun firing at long range by the end of 1995, 'so we can show the general a nice hole in the target – that should please him'. According to David Hull of the Novel Weapons Division, which has overall responsibility for the gun, it is conceivable that the weapon will be so powerful and so precise

173

that there will be no defence against it. 'You might only need a few of them; it could end tank warfare.' The prospect of such a weapon in British hands is clearly appealing to the army. But there is also the risk of the reverse happening. With technological knowledge spreading so rapidly around the world – and other countries known to be researching this particular avenue – the work is as much to see what others may be able to achieve as to reach the goal of a serviceable EM gun first. 'You have to assume that other countries will get better tanks,' according to David Haugh. It is an assumption the army is ready to make.

If the three-year study is successful though – and the scientists involved are quietly confident that it will be – there will still be another two decades of development work at a cost of hundreds of millions of pounds before the weapon will be deployable. Even the most fundamental problems are legion. No one is sure precisely what happens to a projectile fired at such high speed through the densest part of the atmosphere – whether its fins melt or its flight is stable or it penetrates the enemy's armour effectively. Nor is anyone sure how many times a barrel can endure the pressure. Until those issues are resolved, the task of turning the gun into a manageable weapon fitted to a tank will have to wait. The principal difficulty is miniaturising the power supply. The capacitor tank at Kirkcudbright, which can generate a burst of nearly four million amps of electrical power, is about as large as a pair of terraced houses – hardly mobile.

But army chiefs seem to have faith in the project. Power plants are shrinking, partly as a result of the demands of spacecraft, and it is thought to be a reasonable assumption that breakthroughs in size and weight will emerge soon. That would pave the way for the fitting of an EM gun to a tank perhaps in twenty to thirty years' time. But this raises two awkward possibilities for the army. If it turns out that the EM gun cannot be integrated into a tank – because of unforeseen physical problems or size or cost – the future of the tank itself could be in jeopardy, lacking a source of guaranteed superiority in firepower. On the other hand, if the EM gun does work effectively, it may well require a new kind of vehicle altogether – possibly with a novel shape and new methods of operation. An EM-armed vehicle would certainly require fewer crew, cutting by at least half the army's current crews of four per tank; it could conceivably be run without any crew at all. The days of the tank, with its familiar shape and role, could be drawing to a close.

If technology continues to advance along the path of the last decade – smaller, smarter, more accurate and with ever greater range – it will become steadily harder for political leaders to justify committing large numbers of soldiers to battle. The growing unwillingness of western democracies to risk the lives of their soldiers in combat is evident from opinion polls – and is therefore reflected in the cautious decisions of politicians as well. It follows then that if technological progress offers decisively accurate fire with weapons managed by machine rather than man, another long-held scientific dream will attract renewed interest: robots to take the place of soldiers.

7

A TRUSTED AIDE

Mass-produced robots will be cheaper and more expendable than humans.

> Frank Barnaby, *The Automated Battlefield*, 1987

Chief Warrant Officer Clifton P. Wolcott was lying dead at the controls of his Black Hawk helicopter, call-sign Super 6-1. The cockpit had been crushed around him. The frantic efforts to free his body were stymied by the armour-plating on the cockpit doors. Metal-cutting saws were proving useless. To make matters worse, the rescue party was coming under intense fire from rocket-propelled grenades and rifles. It was 4.30 p.m. on 3 October 1993 in an alleyway off Freedom Street in the centre of the Somali capital, Mogadishu. The latest American Special Forces' raid was coming unstuck – disastrously.[1] It was to become a turning-point in American political and military opinion about involvement in foreign wars.

Wolcott was one of a total of eighteen American servicemen to be killed in what turned out to be the US forces' single worst firefight since Vietnam. During the fifteen hours of battle which followed the shooting down of Super 6-1, a further eighty-four Americans were wounded. The Somalis said the fighting had left 312 of their soldiers dead and 814 wounded. But these statistics, though appalling, were to have far less impact than what followed: television coverage of the Somalis' treatment of two American bodies and of one American prisoner. It is an episode which illustrates how the world's most powerful nation can be effectively crippled by the supreme value it accords to the lives of its own troops. The last American forces withdrew from Somalia by the end of March 1994 – within six months of the battle.

The raid had begun smoothly. At 3.40 p.m., ten special forces' helicopters had swooped over Hiwadag Street in one of the densest quarters of Mogadishu and landed teams of Delta Force and Rangers troops amid swirling clouds of dust. Their target was a building used by senior members of the faction led by General Mohammed Farah Aideed, one of the most powerful of the Somali leaders, and pejoratively described in the western press as a 'warlord'. General Aideed had been on the run from the United Nations ever since his forces had been blamed for the massacre of twenty-four Pakistani soldiers in June 1993. Though the presence of UN soldiers in Somalia had originally been meant to quell the civil war and so allow the distribution of aid to the tens of thousands of starving civilians, growing hostility between the US contingent and Aideed's forces in particular had changed the atmosphere surrounding the operation. The Americans were becoming increasingly desperate to catch General Aideed and he was stepping up his attacks on them.

It was known that General Aideed himself would not be in the building on Hiwadag Street but an intelligence tip-off had suggested that two of his key lieutenants were there. The American troops, dressed in black body armour and equipped with silenced machine-guns, plunged inside and seized what they described over the radio as their 'PC' – precious cargo. Omar Salad Elmi and Mohammed Hassan Awale were not to be killed; this was a different kind of warfare. The two officials were to be taken away for questioning – a violent arrest for a peaceful purpose – in the hope that their absence would force Aideed himself to become more active and therefore adopt a higher profile. The two men, and others, were loaded in a convoy of US Army vehicles which was to take them back to the main American base.

But at this very moment – 4.20 p.m. – Super 6-1 was hit by a rocket-propelled grenade and nose-dived to the ground. Wolcott and his co-pilot were killed, five others were injured. It was to change the course of the entire operation. The lives – and remains – of Americans were at stake and the overriding priority was now to try to save them. All other objectives were abandoned. Two special forces teams ran from the Aideed building towards the site of the crash; even the convoy carrying the prisoners was diverted towards it (though eventually it was beaten back by impenetrable gunfire). A second Black Hawk helicopter, call-sign Super 6-4, flew to the scene of the crash and delivered reinforcements. But no sooner had the last of fifteen fresh special forces soldiers roped down from Super

6-4 than this helicopter, too, was hit by a rocket-propelled grenade. Super 6-4 crashed half a mile away. American commanders were now faced with trying to defend two crash sites. Further helicopters and two contingents of ground forces were despatched, all of them confronted by well-organised ambushes and grenade fire. The battle raged until dawn the next day; only then had the rescue team at the scene of the first crashed helicopter, Super 6-1, successfully used a Humvee jeep and a tow-rope to prise open the cockpit and free the body of Chief Warrant Officer Wolcott. Despite the scale of the fighting involved, there had apparently never been any question of abandoning his corpse in this foreign battlefield.

Long before, two Delta Force snipers had reached the wreckage of the second helicopter to crash, Super 6-4, but had died trying to protect the sole survivor, the co-pilot, Chief Warrant Officer Michael Durant. The body of his colleague, the pilot, had vanished soon after being hit. Durant was seized by a mob and held prisoner for eleven days. He was filmed in captivity and the television images of his bloodshot, mournful eyes and battered face and filthy clothes were beamed around the world. At the same time, jubilant Somalis were filmed gloating over the wreckage, thin Third-World figures jumping in triumph on the charred fuselages of the most advanced helicopters ever built. Worse, two of the corpses, their faces disfigured, the bodies caked in blood and dust, were pictured being dragged through the streets.

These were sights that made American congressmen see red. Many immediately challenged the very purpose of the US presence in Somalia. Senator Phil Gramm declared, 'The people who are dragging around the bodies of Americans don't look very hungry to the people of Texas.' The comment, of course, missed a key point: that the mobs of militia men desecrating the Americans' bodies were not those most in need of aid but were instead contributing to the internal strife causing the shortages of aid in the first place. But the prevailing perception was becoming far more important than the reality: American boys were being humiliated in a thankless foreign operation and ought to be brought home. The raid had achieved its objective – the seizure of two of Aideed's lieutenants. But it had also handed the Somali general a propaganda victory and had inflamed the deep-seated streak of isolationism spasmodically evident in American policy. The price of this particular foreign commitment had become too high.

It was a reaction manifested most immediately in America's response to the tragedy of Bosnia. The United States, even as the war there had begun in 1992, had made clear its reluctance to commit ground forces to the UN's aid operation. Washington offered satellite reconnaissance photographs, transport planes for aid drops and fighter-planes to enforce the no-fly-zone and to offer air-strikes in support of the ground forces of other countries – but no troops. The reasoning, established by the then President, George Bush, and continued by Bill Clinton, was that US units would only deploy to Bosnia when an overall, comprehensive peace settlement had been achieved there. Even when local peace deals emerged, the White House position was not budged. In February 1994 – five months after the trauma of Mogadishu – when the UN had brokered a ceasefire for Sarajevo and, a month later, when US officials secured another deal between the Muslims and Croats in central Bosnia, the refusal to become involved on the ground continued. The UN was desperate for its member states to offer more soldiers to help police these newly won settlements before they collapsed. Countries as diverse as Jordan, Malaysia and Argentina were providing troops – not to mention the biggest contributors, France and Britain; but not the United States. 'We just don't think we can sell it,' one US defence official told me in March 1994. 'Not now – certainly not after Somalia.'

Not that the United States was alone in agonising over this issue. Two of the factors which have influenced American opinion apply to all western democracies: television coverage and the difficulty of intervening in conflicts short of war. British ministers, for example, who at one stage were heavily criticised within the European Union for advocating a cautious policy towards Bosnia, faced the treacherous dilemma posed by these two factors. On the one hand, advances in broadcasting technology allowed television images of the suffering in this worst European war since 1945 to be transmitted live or at least every day into homes across the country. This meant that government indifference and inaction bore a political cost. Yet, on the other hand, there was extreme nervousness about the prospect of heavy British casualties in a conflict in which conscience rather than national interest was the chief motivation.[2] In the end, a compromise was reached which involved sending a modest force of 2,400 with the very specific mission of supporting the UN's humanitarian effort. The troops arrived in November 1992. But, by January 1994, ministers and officials were becoming uneasy about maintaining the presence much longer. Withdrawal was floated as a possibility, to the relief of many nervous Conservative backbench MPs.

It took a massacre and a new bout of international resolve to change that attitude. A mortar attack on Sarajevo market on 5 February 1994 killed nearly sixty civilians and galvanised NATO into issuing an ultimatum to the Bosnian Serbs to withdraw or hand over their heavy weapons. That international response, combined with a more muscular UN command, convinced the Serbs that a ceasefire was now worth pursuing and the first of the peace deals – covering Sarajevo – fell into place. In turn, this settlement created the sudden demand by the UN for many more troops. The British government's initial response though was negative ('we've done our bit already,' according to one defence official). Even when the UN commander in Bosnia – the distinguished and popular British general, Sir Michael Rose – pleaded for reinforcements in March 1994, the Cabinet was reluctant to agree. The Chancellor, Kenneth Clarke, was quoted as saying, 'not one soldier more'. In the end, with Britain's international prestige and its reputation with the UN at stake, another 900 soldiers were sent. By then though, the argument had yet again revealed the government's reluctance to risk British lives for a cause in which the British interest was unclear.

These circumstances – instant, powerful television pictures of ghastly suffering in complicated, sometimes ambiguous, situations – are more than likely to be repeated elsewhere. Broadcasting technology will, if anything, allow ever more thorough coverage in ever grimmer detail and the tinder-box of central and eastern Europe contains about thirty-five unresolved disputes, including those of former Yugoslavia. For the western democracies, there are two approaches with which to tackle this prospect. The first is political and requires persuasive argument: to convince the electorate either that the conflict in question, though terrible, is not worth the price of intervention or that staying out of the conflict is neither morally justifiable nor in our interest and that, by inference, the deaths of some of our soldiers would therefore be justified. Neither argument will be comfortably won.

Which raises the second approach, a technological one, offered by science. A growing number of military researchers are suggesting that if governments are unwilling to risk soldiers' lives, they should use machines – robots – to perform some of their tasks instead. They hold out the prospect of ever greater automation allowing ever fewer service personnel to be placed in jeopardy. 'The technology is here and now,' according to one British scientist involved in the development of automated vehicles. Missions such as the monitoring of stockpiled weapons or disputed borders, the reconnaissance of dangerous or hostile areas and the clearance of mines could well be carried out by clever machines.

The simplest types of robots have long been employed in automated warehouses and on the streets of Northern Ireland where they are used to tackle terrorist bombs and suspect devices. Yet several different circumstances have coincided with the trauma of Somalia and other conflicts to bring about a far more intense level of interest. First, the proliferation of advanced weaponry is making the battlefield ever more hazardous – whether in a situation such as Bosnia or a full-scale war – and the chances of survival are worsening. Second, most western democracies have experienced severe falls in their birth rates so that the number of potential recruits available to join the military ranks has been dwindling. Third, the acceleration in the miniaturisation of computers has meant that concepts which could only be dreamed about even in the late 1980s are looking far more feasible in the mid-1990s. And fourth, the escalating cost of new tanks, ships and aircraft means that cheaper alternatives will find favour. Frank Barnaby, military expert and former director of the Stockholm International Peace Research Institute, quoting 1987 prices, compared the $25-million price of a fighter-plane with the $300,000 price of an unmanned drone aircraft. The difference is largely due to the cost of providing self-defence measures, an ejector seat and other mechanisms with which to keep the pilot safe. The logic of this dictates that it is therefore better to do without the pilot.

On 9 June 1982 the Bekaa Valley in Lebanon became the world's first large-scale robotic battlefield. The Syrian Army had hidden nineteen anti-aircraft missile batteries in the valley to block Israel's bomber squadrons. Soviet trainers had taught the Syrian operators to keep the missiles' radar systems switched off as much as possible; they knew that the Israelis would watch for any radar emissions and use the information to evade the missiles or attack them. Soon, the first wave of Israeli planes appeared – or so the Syrians thought. They switched on their radars and began tracking and firing at what they thought were Israeli Air Force jets. In fact, the aircraft were drones, unmanned planes, like model aircraft, which were acting as decoys. Each second that the radars were active, Israeli electronic warfare specialists in a second wave of real aircraft could plot the positions of the batteries and loose off radar-seeking missiles at them. All nineteen batteries were destroyed. Not one Israeli life had been put at risk.

One year later, when new anti-aircraft batteries were re-established, the US Navy mounted a reconnaissance mission over the Bekaa Valley. It involved a large number of planes – but no robots. It was a disaster by comparison. Two F-14s were shot down, one pilot being killed, the other captured. The lesson was learned. As the director of one robotic engineering firm put it: 'A manned plane attacking air defence sites is like an elephant attacking an elephant gun – you want to attack an air defence site with something other than its target.'[3]

The potential benefits of robot planes, vehicles and submarines have long been recognised, if only slowly exploited. Aside from the fear of creating a hi-tech Frankenstein, a man-made machine which starts acting of its own volition, the problem has been largely a technical one: achieving a reasonable degree of mechanical reliability and on-board intelligence through computing power to make the machine perform as effectively as the manned equivalent. The US Army's first major venture into robotics, for example, led to the birth of an ungainly, enormous and unwieldy machine called Robox. Ten feet tall and twenty feet long, it looks like a mechanical caterpillar – what at first sight seem to be loosely connected telephone booths mounted on three clumsy sets of legs. Despite the lack of promise in its appearance, Robox can reportedly manoeuvre itself in different directions and can even remember the details of each obstacle it meets so that it knows how to cope on the return journey. The army had apparently envisaged Robox lugging ammunition boxes or even tired soldiers over rough terrain. But the generals evidently got cold feet – maybe the machine just looked too absurd. Funding was abruptly cancelled in 1990 and Robox was offered for sale to timber companies for use in the forests.[4]

A machine with greater promise is the Prowler. Built by a firm in Colorado, this is a robot jeep designed to operate as a sentry. It sees by video and infra-red and has the ability to manoeuvre itself along a perimeter track while watching for intruders. It is one of a number of robotic vehicles built for the purpose of keeping watch or snooping. The US Marines for example have been testing Robo-Spy, a wheeled robot likened to an electric golf buggy with a video camera stuck on top. The machine is connected to an operator by a cable, limiting its range, down which the television pictures and the commands are passed. However successful, Robo-Spy evidently has detractors (perhaps ego-threatened marines) at its base at Camp Pendleton in California: someone slashed its cable one night.[5] Better accepted are the robot submarines employed by the Royal Navy's mine-sweepers which scan the sea-bed for mines, sparing frogmen the task.

It was the Gulf War in 1991 which saw the first widespread use of robot aides. Dozens of pilotless aircraft – what the military call UAVs (Unmanned Aerial Vehicles) – snooped on the battlefield. The US Navy's two battleships, *Wisconsin* and *Missouri*, launched tiny Pioneer aircraft to reconnoitre the Kuwaiti coast for targets. Equipped with a video camera and a transmission link, these propeller-driven drones beamed back television pictures of the ground below even as the battleships' guns opened fire. The gun teams could immediately correct their aim – and the rest of the crew could watch the results and applaud. After as many as 163 flights, only one Pioneer was shot down by Iraqi gunfire; eleven others were destroyed for other reasons. It was evidently a safer way to gather intelligence than committing special forces on the ground. As one Pentagon official involved in robotics research put it, 'The battlefield is no place for human beings.' Even the normally conservative military leadership saw the Pioneers' value. The American commander of naval forces in the Gulf, Vice-Admiral Stanley Arthur, praised the machines as 'marvellous, versatile'. He was especially proud of an incident on 27 February 1991, the penultimate day of the conflict, when a group of Iraqi soldiers, confronted by a Pioneer, tried to give themselves up: 'the first occasion in the history of warfare for human beings to capitulate to a robot'.

Since the Gulf War, interest in robots for use in the air, on land and at sea has grown apace. One estimate says there are currently about 200 projects for unmanned vehicles under way around the world. The British Army, starved of relevant intelligence on the Iraqis during Operation Desert Storm, has bought Phoenix, a remotely piloted aircraft which, like the US Navy's Pioneer, beams back television pictures of potential targets. The CIA has become interested too. Its original plan for a sophisticated and expensive unmanned spy-plane has been scrapped; the aircraft under development was described as being as large and as complicated as the B-2 stealth bomber and involved so much highly classified equipment that, according to one defence official, 'If one had crashed . . . we would have had to bomb it to ensure it was destroyed.' The CIA has instead turned to simpler technology. Since February 1994 it has deployed two Gnat 750 robot planes in the skies over Bosnia, operating from a base in Albania.[6] The Gnats have a range of 500 miles, can stay aloft for twenty-four hours and, from an egg-shaped dome above their wings, can transmit television and infra-red pictures by satellite back to their operators. A follow-on version, being developed at a cost of over $30 million, will be able to relay the images directly to generals sitting in comfort in the Pentagon building in Washington. A fleet of ten drones is planned to be in operation by 1996, each plane costing in the region of $10 million. As one Pentagon official put it: 'I don't want people crying a lot when one gets shot down or crashes.'[7]

But this is the tip of the iceberg of robot developments. The Pentagon is planning to spend at least $600 million before the turn of the century on unmanned aircraft alone. Each of the armed services is grasping the benefits. A high-level study for the US Army for example, *STAR 21: Strategic Technologies for the Army of the 21st Century*, concluded that while this century's core weapon has been the tank, next century's 'may well be the unmanned system'.[8] The study predicts that robots will be 'running and walking' by 2020. The trend towards robotics is already being manifested in many areas of military operations. The US Army has realised that the crews of its scout helicopters are increasingly vulnerable and has commissioned research into robot helicopters. These would probe potential routes for manned helicopters. Under tests ordered in February 1994, the army will use several Exdrone pilotless helicopters, equipped with video and infra-red cameras, to transmit pictures back to the cockpits of the manned helicopters.

Other projects, initiated during the Cold War, have attracted greater attention more recently. A classified US Army reference file, *Next Generation & Future Systems Sourcebook*, produced internally in March 1990, lists at least three robotic programmes. One is for a robotic resupply vehicle, an ammunition carrier, programmed to follow obediently the exact path taken by a manned tank or rocket launcher and so be in position to offer fresh supplies at the right moment. The document, which predicts full-scale engineering development beginning in 1999, envisages up to ten of the vehicles operating in a convoy. Among the virtues highlighted for this project are 'reduced soldier vulnerability' and 'reduced manpower requirement'. Another proposal is for an 'integrated deception system', a robot trickster – a device which automatically projects a false image of a tank or other vehicle to confuse the enemy. An accompanying diagram in the file shows an unmanned camera-like object on a tripod transmitting a picture of what looks like a collection of military vehicles. Quite how this would work is not explained in the text; hardly surprisingly, the date for start of engineering development is given as no earlier than 2007.

The US Army file also includes, with characteristic blandness, even nonchalance, a proposal for a large robot gun. This represents the crossing of a threshold – the purpose of most robots being seen as to act as unarmed spies and scouts – and for many in the military it is a step too far. Listed as Project Number N048, the gun is given the title 'Arnold' (though the acronym is left unexplained) and is depicted as something akin to a tank turret mounted on a small trailer. Scheduled for a laboratory demonstration in 1997 and full-scale development in 2002, the gun is described as an 'unmanned ground vehicle mission package with sufficient artificial intelligence in conjunction with advanced optical and acoustical technology to recognise targets and acquire and deliver the required firepower'. Which means the gun, once positioned by its human masters in an appropriate position for an ambush, will be able to choose by itself when and at what to open fire. This will 'eliminate dependence on on-board personnel' while enhancing 'the lethality of the killing zone'. But the document does not specify precisely how the weapon will be controlled – how, for example, it is to be switched off.

The experts assembled to compile the *STAR 21* study addressed the subject of control only briefly – despite their report being the principal guide to the US Army's future investments over the next thirty years. They envisaged that robot weapons would operate 'mostly under computer control with human supervision' – without specifying what this means. It could be interpreted as saying that the 'supervising' human operators would have to give the final authority before a weapon was fired or that they would merely have a power of veto – an override – if they felt the computer 'controlling' the weapon had to be restrained or even that they could merely monitor the robot weapon in operation. In the single example cited in the study, the development of 'robot mines' – computer-controlled bazookas buried in the ground to await passing enemy tanks – the experts made no mention of the precise conditions under which the weapon would be allowed to open fire, let alone how it would be defused safely later.

This is a curious omission because the question of control is the one that looms largest in the minds of many of the military. The potential for weapons like Arnold to open fire unexpectedly or in the wrong direction has long been dreaded and is a continuing cause of military ambivalence about robot weapons in general. Some commentators regard it as no coincidence that it was one of the US Navy's most highly automated warships, the Aegis-class cruiser, the USS *Vincennes*, which shot down an Iranian Airbus passenger plane over the Gulf; the crew had trusted the judgement of their software to identify the approaching aircraft rather than that of their colleagues on other vessels. Yet the issue has divided senior commanders, who are torn between the mounting number of reasons in favour of robots and the nightmare of the machines running amok. As so often in the field of futuristic weapons, science fiction has led the thinking on this issue. The author Isaac Asimov invented laws to govern the actions of the robots featured in his books; the First Law was that robots must be programmed so that they never injure humans. The US Congress, no doubt aware of Asimov's idea and fearful of the direction of some Pentagon weapons projects, ruled in 1986 that no robots were ever to be armed. The prohibition struck a chord with many in the military. As Robert Cooper, the Pentagon's Under-Secretary for Research from 1981 to 1985, explained at the time: 'Military folks don't have a very good feeling about letting anything or anyone who is not in the line of command elect targets. That's an absolute no-no.'[9]

The congressional prohibition has now lapsed but the sense of unease which brought it about still lingers. Yet the prospect of armed robots will not go away – the fact that the Arnold robot gun is still listed as an official project is a case in point. The problem is that logic dictates that for a robot to be genuinely effective it must possess a reasonable degree of autonomy; and for it to take the place of a human in a battle, it must be armed. On top of that, there is now the prospect of the technology allowing autonomous operation, begging the question: we can do it, so why not?

The simplest robots are commanded continuously by means of a trailing wire or fibre-optic cable; this means that the human operator is in charge – remotely – at all times, though once the wire is broken, the robot grinds to a halt. The next most sophisticated machines are controlled by radio, the operator leaving the robot to perform the most straightforward tasks, like getting from one point to another, as programmed, and only intervening to issue a command to change course or to open fire. This system runs the risk of having the radio signal jammed, though the robot could be designed to shut down automatically if no commands are received after a certain time – rather than setting off on its own, out of control.

The most advanced systems would be autonomous. Some weapons have this characteristic already, such as ICBMs and the latest sea-bed mines, but are given very exact descriptions of their targets and lack the computer intelligence to change the plan and attack something else. Now though, science has brought the military to the threshold of introducing weapons that could choose their own targets. It involves allowing robots a degree of discretion which is provoking deep military reluctance, according to John Pike of the Federation of American Scientists. A long-time critic of many of the Pentagon's weapons procurement policies, he says battlefield robots make him 'very, very nervous', a view echoed by many senior figures in the US and British armed forces. Society, says Pike, has mistakenly come to believe that machines perform more perfectly than humans when, in fact, 'to err is human, but to really foul things up it takes a computer'. And given that a robot will only be of any use if it can make decisions for itself on the spur of the moment, the dilemma is obvious. 'To give a robot some flexibility as a soldier, it'll also have to be given some unpredictability – and who wants that? C3PO with a shotgun?' (C3PO is one of the robots in the *Star Wars* series of science-fiction films.)

There are other reservations as well. At a time of deep budget cuts, military chiefs have generally shown themselves unwilling to sacrifice personnel for machines. However good the case scientifically, it is politically impossible to be seen choosing to scrap regiments or squadrons in favour of research into the unpredictable fruits of mechanisation. This has certainly been the case in Britain. Although the Defence Research Agency's scientists have led the field in many aspects of the development of autonomous vehicles, their work has not always been popular.

It was a chilly afternoon at Chertsey, the DRA's vehicle research centre in Surrey, and half a dozen scientists in overcoats were running about in a muddy field. They had three different robots on the go. TOM (Tele-Operated Mobile Test Bed), like a mini-tank without a gun, looked the most promising. Painted army green, it was negotiating a steep bank, its wide tracks gripping the wet surface, its operator struggling to keep up. TOM's television link was not ready for this demonstration (this was in early 1989) so the robot was being controlled by means of an electric cable. The cable turned out to be too short. The scientist's shoes slipped, TOM lurched into some bushes and then the engine stalled. There were embarrassed grins all round.

TOM was part of a special but meagrely funded initiative launched by the Ministry of Defence and industry to explore the development of unmanned vehicles. Another part of the project investigated ways of using a laser range-finder as the 'eye' of a robot vehicle. A device like an enormous trolley crammed with electrical equipment used the laser to assess whatever obstacle appeared in its path and then calculated how to evade it. A third programme involved trying to teach the computers on board a converted camper van how to recognise television pictures of the edges of the road – and to follow them. Although successful in their own way, none of these technologies has attracted the level of institutional interest and financial support required to develop them for practical use. Not only have the military been cautious, if not opposed, to this research but also political interest has been lacking. On one occasion, senior Conservative Party figures, invited to see a demonstration of the vehicles, were openly rude about them. One former minister told me that the sight of 'these fellows charging about after their robots was ludicrous'. He was particularly dismissive of the radio-controlled machines which had, apparently, not proved to be as responsive as designed. 'My little Freddy's got a toy racing car that does better than that. They were pathetic.'

The result is that the scientists engaged in this research find themselves in a strange paradox. Although, in their view, the circumstances requiring investment in robotic vehicles – however clumsy at this stage – are all too obvious, the institutions which fund their activities remain reticent. Instead the army is eager for the DRA to find ways of reducing the number of soldiers required to man each of its vehicles, stopping short of taking the step of removing soldiers from the scene altogether. Under a programme known as VERDI, the DRA has designed new work stations in combat vehicles which would allow two men – or even just one

– to do work normally undertaken by four. According to one of the scientists involved, the technology would allow the same tasks to be performed without any crew at all, except for an operator issuing commands from a safe distance. But the military, he said, 'have to make a conceptual leap to do that and they can't make it yet'. Though one classified study commissioned by the Ministry of Defence yielded no fewer than sixty-one potential roles for robots, only three of them were selected for further examination (they are believed to include reconnaissance, perimeter monitoring and mine clearance). And even those are constrained by limited funding.

It is a situation which leaves the DRA scientists bemused and struggling to make progress. As one described it: 'If you ask a soldier how he feels about the idea of armed robots, you get a look of horror and an answer which expresses the fear that the weapon could fire at any angle. Yet if you also ask him if he thinks there will be armed robots on the battlefield in thirty to forty years' time, he says, "Oh yes." There's a gap in their logic which they haven't realised. If they want robots in the future, we need the funding now. We are on the brink, I am sure of it, but there's no will yet to go over it.'

Yet the military may be forced to contemplate this radical step. The age of robotics is only just beginning and the manner of its emergence may prove decisive. The fact is that the most significant advances in information technology – the core of any robotic system – are now led by commerce rather than by the military and are therefore available world-wide. There is now the threat that others may develop or acquire some new 'intelligent' robot weapon first. So suddenly has the electronics revolution come about that the armed forces of countries like Britain and even the United States are now often equipped with far older, poorer computers than those available in the average High Street. The normal post-War process under which the military paid for the research and development of new systems which later had a commercial spin-off has been turned on its head. Civilian electronic engineering companies have miniaturised, speeded up and generally transformed every aspect of computing and the military are desperately trying to catch up. The risk, in military eyes, is that this revolution is a free-for-all. Potential adversaries which are militarily inferior now could leapfrog ahead by acquiring the latest computer aids.

One study on robotics and electronics developments for the Pentagon has calculated the speed at which computing power has increased.[10] Between 1950 and 1980, the number of computer instructions per second which could be bought with one dollar doubled every three years. Between 1980 and 1990, the number of instructions per second available for one dollar doubled every sixteen to twenty months. Since 1990, that rate has accelerated. The first IBM personal computer, introduced in 1981, contained a chip which could run 250,000 instructions per second; the latest Pentium chip, introduced in 1993, handles 30 million instructions per second. Over the same period, the amount of memory which could be stored on an IBM hard disk expanded sixty times while the size of the unit itself shrank by half. While it is conceivable that this acceleration in development may slow down as physical limits are reached in the manipulation of the silicon used to make the chips, there is every sign that this growth will continue. Constantly improving software will make progressively more effective use of the new hardware and, as costs continue to fall, an ever greater number of users will bring about a further round of investment and improvements.

To add to the fact that cheaper, smarter and faster robot computer 'brains' are increasingly available is another factor in this electronics revolution: miniaturisation. Computer developments have turned the normal economic theory that 'big is beautiful' upside-down. Unlike the economies of scale which can be achieved in car or steel production, the handling of information operates under different parameters. The processors in smaller computers are now coping with more millions of instructions per second per dollar than those of far larger supercomputers. It has become more cost-effective to employ a large number of small computers than a single large one – especially since the information being handled by the system is more easily distributed to those who need it via a network of smaller machines. Even if a network of smaller units is more expensive than one large machine, the network's ability to spread computing power to where it is most required gives it the edge – especially for the military. Martin Libicki, of the National Defense University in Washington, who wrote the Pentagon study quoted above, has coined a new phrase to describe this change: 'victory of the small and many over the large and few'.

In his report, circulated in senior military circles, Libicki gives three illustrations of his argument. A telephone exchange with 100 phones may yield cheap calls but it is far less convenient for users than distributing those phones to their homes. A single large radar may be cheaper than a network of 100 smaller ones but the latter may prove just as effective without requiring as much maintenance or security – 'a hundred pairs of eyes can always find something in the field most easily if they are spread around rather than bunched up'. The Washington Beltway ring-road can carry more traffic than four individual country roads but a single overturned lorry can close it – while four identically timed crashes are needed to close the country roads. The greater the need for reliability, the stronger the case for distributing the burden.

Martin Libicki produces two further points in his argument for the 'small and many'. First, one large object is more easily spotted by the enemy than 100 smaller ones and far more effort and skill is needed to detect and hit the latter. Second, the more valuable a single item, the more protection it needs and therefore the more expensive it becomes – and only a few become affordable. 'The fewer are made, the more important each is, thus are more worth destroying, thus the more protection they need and so on.' An American aircraft carrier, which can launch twenty-four attack jets, also needs for its own survival and protection air-defence fighters, anti-submarine helicopters, accompanying warships and a submarine: a $10-billion armada to support twenty-four fighter-bombers.

In Libicki's view this leads to the prediction that if robots are to be the weapons of the future, it would be better if they were miniature electronic creatures not large ones. 'Robots,' he says, 'replete with sensors, silicon brains and artificial legs are not impossible. But why must all these be integrated into one package, let alone a man-sized one?' To combine all the various components needed for a walking, talking, fighting robot into one system would be expensive and difficult, and the robot would be as large and as easy a target as a human. 'And far less capable than a network of cheap objects suitably dispersed.' Libicki predicts millions of mini-sensors, 'microbots' and mini-projectiles will act in concert to overwhelm any vehicle large enough to carry a human. It will be an age, he says, of robot ants. There are many other influential voices agreeing with him.

Imagine a tiny whisker of silicon about one millimetre long. It is coated with a thin film of 'piezo-electric' material which has the characteristic of moving in response to an electrical charge. One end of the whisker is fixed, the other is free to wriggle. The electrical power supply is switched on. The whisker twitches forward; when the power is turned off, it swings back to its original position. The electricity is switched on and off repeatedly and the whisker flicks forward and back. It has become a little leg. Picture six of these little legs attached to a 'body' about four millimetres long. The body is not just another sliver of silicon. It is a microchip, crammed with computing power. On its back rests a miniature battery or even a solar cell. In the position of its head is a tiny microphone or chemical detector or camera. Or a pair of sharp-toothed jaws powered in the same way as the legs. It is a robot soldier-ant – outlandish but feasible. It can spy or chew through electric cables or foul up an engine or gun. The technology required is either available or within sight. Versatile, cheap and expendable soldiers may only be a decade away.

The soldier-ant is the brainchild of a Dutch-born scientist at Boston University, Professor Johannes Smits. He is not insane; the findings of his experiments with robot ant-legs have been published in a string of respected academic journals. 'Just think about it,' he says enthusiastically, 'what you could do with ants that crawled into Saddam Hussein's bunker and told you what he was doing or destroyed it.' He admits his work is bizarre, to say the least. 'Occasionally people do laugh at me, at my stupidity or just in amazement, but I don't really mind.' His prominence at the forefront of electrical engineering research in the United States, backed by a long list of honours and awards, guarantees that he is taken seriously. This is especially the case since Smits is among those to have created an entirely new subject of research which only emerged in the late 1980s – micro-electro-mechanical systems (MEMS). It is a field in which the word 'micro' is being attached to a whole host of applications: micro-sensors (tiny devices which see, smell, listen or detect movement or metal fatigue); micro-motors (which power miniature legs or pumps or even wings); micro-power sources (such as thin-film batteries and chip-sized solar cells); and micro-emitters (which transmit radio signals or television pictures).

As with computers, the research has been commercially driven. It is a market already estimated to be worth about $1 billion a year and expected to grow to $3 billion a year by 1997. One expert has called micro-technology 'the industrial base of the twenty-first century'.[11] In Japan, where the largest sums are being invested in this field, most of the funds for a $200-million investment initiative sponsored by the

Ministry of International Trade and Industry have come from private companies. One Japanese project to develop micro-manufacturing techniques has exhibited its skills by producing an intricately detailed model car the size of a grain of rice. Those involved in Japan and the United States are taking their micro-world seriously. They see benefits for everything from safety standards to cellular telephones to industrial processing. Air-bags in cars are one current example already in use. These detect the sudden deceleration of a crash with the help of a tiny chip (rather like the ant-leg) which senses the change in pressure. For the future, a computer printer would run more smoothly if the paper, rather than jamming on a large roller, was fed through the system by thousands of miniature ant-legs. Aircraft manufacturers and airlines have long wanted an infallible method of spotting structural weaknesses and metal fatigue: embedding hundreds of micro-sensors, equipped with micro-transmitters, in the wings and fuselage would far more easily spot potential trouble and sound a warning than lengthy checks by maintenance teams.

Fluids in braking systems or engines or hydraulic lifting-gear could be more efficiently circulated by hundreds of mini-pumps than by one large one. A tiny pump, implanted in the body, could deliver a drug evenly and efficiently for the required period. Similarly, thousands of tiny adjustable panels positioned over the surface of an aircraft could be far more efficient than normal wing-flaps. The key to aerodynamic control is the thin 'boundary layer' of air just above the surface of the aircraft so its manipulation by a microscopic field of wing-flaps could lead to much more agile flight. The USAF clearly believes this holds promise and is funding research into the subject at the University of California in Los Angeles and two other institutes.

Johannes Smits, though primarily concerned with promoting micro-technologies for civilian uses, has conjured up a vision of the military usefulness of robot-ants. Although the practical achievements of his own research have been painstaking – by spring 1994, he had his ant-legs working but had yet to attach them to the ant body – he has only managed to attract faltering interest from the military. 'It's too new, too revolutionary,' he remembers being told by Pentagon officials responsible for research funding. His first contract was instead for one of the more prosaic roles: he was funded to develop micro-strain gauges – sensors to detect metal fatigue – for the US Army. Finance for the more esoteric research has proved hard to obtain. When Smits first floated the idea of robot-ants to the

National Science Foundation in 1989, he 'met a lot of incredulity'; 'it couldn't be done, it's ridiculous,' he was told. Only slowly is that attitude changing. In 1992, he was asked to give a presentation at the US Army's research laboratory in Fort Monmouth, New Jersey where he outlined his plans for the robots. 'They were very impressed – they weren't laughing, you could see a sort of gaze in their faces.'

The plan he outlined is borrowed in part from the natural world. Ants make up a staggering 9 per cent of the earth's biomass – that is, nearly one-tenth of the weight and volume of all living material consists of ants. As a measure of their ability to survive, compared to mammals, it was a statistic that impressed Smits. So did the facts that ants can carry sixty times their own body weight and are organised into a highly effective colony with a series of specialist roles. He envisages his robot-ants specialising too, perhaps performing as many as sixty-five different roles. Some would be endowed with large memories or computer power, some with strong limbs; others would be equipped to detect the movement of certain vehicles or people or the presence of particular toxins or chemicals in the air. One group could be given responsibility for transport: faced with an obstacle such as a trench, they would be programmed to form themselves into a bridge over which their fellow ants can cross. Another group could be designed to operate the communications system to relay information back to the human masters. These ants would line themselves up end to end to act as an aerial. A third team could form themselves into a video camera: one ant, fitted with a tiny lens, would stand in front; another, with the video sensor, would be behind; a third member of the team, with the best memory, would store the image. 'It sounds futuristic,' admits Smits, 'but really each of these processes is manageable.'

He does not stop here. Some ants could act as fuel-tankers, fitted with large batteries or solar cells, to 'top up' other ants stalled in the dark through lack of power. Some could be made large enough to carry their colleagues faster over longer distances. Some could act as messengers, programmed to touch other ants and 'collect' whatever information they have gathered. A final category could involve kamikaze ants – mini-robots programmed to hurl themselves into the exhaust of an engine as soon as they hear it starting. 'You could stop a million-dollar tank with a bunch of ants that may cost you as little as a dime each.' Further possibilities are opened up by Smits' analysis of the way his ants' legs move. At one speed setting, they could carry the ant about two centimetres per second. But at their highest speed, fluttering up and down at 140 times per second, they generate the same aerodynamic power as a flying insect. 'They could sort of hover along at about four metres per second.' The ants could become airborne. 'Once I get it working,' Smits believes, 'seeing is believing and they'll start paying big money.' A chip that walks or, better still, flies will be irresistible, he says.

Smits' research is just one part of the micro-revolution under way. Other researchers, notably in Japan, have been concentrating on what is called micro-flight. They have established that when insects fly, their minuscule mass means they are not subject to the same aerodynamic restraints as a bird or aircraft. They can hop and drift and float vast distances. Under the Japanese government's ERATO research programme (Exploratory Research for Advanced Technology), Professor Keiji Kawachi of the University of Tokyo has begun a five-year study of 'millibioflight'.[12] In a summary of the aims of the project, due to be completed in 1997, Kawachi explains that 'many structures in nature . . . take superb advantage of aerodynamics to ride the wind'; and that 'engineers can design wings which can carry the 350 tons of a Boeing 747 jumbo jet thousands of miles . . . yet they are at a loss to explain how tiny insects fly'. In particular he wants to focus on how insects maintain a stable position even when confronted by powerful gusts of wind. The housefly, he notes, has vibrating bars on its body which act as gyroscopes and help guide the speed with which the wings beat; other insects make use of drag and lift in unique ways to control their flight.

The aim is to understand how insects fly – and then replicate it. Researchers at the University of Michigan have already calculated that the manufacture of micro-aircraft 'should be possible'. In an international conference paper, they say that components only one-third as thick as a human hair are already available; that micro-batteries with enough power for nineteen hours' flight 'may be available commercially in a few years'; and that miniature electrostatic motors could produce enough energy to propel an insect-size device up to 400 microns long – about the same as the thickness of the average cotton thread.[13] The technology for pin-head-sized robots, whether the military want it or not, is approaching.

In another corner of the micro-industry, the technology of computer brain-power is advancing too. One problem with the miniaturisation of computers has been the physical limit on the amount of information that can be stored on a silicon chip and the speed at which it can be extracted when required. The chip can only handle a single 'layer' of information which has to be inserted and extracted from above or below. This is like the pages of a book all lying side by side on the same surface – using only two dimensions.

A new proposal to break beyond this constraint is to turn away from silicon and use other products that allow a three-dimensional approach for data storage instead. Professor Robert Birge of Syracuse University, in New York State, has managed to do that by coming up with the 'data cube'. It is a lump a little larger than a sugar-cube on which can be stored up to twenty gigabytes of information – roughly the equivalent of 4,000 Bibles. With modifications, Birge eventually expects to be able to store 512 gigabytes of data; then the equivalent of 100,000 Bibles would be contained in a device measuring 1.6 centimetres by 1.6 centimetres by 2.7 centimetres. The key ingredient is nothing more than a particular protein found in a form of algae – 'pond-scum', according to one USAF officer. The protein, bacterio-rhodopsin, contributes to the purplish colouring, visible from the air, of the marshes around the edge of San Francisco Bay. It was selected for the unusual consistency with which it reacts to light. When a finely tuned laser beam fires just one photon at one of the bacterio-rhodopsin molecules, the molecule changes colour; another flicker of light and it changes back again, thus recording a 'zero' or a 'one' in the binary system. With billions of protein molecules in the data cube, each one accessible to a pair of laser beams mounted around the outside, the device is held up as offering yet another factor in the transformation of computing and automation. A future mini-robot could be given the brain-power of a current-generation supercomputer.

In 1992, the Pentagon's Advanced Projects Research Agency, ARPA, realised that civilian-led developments in micro-systems and information technology were leaping beyond the military's grasp. In response, it took two steps. First, it embarked on a three-year investment programme worth $24 million to try to capitalise on the civilian advances in micro-systems; second, it commissioned the RAND corporation, the Pentagon-funded think-tank based at Santa Monica in California, to organise a workshop where academics, industrialists and military experts could thrash out ideas that might guide that programme and others in futuristic technologies. The workshop, held in December 1992, was to encourage civilians to explain to the military the advances they had made and advise on the next likely directions. ARPA wanted to know where best to spend its seed-corn research money: projects listed in the defence budget under category '6.1' are meant to bear fruit as viable weapons only in twenty to thirty years' time, those in category '6.2' a few years sooner. The workshop was given the title, 'Technology-driven revolutions in military operations'. It was a measure of how much the military had lost the lead in scientific research since the end of the Cold War.

There were sessions on 'Cyberwar', how battles could be fought by computer, with one side trying to disrupt and defeat the other by accessing its electronic information network; on futuristic engine systems; and on the 'Jedi Knight', a project to equip the infantryman of 2030 with new means of transport, armour, camouflage and weapons. But it was the session on micro-electro-mechanical systems (MEMS) which caught the imagination of many participants.

By the time of the workshop, RAND researchers had themselves carried out a study of the micro-industry and had begun to dream up military applications.[14] Although they found the field was still in its infancy, it was evolving at a 'rapid pace' and design techniques 'unthinkable only a few years ago' could allow the cheap mass-production of rugged micro-systems. Their report, sponsored by the US Army, the US Air Force and the Office of the Defence Secretary, is filled with photographs from this improbable micro-world: cog-wheels the size of a speck of dust, entire motors no bigger than a grain of salt. The authors, Keith Brendley and Randall Steeb, suggested that these technologies could be exploited in several different ways. A microscopic sensor with which to detect chemical weapons would be useful for every individual soldier, no longer dependent on the more expensive and more cumbersome devices now in service; a mini-mirror which responded to laser light could be carried on every vehicle to help identify it as friend or foe; and micro-dots, with the ability to change colour, implanted in huge numbers on the surface of a tank could create the possibility of rapidly changing camouflage.

But the greatest potential, in the study's view, was for micro-spies. Sensors the size of a peppercorn would be scattered in their millions over a huge area of enemy territory or near a disputed border to listen and watch and smell for military activity. Each device would carry several different sensors: thermal, acoustic, magnetic (to detect vehicle movement), chemical (to spot tank exhaust). Each device would also be fitted with a version of a microscopic mirror system which, when illuminated by a laser from a robot-plane flying above, would transmit the information gathered (much as the laser scanner at a supermarket 'reads' the bar code on each product). If this was ever made to work, it would represent a significant step beyond the 'jungle monitors' dropped into North Vietnam to listen for Vietcong activity. These Remotely Monitored Sensors were the first of their kind: microphones with a radio transmitter left in strategic locations. But they were large, expensive and unreliable. Even the current generation of battlefield sensors, known as REMBASS, in service with US Special Forces, weigh 6.5 pounds and are about eight inches long; they are complicated to operate and, as a result, are unpopular with the soldiers. Micro-sensors, three millimetres long, may prove far easier to use and be far more effective. Scattered over southern Iraq in July 1990, for example, they may have provided better warning of the Iraqi invasion of Kuwait on 2 August that year.

The RAND researchers envisage their micro-sensors being of most value in difficult terrain where the enemy is hard to find – above all, in cities. Ever since the ferocious battle in Mogadishu, they have been aware that the US military have become exceptionally wary of urban warfare. One senior military officer even told Keith Brendley: 'We don't really do cities.' It was a comment that led him and his colleagues to 'test' the use of micro-sensors in war-games, simulated on computer. They assumed a miniature robot-plane could be sent to fly through particular buildings, dispensing sensors as it went, each sensor then relaying back intelligence on the presence of enemy forces and the locations of their weapons. On the assumption that the system performed as planned, the micro-sensors made a huge difference to the conduct of the simulated battle. Brendley admits though that 'there are any number of problems to do with communications, dealing with all the information coming back'. But he remains confident. 'It may never come to pass but the technology is heading that way and I think it will happen.'

Less bullish is his prediction about micro-weapons. The study describes the scenario of hordes of tiny robots moving towards a weapons system or a radar and disabling its electronics systems as 'a tall order'. A robot-plane would drop small canisters – 'aerobots' – which would steer themselves to within a few metres of the target and, ideally, land upwind. The aerobots would disgorge their loads of micro-weapons and these would hop, fly or drift towards and into the target. Each weapon, armed with a 'kill mechanism', would dispense a tiny quantity of acid or conducting fluid to short-circuit the electronics and disable them.

A different approach for the use of micro-robots was suggested by one of the enthusiastic participants at the RAND workshop, the military consultant Sam Gardiner. He coined the term 'intelligent fly' for devices which could be 'seeded' across the runway of an enemy airfield and programmed to listen for a particular engine sound; on hearing it, they would simply hurl themselves towards the engine and, in their millions, foul it up irredeemably. Martin Libicki, the National Defense University analyst, has yet more suggestions. The robots, faced with an enemy tank, could either broadcast its position for another weapon, such as a precision-guided missile, to come and attack; or jump on top of the tank (like a flea leaping on to a dog) and act as a homing beacon for a weapon; or attack the tank themselves by eating their way through its most vulnerable components (its electronics) or by smearing the driver's window and optics. Libicki envisages micro-aircraft performing the same tricks against jets. Hovering in a swarm, they could either announce the exact location of an enemy aircraft or illuminate it with their own mini-radar systems; or, acting more decisively, they could explode, generating a storm of carbon fibres or ceramic shards to clog the jet's engines. At sea, hordes of robotic torpedoes could chase entire enemy fleets towards minefields. The ideas have only just started.

The RAND study, in a note of caution, identifies navigation, mobility and power as the three biggest problems with putting the concept of robot weapons into practice – making sure the robots can actually get to the right place. Yet it offers a rather disturbing solution, dredged from a particularly murky corner of science: the creation of creatures which are half-insect, half-robot. 'Rather than try to recreate these capabilities [of navigation, mobility and power], one option may be to harness insects as platforms for micro-electro-mechanical systems.' According to the study, researchers at the University of South Hampton have used minute neural probes to map the central nervous system of a honey-bee, establishing which parts of the system control the various key limbs and movements. Building on this work, Brendley and Steeb envisage fitting insects with micro-computers and using neural probes to direct them – Pavlovian stimuli of reward or punishment being administered through the central nervous system according to the insect's actions. 'One may be able to use the insect as a power source, like a self-winding watch,' they predict. Even the 'kill mechanism' could derive from the insect. They suggest that 'one could dope a spider's web with a conductor' so that when the computer-controlled insect has crawled inside vital enemy electronics it can spin a web which causes an immediate short circuit.

Brendley and Steeb concede that this approach is unprecedented and 'may simply prove unfeasible'. But they make no mention of whether the military would ever want to harness insects in this way. Arguably, such a move is no more distasteful than using horses to haul ammunition across the killing-fields of the First World War. Instead they take a grander view: that the time of micro-machines is upon us and that, if they can be made to work, micro-robots would offer 'military planners and political leaders a weapon yielding strategic gains within politically acceptable constraints'. The authors believe the weapons could 'develop into a trump card' for the United States; none of their concepts for military use were rejected as impossible by the experts consulted for the study. Yet they also sound a warning. Since other countries, especially Japan, are investing far more heavily in this field, the key technologies may well be developed first elsewhere, and could even fall into the hands of terrorists. For that reason, they recommend that the US should at the very least monitor the progress of micro-industry research and start conceiving of counter-measures.

The Pentagon's Advanced Projects Research Agency has taken note, as evidenced by its sudden decision to invest in micro-technology. Interest is growing, if only to prevent others getting ahead. If potential adversaries can find ways of using robots to inflict defeat on American forces with no loss to themselves, the price of launching an attack may become worth paying. At the same time, the lesson of Mogadishu is that for the United States almost any course of action is preferable to one that leaves Americans dead or their corpses abandoned. The combination of a fear of enemy automatons, of political squeamishness about combat and of the inexorable advance of technology may produce an unassailable case for robot weapons. Concerns about control will eventually be submerged; technologists will argue that the smarter the software and the more reliable the hardware, the greater the possibility of preventing robotic disaster.

Technology which permits less human oversight does not necessarily compel it.

The primary objective will remain that of keeping American and other western soldiers safe. Yet this ambition does not stand alone. It is mirrored in a parallel development of weaponry: one that seeks to keep the enemy safe as well.

8

BLOODLESS VICTORY

The military only understand a weapon if it leaves a smoking hole in the ground. We can move beyond that era of warfare now.
John Alexander, Director of Non-Lethal Weapons, Los Alamos National Laboratory, BBC interview, 28 March 1993

We were driving against Atlanta's early morning rush-hour traffic towards Stone Mountain, a bare lump of rock which rises from a choking sea of suburbs and high-technology industrial estates. I was having a difficult time, frequently experienced by television reporters, trying to sound convincing to the film crew about the purpose of our next stop. It was to be at a tiny engineering firm where we would film its latest product: a non-lethal weapon.

'A what?' Several voices cried out in annoyed disbelief. 'Non-lethal?' The idea seemed a contradiction in terms, a notion too eccentric to be taken seriously.

'A non-lethal weapon is a weapon that doesn't kill anybody,' I replied, 'a weapon that allows you to win a war without killing your enemy.'

I was sure my voice was rising to cover my own scepticism. I remembered a general admitting he had once written a note in the margin of a speech: 'Weak point, speak louder.' I had to press on regardless; we were going to see a newly invented gas that could stop engines and I felt obliged to justify asking the crew to film it. A non-lethal weapon would let you win without casualties, I said. It would let you force armies to stop whatever they were doing – ethnic cleansing, genocide, invasion – short of actually having to bomb them into submission. Many experts, I continued, regarded this concept as representing the next generation of warfare.

The problem, in researching this report, had been finding examples of non-lethal weapons: the most promising were highly classified. The device we were about to film was in a curious stage: it was being studied by the US Air Force but had not yet been formally accepted. It was in pre-secret limbo and I was anxious to take advantage.

I then had to explain what the device was. I was dreading this: I knew that most ideas for non-lethal weapons provoked gales of laughter. They had certainly had that effect in the newsroom back in London when I first proposed reporting on this subject. I knew few of the ideas would be taken seriously. I myself had found it hard not to laugh when first reading about non-lethal weapons in a restricted Los Alamos briefing paper, obtained from an American source. Not that the document itself betrays the slightest trace of humour. Billed as a 'comprehensive defense strategy providing commanders with new options', it lists a bizarre variety of 'technologies that allow force to be projected while minimizing the potential for lethal consequences'. The document is a blueprint for 'weapons that disrupt, destroy or otherwise degrade [the] functioning of threat material or personnel without crossing the "death barrier"'. It says the mission of non-lethal defence is to 'effect control over people and situations in which the application of lethal force is undesirable'. Worthwhile stuff, as one analyst put it to me, but there was no avoiding what he called a 'giggle factor'. I ran through the Los Alamos list as we drove out of Atlanta that spring morning.

It starts with electromagnetic weapons. These include an explosive pulse-power device, the size of a small parcel, which gives off 100 megawatts of electricity in a single flash. An accompanying diagram shows the device fitted to an enemy electricity pylon while a neigh-bouring picture has a puzzled team of enemy electricians trying to repair a roomful of blank computer screens. One better than de-stroying the pylon itself, this electricity bomb will damage everything connected to it – high-technology sabotage. The document says the device, weighing ten to forty pounds, will be 'man-portable', will work as much as four kilometres away from its target and will use 'mature' technology – meaning it could be ready in a few years' time. The document suggests that centres of communications, computers, radar and economics would be potential targets.

Another electromagnetic weapon is an isotropic radiator – a 'light bomb'. This device explodes in a flash of light and heat so intense that it will temporarily blind all optical devices, from the binoculars of an enemy general to the infra-red night-sights of his troops. The document suggests that this could be fitted to a remotely piloted vehicle – a robot aircraft – to sneak up to enemy positions in a 'silent assault'. Less subtle is the plan for a high-power microwave weapon. The picture accompanying this suggestion shows a cutaway of a well-defended enemy bunker, brimming with electronic equipment deep underground, with a handful of aerials rising above it. Along comes a cruise missile which, rather than attempting to attack the bunker itself and killing those inside, blows up near the aerials, showering them with microwave energy. The microwaves are passed underground, via the aerials and their connecting cables, where they shatter the enemy's electronics. In theory, the machinery would be rendered useless but the personnel would survive. According to the Los Alamos document, the warhead needed to achieve this effect could be developed at a cost of $20 million over three years, sooner if needed.

Next on the list is 'information sabotage' – 'to disrupt or distort information flow through surreptitious entry' into the enemy's command and control system. This is computer-hacking on a grand scale and by another name, the US armed forces learning to turn the tables. They themselves have had their computer systems repeatedly penetrated by hackers ranging from German schoolboys to the KGB. Now, this process – in reverse – is being elevated to the status of warfare. The document talks of 'subtle distortions of data' as the most benign intervention. A diagram shows computer-operators waiting for a technician to solve a mysterious problem: a close-up of one screen shows it reading, '2+2=5'. Nastier 'command-activated viruses' would disrupt a computer network at a particular moment, such as after a diplomatic warning has been ignored. 'Predictable system failure' involves the collapse of an entire network at a preset time.

The atmosphere in the car was warming up; the image of generals fighting with computers caused general merriment. More amusement was to come though.

'Super-reagents' provide the next group of non-lethal weapons on the Los Alamos list. This time the accompanying diagram shows a lorry driving over tiny capsules; a close-up shows the crushed capsules releasing a fluid which melts the lorry's tyres. The idea is to 'seed' a convoy route to prevent vehicles from using it. Other agents, described as 'super-oxidisers, solvating agents and depolymerisers', will accelerate rusting in metals, making them so brittle they snap, and will attack the polymer structures making up plastic, causing them to decompose instantly. Axles, engines and instruments would suddenly stop working or collapse. Another category of chemicals acts as superglue or an instant skid pan. Sprayed over roads, bridges and runways, they will make the surface either so sticky that vehicles would be 'glued' into place or so slippery that wheels would be denied any grip, an 'anti-traction' weapon. The document concedes that some of these ideas are years from being realised: 'basic chemistry needs to be done'.

More sophisticated still is the suggested use of microbes to 'enhance biodeterioration' in key components – bugs that eat fuels, explosives and the solder holding weapons together. To head off the criticism that this would be a flagrant breach of the convention banning biological weapons, the document notes that the use of microbes is well advanced in environmental areas such as tackling oil spills. Use would therefore be 'legal', the document asserts. In this instance the diagram shows a distinctly illegal-looking agent in a raincoat spraying an invisible substance at a bank of computers. The close-up shows cartoon-style bugs greedily eating the silicon circuitry. Because these organisms would be 'naturally occurring', they would be 'relatively low cost'. They could also be bred to resist pesticides and to react within a chosen time-scale of hours or months. There would be the potential to 'freeze-dry' them for storage and, as with any secret agent, human or otherwise, there could be 'plausible deniability'.

The final weapon detailed in the document is a 'sonic system', a noise bomb that 'causes non-lethal disruption, disorientation or incapacitation to humans'. The calculations for such a device have already been done. From ten kilometres away, the weapon yields 110 decibels and would merely 'alert' the enemy. From one kilometre away it produces 130 decibels and causes 'pain' (the document notes for comparison that an aircraft at 100 metres generates 120 decibels). While from 100 metres away the device would produce 150 decibels, enough to cause 'physical damage'. The sound will be directable and would rely on 'nineteenth-century technology with [a] twenty-first-century application'. Of the precise effects on humans, the document remains coy. Not so a draft of an internal US Army training document. The *Operations Concept for Disabling Measures*, dated 4 September 1992, is explicit. The noise weapon, it says, can cause 'nausea, vomiting or bowel spasms . . .'

The crew's laughter at what one American colleague called a 'bathroom bomb' lasted almost until our turn off the highway. There were jokes about catching the Serbs with their trousers down and about the unpleasantness of accepting the surrender of the victims, however non-lethal their suffering might have been. The concluding assertion in the US Army's document, that 'the effect [of the noise weapon] ceases as soon as the generator is turned off, with no lingering physical or environmental damage', beggared belief. Yet the jollity was short-lived: I still had to explain exactly what we were about to film.

The device, I said, is a gas that stops engines without harming the people near it – a non-poisonous gas which is supposed to stop convoys. It inhibits the combustion of most normal engines. Imagine it bringing the Serbs' military supply trucks to a halt or freezing the Iraqi tank columns before they crossed into Kuwait.

But my attempts to explain the device's potential value fell on deaf ears. By the time we arrived at John Astleford Inc., an engineering workshop not much larger than a barn, the camera crew were looking distinctly uneasy. The firm's director, John Astleford jnr., an impish figure with an endearing smile and a mind bubbling over with ideas – 'I just think 'em up' – did his best to reassure us. He would not reveal the ingredients of the gas because 'it's kind of proprietary, you know, and I'm only a little guy'. But it is perfectly safe, he said. When pressed though he did admit to one problem: 'there can be a pretty bad smell, in fact pretty awful'. We were warned.

Astleford had arranged a lawnmower engine on a workbench; and beside it a canister of his secret gas. There was no more to it. As a glimpse of the future direction of weaponry, it was hardly promising. The producer, David Coxon Taylor, and the crew had to work hard to transform the scene into one which would look even remotely interesting on television. It meant employing some clever lighting. But that, in turn, meant covering a skylight with our coats and closing all the doors. The workshop was soon dark and airtight, an arrangement we were to regret later.

We were soon ready. Astleford reached out gingerly, to avoid dirtying his tie, and started the engine. It was shatteringly loud in the confined workshop. Astleford lifted a pipe connected to the gas cylinder and pointed it at the air intake of the engine. He twisted the tap on the cylinder. With a piercing hiss, out squirted a large blast of gas. Within a second or two, the engine came to a halt: silence, no failure, no bad smell. A demonstration of a non-lethal weapon.

'There, David, it worked,' he beamed. John Astleford, the irrepressible inventor with twenty-two American and over fifty international patents to his name, was having fun. He has never stopped. Even at high school he designed a device for warming the seat of his car on winter mornings. While a sergeant in the US Army, specialising in communications, he managed to mend the most badly broken radios in the field, much to the fury of his superiors, who wanted to avoid the encumbrance of front-line repairs. After dividing his career between the two giant electrical engineering firms, Westinghouse and Siemens, Astleford, late in life, set up on his own, turning his kind, wrinkled face to a world he sees as brimming with enjoyably soluble problems. Washington State fruit-growers needed to be able to check the ripeness of their produce: Astleford designed a sensor that could age fruit more accurately than any other technique. Local dentists asked for an easier way to crown teeth: he designed them a unique pin device which suited perfectly. And when he saw a report in the *Wall Street Journal* about the growing interest in non-lethal weaponry, he started thinking. It did not take him long to see the point and devise a proposal.

'I see the air force using my gas in mines which they could air-deliver along a road, say, and whenever vehicles went over them they'd be shut down by the gas. It wouldn't hurt them, just halt whatever they were doing for a while.'

Astleford had rung the Pentagon and succeeded in tracking down the air force colonel responsible for handling new proposals: no mean feat in that labyrinthine building. The response was favourable and Astleford was asked for a formal report. When I later contacted the colonel by telephone, he confirmed that of all the non-lethal ideas on his desk, Astleford's was one of the most promising. Air-dropping mines that would immobilise a convoy rather than destroy it was a useful new option, he said. But the Pentagon's procurement process is clumsily slow and John Astleford realised that whatever the level of interest, it may take years to extract the necessary funding to develop his gas into a deployable weapon. Perhaps that is just as well: the gas did not appear ready for use now.

We needed to film the process from different angles and had to ask Astleford to perform his engine-stopping act several times. The second attempt was disastrous. Astleford squirted the gas from too far away and in his panic he missed the engine's air intake. The engine kept running and Astleford persisted in squirting the gas inaccurately towards it. With all the doors tight shut, the fumes from the engine exhaust were quickly becoming intolerable. They were then made immeasurably worse by the addition of a penetratingly unpleasant stench. Some of the gas had been sucked into the intake and was producing the very smell Astleford had warned us about. Suddenly, by unspoken mutual agreement, the workshop became too claustrophobic, dark and noxious and we abandoned our equipment, dodged past the sputtering engine and ran for the doors. We were gasping for fresh air by the time we made it outside. As we stood, trying to laugh it off, the smell followed us out, a sickly, deeply sulphurous invisible cloud.

'This is only the first version, David.' Astleford had joined us by the workshop door. 'There's a lot of work to be done.' Quite, we all thought. Not only could the smell be considered near-lethal but also, even if the gas did work, it was only inhibiting the engine from running for little more than a few minutes. A brief wait and a slight breeze would clear the gas and allow the Serbs, Iraqis or whoever to start up again, just as we had done. I put this to Astleford. 'We're working on it, David, a longer-lasting version's what we want next.'

Further attempts did prove successful and we got the shots we needed. But as we prepared to leave, we decided to lay down a challenge: try it on our hire car. Astleford agreed and, when the cameraman was ready to start filming, he fired his gas under the bonnet. It worked. We said our goodbyes and left. But, as we drove off, we could tell that our engine was producing the now-familiar smell. A cloud of it must have wafted into Astleford's workshop as we pulled away. Even several miles down the road we wondered whether the people in the car behind us were suffering as we were. We all felt a little queasy over lunch. The cameraman asked for the umpteenth time: 'Are you sure that stuff isn't poisonous?'

The idea is not new. The Book of Joshua records that nothing more than the blowing of trumpets and 'a great shout' brought down the walls of Jericho. Various other historical references are cited in a Pentagon document on non-lethal weapons. The ancient Greeks, fighting the Peloponnesian wars between 431–404 BC, tried to impede the enemy with smoke. In the Second World War, the

Yugoslav Partisans scattered spikes along main roads to puncture the Germans' truck tyres, and Soviet anti-aircraft gunners shone their searchlights at German tanks to blind the crews. And at the height of the Cold War, the chief American arms control negotiator, Paul Nitze, wondered if a 'love gas' could not be sprayed over the Soviet Union to induce its people to become more peaceful.[1] Most of these cases though, the improbable gas being the exception, no doubt arose for want of better weapons. They could hardly be considered to have been non-lethal in intent since their use from Jericho onwards was usually followed by massacre.

It is police forces, usually more sensitive to the political cost of applying force to civilians, which have pioneered a more sincere non-lethal approach. CS gas, the choking, tear-inducing agent, and electric batons or cattle prods are widely used to disperse crowds. In Northern Ireland, where the security forces are instructed to use minimum force to avoid causing casualties, there has been much trial and error in the effort to develop means with which to restore order without killing the offenders. Bitter experience has taught the authorities that fatalities only further antagonise the bereaved community, add a new name to the list of martyrs and create a further opportunity for conflict during the inevitably highly charged funeral that follows.

Rubber bullets and later plastic bullets were one answer. Yet it rapidly became clear that these weapons were only non-lethal at certain minimum ranges. If fired in close quarters in a riot, deaths could result, and did. According to one source familiar with research in the early 1970s, other ideas were considered and rejected. Various noise weapons were tested but were found to be useless in the narrow, echoing streets of urban Ulster. Large nets with which to trap groups of rioters were studied but also turned down on grounds of impracticality. The result is that the best non-lethal weapon available to British troops in Northern Ireland is restraint. That has become a governing principle in far larger military operations elsewhere as well.

There is an unwritten expectation that military operations conducted by democracies – especially under the auspices of the United Nations – will involve as little bloodshed as possible. Although the Security Council's Resolution 687 authorised the use of 'all necessary means' to eject Iraqi forces from Kuwait, the then US President, George Bush, felt obliged to halt the fighting when the first television pictures emerged of the rout of the fleeing Iraqi army. He clearly had a sense of how violent allied forces could be seen to be. 'We weren't in the business of slaughter,' he said. His decision to call an early end – the British said it was premature – arguably marked a watershed in modern warfare. Television images, public opinion and politicians' nerves were combining to demand that if combat should take place at all, it should ideally be bloodless.

In a paper, *War Without Killing*, delivered to an American academic forum on future strategy in September 1992, Professor Harvey Sapolsky, arms control director at the Massachusetts Institute of Technology, says that Americans not only spend more on reducing the risk of death by war than most other people but also are experiencing 'growing qualms . . . about killing enemy soldiers'. He traces this back to the Second World War. 'Self-imposed restrictions' have intensified with every conflict following the strategic bombing campaigns that killed 300,000 German and 330,000 Japanese civilians. The United States, he says, has not wished to repeat that level of destruction and no longer considers residential areas, hospitals, crops, dams, religious sites and markets to be legitimate targets. 'Most likely we have long ago sunk our last oil tanker and our last troop ship – all civilian casualties have to be unintentional.' From the 'distaste for body counts' in Vietnam to the 'doubts about killing' the enemy in Grenada and Panama, that self-restraint has become more insistent. The bombing of the air-raid shelter at Amiriya in Baghdad, in which more than 300 civilians died, though 'arguably permissible under international law' because it was thought to be empty of civilians and to house a military communications centre, prompted closer supervision by Washington of the air war. It even 'nearly resulted in its early termination'.

Professor Sapolsky argues that America's ability to wage war is effectively being undermined by this squeamishness. Though the country has been superior at 'producing mass destruction and . . . precise destruction', this will count for little against an aggressor who knows Americans 'like neither to receive nor to give casualties . . .' Certain operations with which America used to threaten potential adversaries – amphibious landings, massed parachute drops – are 'losing all credibility'. With enemy military facilities increasingly sited beside civilian areas and with western television reporters more frequently on hand to witness the aftermath, restraint will become an ever greater factor. Professor Sapolsky offers a bold prediction:

that the development of non-lethal weapons will 'become central to American thinking about war'.

This is certainly the fervent hope of the couple who have campaigned hardest to have non-lethality adopted as a new national strategy. On the Washington lobbying circuit, Janet and Chris Morris, both professional military analysts, are the most vocal champions of non-lethal weapons. They see America becoming increasingly helpless and isolationist without them. It is an unfamiliar argument for most people and initial responses to it are not helped by the distinctive appearance of the Morris duo. One colleague, on meeting them, described them as 'definitely weird'; then later, in a kinder and much more accurate assessment, as 'interesting, genuine, they have a point'. Janet Morris is thin and hard-talking; her grey hair hangs down the length of her back and she swishes it to emphasise her arguments. She speaks at high speed and dilutes her military jargon with no-nonsense phrases like: 'acoustic weapons hold a lot of promise, you just keep using them till [the people threatening you] are sick to their stomachs'. Her husband, Chris, a former musician, who until recently sported a pony-tail, is the quieter of the pair and is fond, in reverential terms, of tracing his ancestry back to the pilgrims who first reached America on the *Mayflower*.

The Morrises think, work and speak as a pair. They have written thirty-five books together, most of them science-fiction thrillers based around high-technology weapons. When they speak, their sentences overlap. Even on the telephone, both will take part in conversations using separate handsets. In calls to their home in Massachusetts, I became used to hearing one of them answer the phone, only to have the other join in without warning, as if it was entirely normal. They share the same belief – that the American military establishment is failing to adjust to a new era – and they sense that their public strength is more than doubled by working together. In a way that is only possible in Washington, they have become an unofficial but highly effective force for change. They inhabit a twilight zone peculiar to America. They seem to have access to key information and personnel yet have remained outside the Establishment.

The collapse of the Berlin Wall in November 1989 spurred them into action. They realised that the weapons with which America was equipped were simply wrong for the challenges of the future. Arms acquired during the Cold War years were designed to maximise firepower when there was little public expectation for any quarter to be shown. These were becoming less suitable now, as Janet Morris explained in an interview with me in March 1993:

'The western world doesn't like seeing casualties on the *Six O'Clock News* every night – they don't like seeing the US beating up on the little guy. The point is to give the warfighter new options that are acceptable, new weapons with which to meet life in the future. We have no enemy our own size any more and we're now so overpowered, we're actually unarmed. It's ridiculous.'

They turned to Ray Cline, former deputy director of the CIA, who now runs a think-tank, the Global Strategy Council, in Washington. The walls of his office are festooned with photographs showing him with several past presidents. Most of his staff are former intelligence officials. Cline, a man well disposed to novel thinking, saw the merit of the non-lethal idea and helped establish a committee of twenty-one retired military chiefs to examine it. The chiefs endorsed the concept. One of them though, who asked to remain anonymous, realised there would be an uphill struggle convincing the military. In a telephone interview, he told me: 'People say, "that kind of stuff is for cissies".' But with the support of such a prestigious group, momentum was building. Ray Cline sent President Bush a summary of the findings – ironically, on the day Iraq invaded Kuwait, on 2 August 1990. The President was too distracted, as was the then Defense Secretary, Dick Cheney, to give the issue any immediate attention.

Yet within two months of the end of the Gulf War, the Morrises' lobbying was beginning to pay off. An internal Pentagon policy planning paper on non-lethal weapons, dated 29 May 1991, was prepared by one Captain M. D. Martin in the Office of the Under-Secretary for Policy. It was a distillation of secret work commissioned by Dick Cheney, involving contributions from special operations, the Joint Chiefs of Staff, the advanced research agency ARPA and the Defence Intelligence Agency. The paper offers a formal definition of non-lethal weapons – in itself an important milestone in the Morrises' campaign to get the idea on the national agenda. 'A non-lethal weapon,' the paper declares, 'is . . . designed to achieve the same . . . ends as lethal weapons but [is] not intended to kill personnel or inflict catastrophic damage to equipment.'

The paper offers a ringing endorsement for this concept. Non-lethal weapons, it says, are 'operationally attractive', offering new options with which to respond to crises. They are 'legally and morally defensible' since responses to aggression can be more proportionate and discriminatory and these may enhance 'US leadership and prestige'. They are 'technically feasible, although few are currently available or in advanced stages of development'. Finally, the paper says, non-lethal weapons are affordable in an era of tight budgets and offer a 'satisfying . . . richness of possibilities'.

Then the paper explores a central dilemma: how secret should the research be into this area? If it is too open, one argument goes, potential adversaries could devise counter-measures; too secret and there will be no chance of devising a common strategy. A certain amount of highly classified development has taken place already. According to one of the retired chiefs on the Morrises' panel, 'Each service has little groups working on this in secret.' Certainly Los Alamos laboratory officials refused to discuss any technical details of the systems they were studying. And the Pentagon paper acknowledges that there are 'a few production non-lethal systems . . . confined to special forces applications'. It goes on to argue in favour of keeping some of the work secret. Many non-lethal weapons, it says, should be maintained in 'LIMDIS status' – Limited Distribution, in what is known as a 'black' program, the detail of which is not even revealed to most members of Congress. This would 'preserve their special character and protect them from counter-measures'.

However, the paper also stresses that it would be 'counter-productive if non-lethal weapons were perceived as a placeholder for black programs'. Translated from the curious jargon of the Pentagon, that means the paper's author recognises the potential for corruption. A particular project could be described as non-lethal purely to help cloak it in the 'black' secrecy that precludes too much of the resented oversight by politicians. On balance, the paper comes down on the side of greater openness and suggests a bold course of action. It says the time is right to launch a major new drive in this area – a Non-Lethality Initiative, reminiscent of the 'Star Wars' Strategic Defence Initiative. This would 'exhibit political leadership', 'pre-empt another nation claiming this appealing issue' and build the necessary support to 'effect a change in the way warfare is conducted'. The next step, the paper says, should be to draft a National Security Directive, a presidential statement of intent. It even suggests a declaration in the President's next State of the Union speech may be 'appropriate'. The President could use the opportunity to present 'a new doctrine which emphasises attractive political and moral attributes as well as new options for the low- and mid-range of conflicts most likely in the next decade'.

But the recommendation was not to be seized on that rapidly. The next State of the Union speech passed without reference to the concept. Despite the enthusiasm of the paper's author and of many senior officers as well, the initiative never got off the ground. A draft of a National Security Directive on non-lethal weapons was prepared but then blocked; renewed interest would only emerge several years later.

According to Janet Morris, the idea had run foul of entrenched interests in the Pentagon. A new Star Wars-style crusade would have sucked dwindling resources away from more established conventional weapons programmes. It was preferable to the forces and to the weapons-buying bureaucracy to keep non-lethal weapons modest and, above all, secret. Faced with a choice between buying a 'large, glamorous but utterly useless lethal weapon like a B-2 bomber' and non-lethal weapons which 'you can actually use in the world today', the Pentagon had opted to stick with its traditional approach.

The decision not to launch a new initiative had a further drawback, in the Morrises' view. It was evident that if the term 'non-lethal' ever became fashionable, it would be applied to a whole host of weapons projects, many wholly unsuitable, in a gold-rush search for funds. Without a coherent national strategy to guide the process, money would be wasted and opportunities lost for developing a coherent doctrine for the use of these weapons. Already the Morrises challenge the funds allocated to Los Alamos for its highly secret microwave weapon, described by the laboratory as a non-lethal project. Microwave-weapon research has been running in different guises for decades and, as Janet Morris said, 'I wouldn't put my baby or my cat anywhere near a microwave, would you?'

That kind of dubious billing has happened before. In the late 1980s, the vogue Pentagon policy was 'competitive strategies'. This called for the most intense competition with the Soviet Union in the technologies in which Moscow was weakest. Overnight, long-standing proposals for weapons were revised to include this key phrase. 'As if by pure coincidence,' according to one official, 'there was suddenly a whole host of projects billed as ideal for competitive strategies funding.' The same has happened with peace-keeping. It has become a running joke that for a bid for a new weapon to have the slightest chance of succeeding, it must be touted as ideal for UN operations. The Morrises were determined that non-lethal weapons would not suffer the same fate.

Their view remains that though the individual technologies for non-lethal weapons are important, the need for an overarching strategy or national policy is paramount. They point out that the primary security mission of the United States has hardly changed since the start of the Cold War. Then, National Security Directive number 68 set out the objective of containing Communism. It was the guiding principle for the next forty years. Now, the Morrises argue, the West needs a new guiding principle: the objective of containing barbarism. It is, they say, barbarous behaviour that the western world now finds threatening and, at the same time, so confusing. Faced with this challenge, the answer lies not in taking sides – because the cause of conflicts of the sort raging in Bosnia are so impenetrable – but in smothering the barbarism itself. 'All you want to achieve is to stop aggression, that's what non-lethal weapons give you the chance to do,' said Janet Morris in her interview. 'For the first time technology allows us to stop someone from doing something without hurting him.' With the battlefield effectively frozen – vehicles immobilised, radios jammed, key fighting units feeling ill – there would then be a far better chance of political talks achieving a lasting settlement.

The Morrises have considered the industrial implications as well. The huge arms industries which have been geared to producing lethal weaponry – and are now suffering as a result, laying off workers in their thousands – would be encouraged to produce non-lethal weapons, if they assessed that there was a growing market. The same level of expertise, engineering skills and familiarity with military standards would be required for this new role. The Morrises call this a 'step-down conversion' for the defence contractors, a reorientation of their current – but dwindling – output. And if the concept of non-lethality was endorsed by the United Nations, the ingenuity of other arms-producing nations could be tapped as well.

It is a compelling argument and finds widespread support. But it depends on a commitment to openness and public discussion, and this is far from agreed. Some of the most influential proponents of non-lethal weapons insist that American interests are best served by developing them in secret. One such figure is John Alexander, a man well accustomed to the highest levels of secrecy. After a long and discreet career in special forces, including tours with the Green

Berets in Vietnam, and as the Head of Advanced Concepts for the US Army, he only recently chose to allow his name to appear in print. He is now the director of Non-Lethal Weapons at Los Alamos and was the author of the leaked list of suggested weapons. He organised a two-day conference on the subject in November 1993 and although the event was publicised, many of its sessions were listed as 'classified'.

John Alexander comes with a reputation. 'Kind of strange,' one of his colleagues had warned me. 'Alexander? Ooooh, spooky!' another had exclaimed. He's into near-death experiences, UFOs, alien kidnap-victims, you name it, said a defence analyst who chose to remain anonymous. A Los Alamos public relations officer had advised me against pressing Alexander too closely on the details of the various weapons. 'He'll talk policy but he'll just clam up if you ask about the systems themselves.' Given what others had said, this advice made me wonder, not a little nervously, about the likely response of this mysterious figure to unpalatable questions.

We met in the lobby of my hotel in Washington. John Alexander stood tall, neatly dressed, the picture of an anonymous businessman. I found myself being overly polite. And, as our interview got under way, two characteristics of John Alexander left more of an impression than they might otherwise have done.

The first was that whenever the subject of avoiding death came up – which happened in nearly every answer – he would stress each point with an unsettling widening of his eyes, stretching them open as if to reinforce his message. The second impression was left by the curiousness of his language. Although he explained his view of non-lethal weapons with great fluency – no doubt the result of innumerable briefings to the military – he produced some startling phrases. For example, in one of his earliest answers, he began straightforwardly to outline the rationale for non-lethal weapons. The US, he was saying, understood war and it understood sanctions and it now needed options in between. The problem was that the military had too much firepower in an age 'when it's no point using a sledgehammer to kill flies'. The military still believed that their classic mission was to locate a target and kill it without reckoning on the cost of the aftermath, even though it was always the winner of any conflict who had to foot the bill for reconstruction. A logical enough argument, yet what followed left us stunned:

'If you go to keep the peace in a country, you don't want to antagonise the local population. You want to be friendly towards them and killing them doesn't do that. Death is an irreversible process in most cases.'

Death irreversible in most cases . . . The very notion made me wince in morbid fascination. The moment passed and Alexander was producing yet another oddity. I had asked about the applicability of his ideas to Northern Ireland. Alexander had briefed the Chief Scientific Adviser to the British Ministry of Defence only weeks before and Northern Ireland had come up. If your young soldiers were confronted in an ambiguous situation, he said, and were unsure whether a hostile group was armed, it would be much better if they could make the group uncomfortable rather than kill them. 'Just slime them and then sort it out,' he concluded. 'Sliming' was to become a catchword for the next few days.

Alexander however saw nothing remotely strange or humorous in any of this. When I suggested that some people might find the idea of bugs that eat plastic or sound weapons that disrupt the enemy's bowels as bizarre, to say the least, he replied with a stony face. 'I'm not sure I would call them bizarre at all.' There was no alternative. It was the way the West was being driven 'because of the requirements of national security in the future'. Here was a man who evidently believed time was on his side, that there was little point engaging in a public debate on a strategy the military would inevitably come to accept, if slowly. He had said all he wanted to; our interview came to an end.

Ten thousand feet above the misty-green fields of Pennsylvania, we were scanning the clouds for our first sight of one of the few non-lethal weapons in the American arsenal. We were on board a tanker aircraft, a converted Boeing 707, lying on narrow mattresses at the back of the bare fuselage, peering through the rear observation windows. An airborne rendezvous was due any minute with an aircraft which, until that morning in April 1993, had never been filmed before. We were the first journalists to secure access to the still-secretive 193rd Special Operations Group, specialists in psychological warfare. Their motto: 'We fire electrons not bullets'.

Suddenly the clouds parted. Hollywood could not have staged an entrance more dramatically. Just a few hundred feet behind us was the vast pale-grey shape of an EC-130E Commando Solo. Although based on the airframe of a Hercules transport plane, it bore little resemblance to one. From almost every surface, weirdly shaped bumps and aerials protruded. The tail-plane sported what looked like double horns. Beneath the wings hung large discs. And from the spine sprouted numerous spikes and fins. As the plane edged ever closer, manoeuvring into position to refuel, it was hard not to be awestruck by the ingenuity packed into the machine that gently swayed below us. For this was the world's most advanced airborne television and radio station, the latest word in the dark art of 'psy-ops'.

Such is the secrecy surrounding the Commando Solo and its sister aircraft that permission had taken months to arrange. When it came, our visit to their base at Middletown, Pennsylvania turned out to be a major local event. We were ushered into a conference room and saw some thirty of the senior staff leap to their feet. Then the camera team, the producer and myself were invited to meet every single officer, a task which involved advancing in a stately procession around the room shaking each outstretched hand. Dressed in jeans, we felt like shabby royals and, soon after the first dozen hellos, I ran out of original things to say. But, ever enthusiastic, our hosts produced an endless variety of meaningless greetings: 'way to go, Dave'; 'never seen, always heard'; 'go for it'; 'have a good one'. By the end of the round, the coffee and doughnuts we were offered seemed woefully inadequate.

In the briefing that followed, most of my questions were answered with a polite, 'we can't talk about that, I am afraid'. Because the aircraft carry electronic warfare systems, as well as their propaganda-broadcasting equipment, we were denied the opportunity to see inside them. The only glimpse of the equipment came in a photograph which had been included (inadvertently, I later learned) in a bundle of information given to me on my arrival. The picture shows two rows of seats for eleven crewmen facing sideways towards massive racks of transmission gear. A few of the units are recognisable as television cassette-players; most are indistinguishable banks of buttons and dials.

The planes can broadcast propaganda on AM, FM, shortwave and military radio frequencies. They can also transmit television programmes on six different technical systems to be able to dominate the airwaves and reach television sets virtually anywhere. That includes the NTSC system which is common throughout the Americas, the

PAL format used across most of western Europe and the Russian SECAM format found in the countries of the old Warsaw Pact. Only the French SECAM television broadcasting system is not catered for: 'it's too obscure' to bother with, one of the operators said. France and its former colonies aside, the rest of the television-viewing world is vulnerable to being bombarded with the messages broadcast by Commando Solo and its earlier version, Volant Solo. It has led the commanders of every major American military operation for the last three decades to use the planes. Their propaganda output was heard or seen in Cambodia in 1970, Grenada in 1983, Panama in 1989 and Iraq in 1991.

That last operation, Desert Storm, saw a massive psy-ops campaign. Specific Iraqi army units were sent messages on their own frequencies while millions of leaflets were dropped on them as well. Both forms of propaganda carried warnings of impending air raids by formations of B52 bombers. As an incitement to surrender, it was judged a success. Word was soon passed around the various Iraqi units that the warnings were not only proving to be accurate but also worth heeding. Each formation of three B52s was dropping a total of 153 bombs, each bomb containing 750 pounds of explosive. The impact on morale, as became clear from interviews with Iraqi soldiers later, was devastating. It was a macabre case of non-lethal carrot and lethal stick: not 'surrender or we bomb you', but 'surrender while we bomb you till you leave'.

'They got the message, it worked.' Colonel Reed Ernst, Commander of the 193rd Special Operations Group, was smiling. Thickset in his leather jacket, a stiff-legged swagger from over 9,000 hours' flying secret planes, he has the air of a film-star bomber pilot. With fourteen military awards and a long career in psy-ops and intelligence-gathering, Colonel Ernst displays a trait common in the American military of unceasingly stating pride in the value of his work. Slogans come thick and fast. 'Air commandos, quiet professionals.' Or: 'we own the airwaves'. And at every opportunity, the much-repeated: 'we fire electrons not bullets'. It was therefore only mildly surprising when he declared without a blush: 'psy-ops got a bad name with Goebbels but now they're coming into their own'. Like many of his colleagues, Ernst has judged correctly that his kind of warfare – psychological – neatly fits the gap between diplomacy and combat.

Its use in the Gulf War might not have been as purely non-lethal as some might have wished. But the essential idea of targeting minds rather than bodies holds appeal for the military. Propaganda leaflets, loudspeaker announcements and special radio and television broadcasts have long had an acknowledged role. Now though there is growing interest in using psychological warfare far more specifically and effectively. Notable for his endorsement of that concept is Colonel Jamie Gough of the US Air Force. At one stage deputy director of long-range planning for the USAF, Gough is urbane and sincere in his belief in the need for radically new approaches to warfare, a message he has gone on to preach at the National Defense University in Washington. He wants to see the military build on the experience of psychological operations and develop them more precisely into non-lethal weapons. 'You have to think in terms of addressing targets, not in a physical sense to be attacked with bombs, but targets like people's minds.' Gough identifies nationalism in particular as the root cause of many of the current conflicts. 'Nationalism is a target and that's where those non-lethal technologies need to be exploited.' In short, he wants mind-bombs with which to convince people not to fight.

That may not be as far off as it sounds. The ultimate in non-lethal weaponry – a mind-control system – has long been under development in Russia. It has potential that is both benign and terrifying. The device was discovered in Moscow by Janet and Chris Morris, during a hunt for previously secret technologies soon after the failed *coup* attempt in August 1991. In an establishment with the disturbing title, The Department of Psycho-Correction, at the Moscow Medical Academy, they witnessed a demonstration of the system. They saw how it could provide an unprecedentedly accurate analysis of the human mind. Then they were shown how, using the information obtained in the analysis, the system could surreptitiously target an individual's weaknesses and shape his behaviour. Tailor-made messages or instructions could be disguised in music or static-like 'white noise' or even transmitted in the audio 'shadow' of a radio or television programme. The Morrises were convinced it worked.

The designers, Igor Smirnov and Sergei Kavasovets, stress the positive aspects of their research. By building up a 'picture of the mind', they then know which key words, phrases or sounds would produce a constructive reaction. They envisage the technique helping mental patients and alcoholics and they quote a particular case. A fourteen-year-old Russian boy had been repeatedly assaulting his sister sexually. He was put through the analysis process and the researchers, having identified the factors contributing to his behaviour, prepared a cassette-tape of appropriate sounds and signals to penetrate his subconscious and cure the problem. The boy was instructed to listen to the tape every day. It is claimed that the attacks stopped – until the day the tape snapped.

More significantly, Smirnov and Kavasovets claim that if enough members of a particular country or ethnic group are analysed, common vulnerabilities could be identified and large-scale influence achieved. This too could have positive roles, it is said. If a fire started in a crowded cinema, for example, the Tannoy system could covertly broadcast messages instructing people to remain calm. What the two researchers will not address though – even when pressed – is the potential for the opposite to apply as well. Such a system could presumably be used to urge people to fight.

It is believed in western intelligence circles that such a technique was applied to certain key Soviet units in Afghanistan. The open scientific literature certainly reveals a highly active research programme in this area and, with morale low among the occupying troops, a device for encouraging a robust performance would have proved useful. One former Soviet paratrooper sergeant confirmed as much to me, in an interview in Minsk in February 1992. He said that before particularly unpleasant missions, such as a search-and-destroy operation, he and his colleagues were sometimes ordered into a dark room to watch swirling coloured shapes projected on to a screen and to listen to 'strange noises'. He was not at all sure this had any effect. Like many Soviet soldiers at that time, this one said he was either too high on marijuana or too drunk to pay much attention. Yet it is this kind of application of mind-control devices that triggered immediate interest in the technology unearthed in Moscow. The Morrises, worried their discovery might be snapped up by the highest bidder, possibly with disastrous consequences, quickly made arrangements for the machine and its designers to be brought to the United States.

Officially described as an aid for psychiatric care, the device was immediately seen as having valuable potential as a weapon. That its origin remains unclear was of little concern. Though it is thought that the device might have been developed to 'correct' the views of political dissidents, some of the American military and intelligence officials who scrambled to see it wondered if it might eventually fulfil a much larger role, trying to 'correct' the scourge of nationalism. The device provoked intense interest when it arrived, with the CIA, the Defence Intelligence Agency (DIA), the FBI, the armed forces and the Special Operations Command all sending representatives to inspect it. The hunger for a wonder-weapon to answer their fears was all too evident.

The Morrises had anticipated such a reaction. Ever distrustful of the motives of the more secretive organisations, they had set up a company to import the device and to hold the rights to it (though without claiming any future profits). This ensured that no single organisation could seize it and remove it to the world of secret unaccountability. The Morrises wanted to avoid losing the device to the wrong hands – above all, to hands that were likely to avoid any public scrutiny or debate on the issue. The merits and dangers of a weapon of this potential power, they decided, needed thorough examination. Firm democratic control was essential.

'I wouldn't put anything past any of these people,' Janet Morris said. Part of her strategy to force an open debate was to invite us to film the device. (Indeed, the Morrises' help with my report on non-lethal weapons for *Newsnight* provided an insight into one of the mechanisms by which Washington functions. Having opened several important doors for us, the Morrises then circulated video copies of the broadcast report as part of their campaign. The report was shown to some highly influential audiences, including staff members of the Senate Armed Services Committee, officials on the long-range planning staff in the office of the Joint Chiefs of Staff in the Pentagon and middle-ranking officers of the National War College.)

We arrived at one of the sleek modern buildings clustered around the CIA's headquarters at Langley, just outside Washington. It was think-tank country. Signboards bore names like 'Defense Systems Inc.' and 'Systems Technology and Control' which reveal little except an association with the military and the intelligence services. The first people we saw had that giveaway combination of disciplined stature and neat suits. One, who ushered us to the right office, almost immediately rattled off the names of the people he claimed to have met in the SAS. We were among people whose interest in weapons other than those of the most lethal kind was not immediately apparent.

The device, when we eventually saw it, was hardly impressive in appearance: a few pieces of computer equipment. Chris Morris had volunteered to let us film him being analysed by it. He sat still while electrodes were taped to his head, one in the centre of his forehead, one above each ear, one on each lobe. These were connected to an electroencephalograph (EEG) which would register the impulses in his brain. In front of him was a computer screen and, suspended across it, a large wire circle adorned with little red lights. It might have seemed farcical if the two Russians had looked a little less evil. They muttered darkly to each other, reeking of smoke, as they fussed over their equipment: Igor Smirnov had a dark beard and never smiled, Sergei Kavasovets' cold, pale-blue eyes were similarly humourless. We dimmed the lights; it was time to start.

The computer screen came to life. A large white block in the centre of the screen flashed on and off, a smaller red block appearing for brief moments inside it. The little lights on the wire ring began to wink, at a different rhythm to the computer screen. Then came a succession of words. Each was at least six letters long; a few made sense but most had the curious characteristic of nearly resembling a recognisable word but not quite doing so:

'Deambutt . . . Jovotree . . . Christoph . . . Ficknell . . . Borotty . . . Bainstar . . .'

Chris remained motionless. The light from the screen flashed across his face, his eyes transfixed by the words. A slight furrow appeared on his brow as he struggled to interpret them in the split-second before they vanished. Some stayed up fractionally longer than others, a few almost seemed to overlap. It was relentless.

'Mistador . . . Seenfirn . . . Cransery . . . Boronate . . . Dillar . . . Decrease . . . Brolloli . . .'

Yet it turned out that there was another, hidden layer of probing taking place as well. When we replayed our videotape several days later, we discovered that sandwiched between the visible words were other words, caught on a single frame, appearing for as little as one-sixtieth of a second. These had a more sinister tone:

'Armed . . . attack . . . defense . . . weapon . . .'

After twenty minutes, the screen stopped pulsating and Chris was allowed up. 'It's not unpleasant, just tiring,' he said, as Smirnov and Kavasovets went to work analysing what they had found. The words, they explained, were merely a device to focus the mind, to distract the conscious while the electroencephalograph gathered the responses of the subconscious. Within minutes the Russians had produced a three-dimensional graph showing the relative importance in Chris's mind of ten different factors including family, sex, job, father, health and anxiety. For Chris, the analysis rang true – so much so that he asked me not to report it. With this level of understanding of an individual's mind, Smirnov and Kavasovets said, they could choose the 'optimal strategy for treatment'. Left unsaid was the fact that 'treatment' might well be involuntary.

The FBI's senior officers were feverishly interested in that possibility. During the single week in which the device was in Washington, in March 1993, they sent experts to study the device no fewer than three times. They had a particularly pressing motive. David Koresh, the self-styled prophet of the Branch Davidian cult, was at that very time successfully resisting a siege of his compound at Waco in Texas. Federal agents had bungled an attempt to capture him and to free the dozens of his followers, some with their children, holding out with him inside. The troops surrounding the compound stood humiliated. The best they could do was to maintain a barrage of noise with helicopters and loudspeakers to keep the followers awake and to try to undermine their morale. As an image of the government's impotence, it could not have been more telling. Hence the FBI's intense discussions with the two Russian 'psycho-technologists', as they described themselves.

The idea, guarded with great secrecy, was to use the Russian device to analyse David Koresh's immediate relations, especially his mother, and any followers who had escaped or who had been close to him. A detailed database of their psychological characteristics would be built up, the hope being that such a mental picture might resemble that of Koresh himself. Subconscious messages urging him to surrender would then be broadcast, hidden in music or loudspeaker announcements by the police. Given the intense pressure on the FBI to end the stand-off, without huge loss of life, this strategy for mind-control had immense appeal. Later, though not confirming this plan, the Attorney-General, Janet Reno, revealed how desperate she had been to find a non-lethal solution, 'some magic weapon'.

After much agonising though, the FBI got cold feet. The Russians could neither guarantee the plan would work nor promise there would not be some unexpected reaction. The FBI officials realised the immense difficulty they would face in Congress if they had to justify using a novel, foreign technique, without assessing it properly first. The idea was abandoned. The stand-off ended in a bloodbath, Koresh and his followers dying in a massive fireball. The Russian mind-control device was shipped back to Moscow, unused but not forgotten.

The concept left an impression on many senior officials. A staff member of the highly influential Senate Armed Services Committee said, after hearing an explanation of the device, that 'it felt like the curtain being pulled back on a new era'. According to one USAF colonel, the system has 'the potential to leapfrog everything we have now'. At the same time, the realisation dawned on many that even if the United States chose not to pursue this approach, other countries may do. One officer feared the device falling into the hands of the Iranians. A CIA official said there was a risk that an enemy could gain access to American communications channels and broadcast subconscious messages to American fighter pilots convincing them that their aircraft were inadequate for the dog-fight ahead. Others worried that, if applied on a national scale, the device could even influence election results. Worse, it could help others to win wars. The only acceptable option, which has yet to be realised, was to secure it for America's sole use; that America must retain its technological lead in war-fighting.

That is the principle on which most of the armed forces tend to judge non-lethal weapons. Their yardstick is not an abstract ideal about a new, more acceptable concept of warfare. Rather, it asks a simple question: will it help us win? To that end, the first few non-lethal projects retain a lethal option as well. As he left office as Air Force Secretary in January 1993, Donald Rice confirmed that trend. 'We're a long way yet from transforming the nature of warfare from something that goes bang to something that doesn't,' he said. One example of this is the Stingray, the US Army's new laser 'dazzling' weapon mounted on a Bradley fighting vehicle. According to one commander who has had to provide crews for the tests, the laser can be set 'to different strengths'. This is reminiscent of the order heard in the *Star Trek* films: 'Set phasers to stun.' Reality is catching up with science fiction. Crucially though, in the commander's view, the US Army's laser, known as Stingray, can be used 'to blind or to kill'. Hardly evidence of a new era in military thinking, it shows that soldiers view non-lethality as simply another option.

That is most apparent in the first draft of a US Army training and doctrine booklet on so-called *Disabling Measures*. This document, written in September 1992, leaked to me a few months later (and quoted earlier in this chapter), begins with the recognition that 'situations will arise where the destructiveness of conventional weaponry is too much and diplomacy is not enough'. It describes how non-lethal weapons could be used to fill that gap and at the same time reduce the risk of 'military overkill, international censure, political repercussions or media criticism'. It then provides the first clues about the military view of how to employ these weapons. The scenarios range from riot control to major wars.

At the very least, the document suggests, non-lethal weapons could help 'disperse dangerous mobs', a popular notion in a military still traumatised by events in Iran in 1979. Few officers have forgotten the humiliation of seeing the staff of the American Embassy in Tehran taken hostage by hordes of militant students. A device to keep crowds at bay – for instance, a noise weapon with a limited range – would shield those inside. Other devices, such as glues and anti-traction agents, could be used in the opposite way, to isolate and 'exert pressure on' a nation trying to evade trade sanctions.

However, more aggressive uses of non-lethal weapons are also disclosed by the document. There could be a role for them in snatch-or-destroy incursions into rogue countries – to try to reverse the spread of weapons of mass destruction. 'US forces may be required to go into a country to accomplish a single objective,' it says, 'such as the destruction of a chemical weapons production facility or the capture of nuclear weapons.' In those cases, non-lethal weapons could be deployed to 'slow the arrival' of the country's forces. American forces could then be extracted 'without a major engagement'. Given the twin pressures of trying to minimise casualties and having to act against nuclear proliferation, this scenario is likely to be one of the most closely studied.

The document sees non-lethal weaponry 'augmenting' lethal force not replacing it. In a section on 'large-scale operations', the purpose of laser-blinders, pulse-power generators and computer viruses is described as being to create 'windows of opportunity' for American forces to attack by more conventional means. A paragraph on operations in 'urban terrain' goes further. One motive, it says, for using 'aqueous foam' to block doorways is to 'channel movement through established firing zones'. In effect, this would involve using non-lethal weapons to increase the killing-power of lethal ones.

The Gulf War produced a revealing example of the use of both forms of weaponry. One of the first tasks of the air operation was to shut down key sectors of Iraq's national power grid. General Schwarzkopf and his commanders had to choose how much damage they wanted to inflict on the electricity infrastructure to achieve that end. Initially, the option they selected was non-lethal. Tomahawk cruise missiles were sent to power stations and switching centres and attacked them – not with conventional explosives but with thousands of spools of carbon fibre. The fibres landed on the electrical components, causing instant short circuits and disruption. A retired American electrical engineer, Warren Piper, visited the power stations at Tikrit, Saddam's home town, and at Arbil after the war and saw the effects for himself. In a telephone interview, he said the fibres had shut the stations down with 'fantastic accuracy'. Yet twenty-four hours later, the Tomahawks returned, this time armed with explosive warheads. General Schwarzkopf had evidently wanted to be sure. According to Bill Arkin, a Greenpeace consultant who carried out a major study of the effects of the Gulf War, the generals 'got so nervous about whether this non-lethal stuff would work' that they chose to bomb the sites conventionally as well.

War-games involving non-lethal weapons shed further light on military attitudes. In one US Army game, designed as a re-run of Operation Desert Storm, the team playing the allied side was given the option of using non-lethal weapons against the Iraqis. Of all the ways in which these weapons could have been deployed – to impede Iraqi reinforcements or supply convoys for example – the team devised a lethal use for them instead. As the forces of the Iraqi Republican Guard were retreating from Kuwait, the allied team attacked them with glues, anti-traction agents and engine-stopping gases. The convoys ground to a halt.

But the allied team regarded this non-lethal act as a mere prelude to what was to follow: a full-scale attack by conventional weapons, more effective for being aimed at static targets. Sam Gardiner, the strategist who led the war-game, concluded that in this case the battlefield had been made 'more lethal, not less'. It was a new example, he said, of General Patton's famous phrase about manoeuvre warfare: 'hold them in the nose and kick them in the pants'.

Another war-game explored the use of non-lethal weapons as

tools for peacemaking. Sam Gardiner called it an 'unwar' game. The scenario was a confrontation between India and Pakistan, with the United States, armed with non-lethal weapons, attempting to prevent the conflict escalating. In the exercise, India attacked first, striking across the border at two key Pakistani divisions. In return, Pakistan launched a counter-attack, seizing a chunk of Indian territory to strengthen its position in the negotiations which could be expected to follow. At this moment, the United States applied the now-familiar glues, slippery substances, rubber-eating bugs and bowel-quivering noise weapons to bring a halt to the fighting. So far so good – but not for long.

The team playing India believed that the American intervention, however well-intentioned and non-lethal, favoured the weaker side in the conflict, Pakistan. Pakistan, as the victim of the initial aggression, did indeed stand to gain from the US action: it halted the Indian attack. Gardiner's conclusion was that any intervention, even with non-lethal weaponry, ultimately involves taking sides. Even if the United Nations, rather than the United States, had undertaken the intervention with non-lethal weapons the effect would have been the same. Non-lethality no longer seems to be such a panacea as a peacemaker.

Just as serious was the war-game's revelation that a decision by the United States not to intervene was tantamount to supporting the aggressor, in this case India. To an extent, that has always been the case. The Muslim-led Bosnian government, for example, has long claimed that the failure of the West to intervene in former Yugoslavia amounts to acquiescence in the offensives launched by the Serbs and Croats. When non-lethal weapons are involved though, the case for intervention is stronger. Since the use of non-lethal weapons entails a vastly lower political cost – because fewer troops are likely to die – than with conventional weapons, then a decision to act should be easier to take. In a paper summarising his findings from the war-game, Gardiner emphasises the impression that would be given by the US choosing not to get involved. 'If the United States could stop this aggression easily and is not stopping it, the United States must want India to defeat Pakistan.' He calls this the 'negative dimension of non-lethal weapons'.

British military analysts have reached similar conclusions. Although British research into non-lethal weapons has been on a far smaller scale – and kept far more secret – the problems identified by Sam Gardiner's war-games correspond with those highlighted in Britain. One leading Defence Research Agency scientist, though supporting further work on the subject, said there was still no philosophical agreement on the purpose of non-lethal weapons: 'What are you trying to achieve?' he asked, choosing to remain anonymous. If the point was merely to freeze an enemy's actions or to paralyse a battlefield – as in the case of the India–Pakistan war-game – what would happen next? The fighting may have ceased but would the chances of reaching a negotiated settlement be any better?

The scientist identified more practical difficulties as well. While it may well be possible to glue tyres or jam engines from short range, it would be far harder to do so from greater distances. Applying these substances to the right vehicles or people from a militarily useful range was no easy task. Nor would it always be safe to use non-lethal weapons against a lethally armed enemy. Only the most sophisticated opponent may tacitly 'agree' to fight non-lethally. 'You can't do much non-lethally if there's a high-velocity round coming towards you,' the scientist said. Even if you did use a non-lethal laser rather than a gun against an adversary, 'is it more humane to blind him or shoot him in the head?'

Yet despite these reservations, there is a gradual acknowledgement in military circles that it is now becoming more likely that non-lethal weapons may have to be acquired. The technologies are available – or soon could be – and the circumstances for their use seem right. Indeed in early 1994, four years after the first attempts to arouse the military's interest, the Pentagon's director of tactical warfare programmes, Frank Kendall, confirmed that plans to invest in non-lethal weapons were now under way; officials, quoted at the time, predicted that as much as $1 billion could be spent in this area over the next few years.[2] A special Pentagon group was established to receive specific suggestions from industry and the laboratories. At the same time, the highly influential Senate Armed Services Committee pressed the military to accelerate its work in this field; the National Security Council became formally interested as well. The ball was rolling.

But non-lethal weapons raise two difficult dilemmas. First, over secrecy: non-lethal weapons deployed secretly will bring the benefit of surprise but will lose the potential value of issuing a public threat of non-lethal action, as a step short of conventional war. Secondly, non-lethal weapons may ironically make war more likely. The Cold

War emphasis on maximising firepower has armed the West with weapons often unsuited to smaller-scale operations conducted under the gaze of the media. To turn to non-lethal weapons instead would make intervention easier to contemplate but at the same time harder to refuse. The use of non-lethal weapons may buy more time for diplomacy by holding off the day when conventional weapons are brought to bear. But the effect may be to make involvement in wars more common rather than less – and there will still be no guarantee about the consequences.

CONCLUSION

The technology critical to defence will for the most part continue to advance undaunted.

An internal Defence Research Agency
document, dated 1993–4

In 1953, in a speech to the American Society of Newspaper Editors, President Dwight D. Eisenhower warned of the dark side of the harnessing of science to military ends. As the momentum of the Cold War arms race was gathering pace, he declared that a 'military-industrial complex' could wield 'unwarranted influence' in national life. He implicitly conjured up an image of a self-feeding, self-serving behemoth which would draw away vital resources from more pressing needs. From the man who had led the allied armies against Nazi Germany in 1944 and who was at that stage leading the West against the Communist bloc, this was powerful, even heretical, criticism. Yet it did not stop there. He went on, in the same speech, to offer what remains the most evocative summary of all that is wrong with the quest for more and better weapons:

'Every gun that is made, every warship launched, every rocket fired, signifies in the final sense a theft from those who hunger and are not fed, those who are cold and are not clothed. The world in arms is not spending money alone. It is spending the sweat of its labourers, the genius of its scientists and the hopes of its children.'

However true, his words went unheeded: the demands of the confrontation with the Soviet Union were overbearing. And, even after the demise of the Communist system, when the popular hope in the West had been that the days of expensive and prolonged investment in the military might at last be over, the unleashing of ethnic and nationalist aggression and the proliferation of potent technology have ensured that a huge proportion of the world's wealth continues to be spent in military competition – and military conflict.

According to World Priorities, a Washington-based institute, there have been 149 wars since the Second World War in which 23,140,000 people have been killed. In 1993, the institute counted twenty-nine ongoing wars. It recorded that more people died in the various conflicts which raged in 1992 than in any other single year since Vietnam seventeen years earlier. Over 90 per cent of the wars were in developing countries which, though receiving a total of $56 billion in aid in 1992, spent at least $36 billion on weapons. The total spent on weapons world-wide that year reached $600 billion and there is no sign of that level of expenditure slowing down. Demand, in a nervous world, remains high and supply eager: attempts to regulate arms exports generally founder in the face of the political and economic benefits of full order books.

It is a period of contradictions. Western governments are trying to meet several apparently opposing goals. They want to realign their spending priorities after the Cold War to devote more money to social causes; they want to minimise redundancies in the defence industries, commonly located in areas in which unemployment is already high; and they want to continue to equip their armed forces with the sort of technology that provides a winning edge in whatever conflict they may face. The least compatible of these objectives is the exacting of a peace dividend at the very moment that involvement in war has never looked so probable. In retrospect, an all-out conflict with the Soviet Union was always unlikely: its implications were too terrifying for both sides. Yet once the Soviet Union collapsed, it was as if a collective decision had been taken that smaller wars could now be fought without an immediate risk of escalation to a catastrophic scale. A plethora of vicious but limited conflicts erupted as a result and outside forces, like the British Army in Bosnia, found themselves involved – not as combatants participating to win but as United Nations referees and linesmen attempting to suppress the most excessive cases of barbarism.

Even in this role, UN troops quickly grasped that the more sophisticated their equipment, the more safely and effectively they could achieve their aims. The Warrior infantry fighting vehicle, with its tank-tracks, heavy armour and powerful Rarden cannon, though designed to fight a high-technology war with the Warshaw Pact in central Germany, turned out to be well suited to the tasks set in Bosnia. Helicopters, though vulnerable, were the only reliable means of transport around the densely packed, hostile streets of Mogadishu.

Not that the Warrior or any of the other weapons systems designed to help win the Third World War could by themselves win the wars in Bosnia or Somalia (in the sense of intervening so comprehensively that they could stop it). But, if possessing the most modern weaponry means minimising the losses suffered by British and other UN forces and maximising the impact on the warring parties, the case for continuing to maintain a technological edge by researching future generations of arms becomes a strong one. If there is a moral argument for western intervention in regional or civil wars, there is also a practical one for equipping the soldiers involved with the best and most modern weapons available.

There is another argument in favour of weapons research as well: high-technology armaments are spreading. Aircraft carriers, submarines, supersonic warplanes, the latest tanks and satellites are all joining the arsenals of a growing number of countries. Even relatively old weapons 'platforms' – vehicles, aircraft and ships – are being transformed into highly capable systems with the addition of the latest sensors, computer-aided guidance and microchip processors. Israel, for example, has been updating its existing warplanes with advanced phased-array radars and fire-and-forget missiles; India plans to give its ageing Soviet-built MiG-21s much greater reach and power by following suit, incorporating western information technology. DRA analyses have found that although updated warplanes will never be a match for the latest generation in one-to-one engagements, there are circumstances in which their capabilities might turn out to be unpredictably potent, especially if large numbers of enemy planes are involved. Add to that the proliferation of nuclear, chemical and biological weapons and the ballistic missiles to carry them and the potential danger of confronting even a medium-sized regional power becomes acute. Yet, if the West wishes to be able to defend allies such as Kuwait against Iraq or South Korea against North Korea, it must somehow maintain a technological advantage.

Achieving that edge poses a highly sensitive political dilemma. It involves a trade-off between the present and the future: between allocating finance to keep alive particular units or squadrons or arms manufacturing plants and using it to promote research into unpredictable but potentially critical technologies for the next generation. The louder voice of the former tends to drown out the quieter protests of the latter: and the scientists whose livelihoods depend on a continuing flow of finance feel the tide is against them, that short-term political necessity is ignoring their long-term contribution. One British military researcher conceded there was 'no way' the government could publicly justify diverting money towards his particular futuristic project in favour of a famous regiment. Not that the defence budget is managed that simply. But political choices are made on a larger scale about whether, for example, the army should be allowed to retain more personnel or the Defence Research Agency given a larger slice of the cake. During the early 1990s, the government seemed to go against the DRA: its budget fell from the region of £700 million to around £600 million, its personnel strength planned to fall from 11,500 to 7,500.

The sense among scientists that their contribution is politically insignificant is exacerbated by changes in their relationship with the armed forces. With the decline in military spending, the pressure to justify the purpose of some of the more esoteric (and complicated) projects has become intense. In Britain, the reins are now firmly in the hands of the military. The weapons laboratories, which for much of their existence were seen to have operated as semi-independent fiefdoms, have recently been brought under the direct control of officers and civilian officials in the Ministry of Defence. About 60 per cent of the DRA's work now comes under the heading 'applied research' which, as is implied, is carefully focused scientific support to meet particular operational requirements, often relatively short-term. About 16 per cent of the effort goes towards advising the Procurement Executive, the weapons-buying department of the Ministry of Defence; about 14 per cent on intelligence and civilian projects. The remainder – only some 10 per cent – is allocated to 'strategic research', what one senior scientist called the 'blue skies stuff'. The days of a scientific free range, once enjoyed by the older generation of scientists, are over.

The projects in the 'strategic research' category include Dick Lawrence's work on developing guidance software to predict an enemy aircraft's next move and Nigel Haig's on devising a robotic eye which responds in the same way as a human's. However obvious the value of these endeavours might seem, they have to win funding like any other. Each scientist is invited to submit an idea and then justify it in a three-minute 'sales pitch' before a panel of outside experts. If the project is approved, the scientist will be given three years in which to prove its validity; within that period, he has to file regular progress reports as well. It is a source of enormous resentment. Yet for the Defence Research Agency as a whole it is a vital mechanism for survival in a harsh financial climate: the system is designed to minimise waste – by killing off unpromising work early – and to reassure the military, who are providing the money, that the scientists, however eccentric, are not out of control.

But the future of military research cannot be justified by internal reforms and cost-saving on their own, however reasonable those steps are. The task faced by the DRA and its counterparts abroad is to explain the need for a research effort across a broad range of technologies, even if at first sight they have little military relevance, let alone social value. An internal DRA document for the financial year 1993–4 gives an example. A next-generation aircraft will depend on the feasibility of a new kind of engine. That will depend on the feasibility of a better composite material (stronger yet lighter). In turn, that might be possible only through the development of a new treatment or coating for the material's surfaces. Each step in this chain requires a body of scientific expertise – yet on its own might seem to have little point. In an atmosphere of intense squabbling over funds for other areas of military activity with a far higher political profile, it is a difficult case to make. It involves moving beyond the Cold War days of pursuing technological advance unquestioningly, for its own sake. A much clearer justification is now required.

One solution has been offered by two experts in the United States. Ted Gold and Richard Wagner argue that continuing military research might be made more affordable and therefore more politically palatable if the results of laboratory work are in effect 'frozen' once proven, not immediately fed into the expensive 'pipeline' of production and deployment. In a paper, they suggest that it may be sufficient to establish that new weapons will work. They talk of the 'long shadow' that military research might cast over potential adversaries, convincing them they would have little to gain from trying to compete.[1] The weapons themselves, developed but not purchased, would act as 'virtual swords' – ready for production, constantly updated and extensively tested on simulators but not actually in service. The authors acknowledge that with the global spread of computer and simulation technology, this process might well be available to non-western countries as well. But 'better a virtual arms race than a real one,' they conclude.

The argument has not been accepted formally but it has contributed to a current flurry of change. The Pentagon's latest technology strategy, prepared in 1994, involves reforming the research effort to reduce costs and to speed up the process of deciding whether a particular project is worth pursuing into service, if not into the proposed 'virtual' status. The traditional system of American military research has established four categories: basic, long-term research (funded under a section of the defence budget known as 6.1); exploratory research (6.2); advanced research (6.3); and engineering development (6.4).[2] Critics argued that the system is cumbersome and unresponsive and allows too many unpromising projects to continue. Under the revised arrangement, weapons selected for Advanced Concept Technology Demonstration will be studied at an accelerated rate: those that pass will be hurried into production, those that do not will be abandoned.

The DRA has tried to adopt a similar approach, if only because of financial pressure from the Ministry of Defence. Here the idea of pursuing research up to the point of production – but not necessarily any further – has elicited a positive response. One official saw its value in the context of the global competition. 'We don't need to build weapons but we do need to avoid dropping behind.' The government seems to have accepted this. The 1994 Defence White Paper, a document notably more pessimistic than the editions produced in the aftermath of the fall of the Berlin Wall, recognises that the 'need to retain battle-winning technological advantage is as pressing as it has ever been'. It highlights the value of the Strategic Research programme with its emphasis on high-risk, high pay-off technologies.

But the test of that is finance – and it is dwindling. At the same time, both the British and the American governments have been investigating the potential value of directing their military scientists towards civilian projects. This can lighten the financial burden of purely military research if spin-offs produce income from the licensing of new products; it also maximises the wider economic benefit of maintaining a military research programme. Officials are fond of quoting examples of how this can work: infra-red seekers from air-to-air missiles can spot fissures within glaciers and so predict avalanches; precision warheads can assist the drilling operations of the oil industry; a genetically engineered vaccine against a biological warfare agent is being offered to medicine as an antidote to gas gangrene, the potentially fatal condition which can follow the infection of wounds. The attractions are obvious yet there are risks too: from one perspective, critics may argue that civilian research should be undertaken by civilian scientists, not by military ones trying to justify their existence; from another, that the scientists who represent the nation's only expertise in weapons development may find themselves distracted from their core tasks, with disastrous consequences in times of crisis.

The fact remains that the scientists whose livelihoods were created by the Cold War have yet to secure their future in its aftermath. For western governments, the dilemma is how to justify maintaining an expensive scientific resource devoted to the military at a time when no single, clear threat is apparent. Put more simply, the challenge is: how to stay ahead in a burgeoning arms race when few wish to contemplate the possibility of those arms ever being used or to recognise that a new kind of race is under way.

POSTSCRIPT

The attack was first noticed when someone heard a hiss from an unusual little box. Immediately dozens of people began coughing and vomiting. Soon hundreds were collapsing. Twelve were dead or dying. These were not soldiers caught by a novel weapon on a battlefield but office-workers in the morning rush hour on Tokyo's underground railway. It was 20 March 1995 and Japanese civilians had become the first victims of a new and dreaded form of warfare: terrorism with weapons of mass destruction. Normally associated with the most brutal conflicts between nations, the category of arms known as 'weapons of mass destruction' includes nuclear, chemical and biological weapons. That March morning, small gas dispensers, smuggled onto three of the subway trains, had released Sarin, a sophisticated chemical agent designed to immobilise the human nervous system; its inventors had meant it to paralyse entire armies. In the packed car beneath the Tokyo streets, it was fortunate that only 12 people were killed. The toll of 5,500 wounded indicates how much more devastating the attack could have been.

A threshold had been crossed: for the first time a weapon with Sarin's potency had been deployed by an organisation other than a national government. The suspected perpetrators were the leaders of a vast and well-financed religious cult, the Aum Shinri Kyo. None of the customary procedures and rules of conflict had applied. This was combat beyond the experience of defence planners and government officials in Japan and worldwide. Suddenly it was no longer sufficient to prepare for wars beyond one's borders; the Tokyo experience showed how easily weapons of mass destruction can be deployed within them as well.

For years there had been predictions that the greatest threat to the world's democracies would come not from other nations but from 'sub-state' groups – terrorist organisations, aggrieved ethnic minorities, even drug cartels, equipping themselves with the same weaponry available to the most advanced nations but not sharing any of the usual political restraints about its use. A small band of military experts, including Carl Builder, the RAND Corporation analyst previously quoted on this subject, has repeatedly warned that military commanders are preparing to fight the wrong sort of enemy – that, in effect, they are looking in the wrong direction. All too often generals have ignored these warnings, preferring to address more traditional military threats and leave sub-state battles to be fought by the police. But now, these established views have begun to change; events have forced them to.

First came the Tokyo attack. Then, one month later, on 19 April 1995, the United States itself suffered one of the worst single acts of terrorism recorded in any Western country. A van bomb planted outside a federal government office block in Oklahoma City exploded, killing 167 people. Among the victims were 19 children; the building had housed a crèche. Although the damage was caused by homemade explosives, Oklahoma's governor, Frank Keating, declared: 'Obviously no amateur did this.' Subsequent investigations of the extreme right-wing activists suspected of involvement in the attack unearthed signs of a disturbing familiarity with advanced military techniques. High-powered assault rifles, night sights, grenades and land mines have become common currency among the most hardline of America's antigovernment groups. The nation-state, it seems, has lost its monopoly interest in dangerous weapons – and its ability to control knowledge of them.

In August 1995 it was revealed that detailed instructions on bomb-making were generally available from a new means of mass communication: the Internet, the global computer network, open to any of the millions of people worldwide with access to a computer and a modem. The Internet is a system for exchanging information over which no government has any authority. And listed on one of the network's bulletin boards is a 70-page document called simply 'Terrorist Manual', which contains precise listings of the ingredients needed for about 30 different types of explosives and incendiary devices. 'RDX', it declares, for example, 'is one of the most remarkable military explosives, with a power 150% greater than that of TNT.' To manufacture RDX, the ingredients must include: '50 grammes of detonator powder, 550 millilitres of nitric acid. . . .' The disclosure of the sheer ease with which these details were available

242

had a particular impact in France. In the wake of a terrorist bomb explosion on the Paris metro in July 1995, in which 7 people were killed and 86 wounded, the French press made much of the fact that the same type of methyl nitrate used in the attack was also found to have been specified in the bomb-maker's manual on the Internet.

Even more alarming were the discoveries made by the Japanese police in their searches of the premises of the Aum Shinri Kyo sect. The organisation was close to achieving a position in the first league of military strength. Detectives found equipment and technical manuals concerned not just with the production of Sarin and other chemical agents – in far larger quantities than was used in the Tokyo attack – but also with the development of nuclear and biological weapons. Although it is likely that the sheer scale of the effort needed to assemble a nuclear bomb would deter most terrorists, the manufacture of biological or germ weapons is an altogether different proposition. Biological agents, which kill by spreading fatal diseases, can be manufactured cheaply and quickly. The tiniest quantities are lethal (one-tenth of one-millionth of a gram of anthrax is enough for a fatal dose), and its effects, if deployed in an environment like an underground railway system, could be catastrophic. Above all, the production of biological weapons can be hidden. It is hardly surprising that germ weapons are now being called the ideal tool for the terrorist.

Aum Shinri Kyo protested its innocence in all this. Senior cult officials maintained that its scientific efforts were for purely peaceful purposes. The biological research, they said, was meant to further understanding into diseases and their medical cures. It is a claim that cannot be dismissed. The difficulty is that the equipment and materiel found at the sect's headquarters – including incubators, electron microscopes, 160 tons of peptone (used to cultivate bacteria) and samples of *clostridium botulinum* (which causes botulism poisoning and has been used in the past as a biological weapon) – could be for either benign or malign ends. The same technology and many of the same procedures are involved in producing germ weapons as in producing antidotes to diseases. In theory, any factory which uses the process of fermentation (bakeries and breweries, for example) *could* be turned to the production of disease-inducing biological agents. In an age when the ingredients and know-how for the most deadly weapons are increasingly available, the purpose behind their acquisition can be ever more readily disguised.

Aum Shinri Kyo is not alone in pursuing biological research – and having a plausible explanation for its efforts. Iraq has long been exploiting the same avenue. Despite intense Allied bombing in the 1991 Gulf War and incessant inspections by United Nations teams since then, Saddam Hussein is still thought likely to be able to produce biological weapons. At the time of writing, more than four years after the end of the conflict, UN officials admit that at best they are unsure about Iraq's plans and at worst have to assume Saddam is getting away with a highly dangerous rearmament. Denied the chance to continue his acquisition of nuclear and chemical weapons – since both involve large and unmistakeable production plants – the fear is that biological weapons, being simpler to hide and to produce, have become the preferred option for Saddam and other national and terrorist leaders eager to obtain the most powerful arsenals.

Germ weapons are 'the special weapon to be most concerned about in the future', according to Lisa Bronson, a senior official in the Pentagon's Counter-Proliferation Office, speaking in a BBC documentary on biological weapons in late 1994. General Colin Powell, Chairman of the US Joint Chiefs of Staff at the time of the Gulf War, told a congressional enquiry that his 'greatest concern' during Operation Desert Storm was 'that the Iraqis had been working on such a capability.' Biological weaponry, he said, was 'the one that scares me to death, perhaps even more so than tactical nuclear weapons.' In part this is because – pound for pound – germ weapons can kill more people than any other weapon invented. Studies by the Pentagon and by Britain's Chemical and Biological Defence Establishment have calculated that, in an attack on a large city with an average density of population, a chemical weapon weighing around 700 pounds could kill 3,000 people. A nuclear weapon weighing about half that – about 400 pounds – would kill up to 40,000 people. But a device containing just 70 pounds of anthrax spores could kill 80,000. Another investigation, by the National Security Council, explored the specific implications of terrorists using anthrax to attack New York City. According to sources familiar with that research, the conclusion was shattering. It found that huge numbers of anthrax spores could be dispersed by an industrial paint sprayer fitted to a small boat sailing off Manhattan. The cloud of microbes would be invisible and odourless, the boat anonymous among hundreds of others – and as many as 400,000 people could be killed within 48 hours. The terrorists would, by then, be well beyond reach.

Little wonder that Iraq and others see the value of working on biological weapons – not least because the outside world can never be entirely sure about their intentions. In the Gulf War, Allied commanders were sufficiently frightened by Baghdad's potential in this area to order their troops to endure the debilitating side effects of injections of antidotes to anthrax. Pentagon war games had shown how vulnerable the Allied forces could be: one computer model deployed a small Iraqi crop-spraying aircraft flying undetected along the Saudi border and successfully infecting thousands of troops. The effects of such an attack would have been horrific. In the few days during which the bacteria take hold, the victims themselves would have become involuntary germ weapons by contaminating the people trying to help them: biological Fifth Columnists, an enemy within. In addition, the very manner of death by germ weapon was enough to unnerve most soldiers in the Gulf: photographs of victims of naturally occurring anthrax show that mild infections cause grotesque inflammations of the skin. If the spores reach the lungs, choking and fever result in a painful death within four days. Even the survivors of a military unit hit in this way would find their morale sapped by the grotesquely distorted faces of dying colleagues.

Furthermore, Allied intelligence about the enemy was at its weakest on this issue. There were few hard facts and even bombing failed to provide answers. Iraqi propagandists, on a raid on one target, made much of a suspected biological weapons plant at Abu Ghuraib in Baghdad. They claimed the factory was for the production of powdered baby milk, a line seemingly accepted by many of the Western journalists taken to see the wreckage. One British correspondent reported somewhat gleefully that she was using the milk powder in her coffee. The Allies stood by their version, that the plant was in fact manufacturing botulinal toxin, and the intelligence was apparently compelling. One senior American analyst who examined the evidence told me that satellite photographs show the Iraqis hurriedly shifting canisters out of the plant and concealing them in the desert outside Baghdad.

After the Gulf War the Iraqis behaved even more suspiciously. As part of the postwar settlement, United Nations inspectors were sent to Iraq to try to clip its military wings once and for all. They have managed to destroy the most prominent weapons – the 'Superguns', the chemical shells, the Scud missiles and the military nuclear plants – but they have encountered endless difficulties in tackling Saddam's biological weapons. The Iraqis themselves have not helped of course. Their plant at Salman Pak, though damaged by bombing, had been bulldozed flat and stripped of its equipment by the time the inspectors arrived. The Iraqis declined to explain why this had been done, and to this day no-one knows where the laboratory apparatus has gone. At first Iraqi officials denied they had a germ warfare programme at all and only in August 1995 – after four years' stalling – were they coerced into producing the first documents about its extent and organisation. Even then, their response was evasive and the details provided were too sketchy to be useful.

A more significant problem, also encountered by detectives investigating the Aum Shinri Kyo, is the difficulty of identifying germ weapons production itself. Iraq's 'single cell protein plant' at Al-Hakem is one example. A UN video of the factory shows highly intricate piping and controls in a series of advanced laboratories. Privately UN inspectors believe that this sophisticated establishment was built to produce germ weapons. Allied intelligence shared the same suspicion and, for that reason, the site was bombed in the Gulf War. Later, the Iraqis declared that its purpose was to manufacture animal vaccines, a perfectly legitimate and laudable use, and made extraordinary efforts, in the face of sanctions, to cannibalise machinery from other sites to reassemble a working plant. The same processes that yield agricultural products also produce the organisms that can be used as weapons of war. The UN's concern is deep enough that time-lapse video cameras have been installed at key points in the factory to watch for any change from its current peaceful use. Similar arrangements have been made at other factories, and several dozen hospitals and universities are subject to regular inspection. As one British inspector put it, 'They could brew this stuff up almost anywhere and we'd never know.' The right fermentation flask, a few commercially available ingredients and a handful of competent scientific staff are all that is required; Iraq of course meets those conditions easily, as do many other countries and organisations.

Although no Western government will publicly identify the countries suspected of running biological weapons programmes, US State Department sources put the total at 'about a dozen.' (Both Britain and the US have long since unilaterally abandoned their biological weapons.) Of those, only Russia has confessed, and few believe Boris Yeltsin's claim in 1992 that all work in this area had been stopped. As recently as June 1995, leading members of the US House of Representatives cited their suspicions of Russia's germ warfare capability as a reason for delaying the handing over of aid. Other likely suspects include Iran, Israel, Libya, Syria, China, North Korea and Taiwan. A far larger number of countries could swiftly adapt their biotechnology industries to military production. The US Congress Office of Technology Assessment, in a report in 1994, estimated that 'well over 100' countries *could* turn to biological weapons if their governments chose to – and there is little anyone can do about it. Biotechnology is spreading around the world, and, as the report's author, Gerry Epstein, points out, it is a development which is simultaneously positive and negative. 'We want health care problems to be solved and we want to improve food production,' he says, 'but . . . some may use the same technologies to produce weapons of mass destruction. One can't have one without the other.'

Biological weapons have been used in the past and few doubt they will be used in the future. Medieval engravings – including one of the battle of Lancaster in northern England – illustrate an old technique of catapulting infected corpses over the walls of besieged cities to spread disease and weaken the will of the defenders. In the Second World War, Japan killed countless thousands of Chinese by releasing cholera and plague, and its scientists performed gruesome germ warfare experiments on Allied prisoners at the notorious Camp 731 in Manchuria. And in July 1995 there were reliable reports that the military government in Burma had deployed germ weapons against the Karen rebels. The British Ministry of Defence's biological warfare experts were quoted in the press as concluding that dispensers dropped into the Burmese jungle released bacteria that caused more than 300 deaths by cholera, dysentery and other diseases. The diffusion of technology and of the knowledge to exploit it appear to have become unstoppable. As Don Mahley, the senior US State Department official dealing with biological weapons, puts it: 'Biological weapons is one of those areas we're trying very hard to keep in the bottle but, once it's out, it's almost impossible to put back.'

In theory, the bottle should not be open at all, because biological weapons have been banned internationally. At least that was what the Biological Weapons Convention was meant to achieve when it was signed in 1972. Yet the treaty must rank as one of the least successful ever agreed in arms control. Two of the five permanent members of the UN Security Council (Russia and China) apparently flouted it. Worse, its provisions have been overtaken by progress in science. At around the time the treaty was being signed, researchers announced the scientific breakthrough of 'engineering' the genetic makeup of biological material. Using what are known as restriction enzymes, they managed to 'splice' the particular genes of one organism with those of another. It was an advance which opened up the vast and profitable industry of bioengineering. Synthetic insulin, vaccines for hepatitis, disease-resistant plants are all products of this revolution. Yet, just as the splitting of the atom was once seen purely as a source of cheap electrical power, the engineering of genetic material has a dark side too, spawning dreadful weapons for the future, unchecked by the Convention.

Bioengineering allows organisms to be modified to resist traditional antibiotics. A Russian defector to the West disclosed in 1993 that Moscow's secret biological warfare establishment, Biopreparat, used this technique to develop a strain of plague which is incurable by currently available means. The new technology also means that biological weapons have become even easier to manufacture; huge quantities can be 'bred' from a tiny starter culture. Even poisons from the natural world, such as snake or spider venom, can be replicated on a massive scale (the US Army produced litres of venom at Fort Detrick in Maryland, 'to see how others might do it', according to one senior officer there). Official sources were unwilling to describe the techniques involved. But one outside expert, Professor Barbara Rosenberg of the Federation of American Scientists, was prepared to summarise it for me. 'In the past, if you wanted to collect enough rattlesnake toxin to use in a weapon, you'd have to have a barn full of rattlesnakes and milk each one regularly, which would take an enormous amount of time. Now we can take the rattlesnake's toxin gene and clone it with *E. coli* or some other simple bacterium, which we then grow in big vats or fermenters such as you would use for making beer. And in a very short time we can produce the quantity you'd want for a weapon.'

Few scientists doubt the feasibility of creating an infinite variety of new biological weapons. In one example, the genes representing snake venom could be inserted into the structure of a virus like flu. The lethality of the poison would then be combined with the infectiousness of the virus, and an untraceable weapon would have been born. Even now identifying existing strains of biological agents in order to administer the correct antidote is arduous. In the future, it could become impossible. With genetic engineering the surface characteristics of bacteria can be modified or coated in subtle, microscopic ways that make them unrecognisable by the usual tests. More alarming still, particular germ weapons may be engineered to target certain racial types – what may be called ethnic cleansing by test tube.

According to British biological defence experts (who keep a large poster of Saddam hanging in their laboratory), a country like Iraq or a terrorist group would see little point in pouring money into researching exotic biological weapons when more ordinary ones will do. Anthrax and plague can cause a massive impact and are far simpler to make. Yet bioengineering is essentially a civilian undertaking, and with companies selling their products and foreign exchange students soaking up the advancing knowledge, the latest techniques are bound to spread. In one of the most recent studies, Professor Malcolm Dando of Bradford University estimates that within as little as twenty years the ability to construct new forms of biological weaponry is likely to be in the hands of more than just a few advanced nations.

This terrifying prospect provokes a mixture of reactions from policy-makers. One senior US officer described it as belonging in the 'too-difficult' in-tray. A more positive approach is diplomatic. The British government among others is pressing to strengthen the hapless Biological Weapons Convention by providing for monitoring. But it has no power to check on cheating. British proposals call for a system of probing inspections of a huge range of biotechnology plants as the only sure way of capping the bio-arms race. Resistance is stiff. The American biotechnology industry fears losing valuable commercial secrets to teams of foreign inspectors. Its lobbying has effectively convinced the Clinton Administration (which initially favoured the British approach) that America's preeminence in biotechnology – and the profits and jobs that follow – count for more than any possible benefits to international security. 'The risk of opening up isn't worth the potential gain', according to Don Mahley of the US State Department. Developing nations argue that the proposed inspections would merely amount to 'neo-imperialist' espionage. In the end, the convention is likely to remain as weak as ever. Which leaves a final approach: new technology.

Until now, biological defence has long been regarded in military circles as one of the more obscure pursuits, with the weakest call on funds for new systems and the worst career prospects. 'It doesn't sound too good to say you've been out fighting the bugs again', according to one American officer involved. Yet in the last few years this field has begun to acquire new status, as commanders and politicians alike become increasingly aware of the extreme vulnerability of their troops. The technology of germ warfare provides a massive advantage to the attacker over the defender. Although the US Army provided its soldiers with protection suits and antidotes to a handful of biological agents during the Gulf War, they would be useful only if timely warnings were given that a germ warfare attack was under way. Many policy-makers were startled to discover after the conflict that the US military had no reliable means even of detecting that a germ attack had taken place. The first firm indicators would have been gruesome and too late: people dying.

In August 1994, during a day with the US Aeromedical Isolation Unit, I observed a team of highly trained military medics whose task is to ferry home victims of germ warfare if all other defences fail. The unit, based at Fort Detrick in Maryland, is one of the few to come under the direct command of the US president. Its role is unpleasant and difficult, partly because of the nightmarish images it provokes of a future war involving biological weapons and partly because the team is the only one of its kind in the Western world – at a time when predictions of germ warfare would seem to demand a far greater capacity.

In a rare opportunity, we were allowed to film the team's rehearsals, which at times had the surreal appearance of a science fiction movie. To approach a victim – a volunteer, lying on the ground feigning illness – the team donned orange space suits. Plastic helmets protected their heads. Battery-powered pumps on their belts circulated filtered air, but, in the sweltering summer heat, temperatures inside the suits quickly rose. The team, sweat pouring off their faces, had to shout to be heard. Taking infinite care to avoid direct contact with the patient, the medics manoeuvred him into a 'high-containment isolater system' – a stretcher completely enclosed in a clear plastic canopy. This was then driven to a waiting Hercules transport plane for the pretend flight back to the US. With the patient safely isolated in the special stretcher, the team could then remove their orange space suits and prepare for the next stage:

arrival at Fort Detrick medical centre and its special germ warfare treatment ward.

The ward is in effect the last line of defence in biological warfare. Like the aeromedical unit, it is the only one of its kind in the Western world; yet it contains just two beds. When I asked one senior official what he would do if – as is likely – there were more than two germ warfare victims in a future conflict or terrorist attack, he simply rolled his eyes and mumbled that the matter was in the hands of those who provide the funding. The ward itself is designed to operate at 'Bio-safety Level 4' – the highest international standard required to contain the most infectious bacteria and viruses. Its walls, floor and ceiling are encased in a protective shell and access is only possible through a double air lock. Air pressure is constantly negative, so that whenever a door is opened air flows in rather than out, to keep microbes trapped inside. Medics working inside the ward wear what look like vast diving suits, huge blue plastic overalls, their sleeves and legs puffed up with fresh air fed in from a pipeline connecting them umbilically to the wall. Once protected in this way, the medics can receive the germ warfare victim and care for him. This elaborate procedure is not only humane treatment of the patient; it also ensures his survival long enough for laboratory technicians to confirm the precise cause of his condition. Only then can the most effective protection be devised for the surviving troops on the battlefront. Evidently far more resources and ingenuity are needed to defend against a germ attack than to launch one.

The Pentagon, acknowledging its weakness, has begun to give biological defence a higher profile by bringing together the disparate efforts of the armed services in this area. The Army and Navy in particular had been pursuing similar but uncoordinated approaches. In 1993, a Joint Project Office was established to oversee the research and development of future defence systems; budgets have seen a modest rise. The immediate task is to field a detection system so that combat units can at least be warned that a germ warfare attack is being launched. The answer is a projects known as BIDS (Biological Integrated Detector System), a mobile laboratory fitted to the back of a large jeep. By August 1994, a prototype was on trial. I watched its two-man team, fully protected in protection suits and gas masks, driving through the woods of Aberdeen Proving Ground in Maryland and going through the drill of gathering air and water samples to run through a series of tests. Since the computers and analysers packed inside are all off-the-shelf, there is little risk of the system failing. Yet the project has only a limited value. The assumption is that BIDS will operate at or near the front line and will therefore only be able to spot a germ warfare attack once the invisible cloud of microbes has reached that area. What the system cannot do is to warn that a germ cloud is on its way.

That task will fall to a more sophisticated and futuristic device known as the Long-Range Stand-Off Biological Detection System (LRSOBDS), which is being rushed into service at unusual speed. The system involves a laser, mounted on a Blackhawk helicopter, whose beam scans the horizon as far as ten to fifteen miles away in a search for biological organisms drifting in the breeze. Any microbes caught in the sweep of the laser beam give off a telltale reflection (they are much larger than the usual particles of dust found in the air). A special camera on the helicopter records the reflections and passes them to a computer, also onboard. The computer rapidly generates a picture of the approaching cloud, plots its course and relays a warning to the forces on the ground below. This remarkable harnessing of technology, due in service in 1997, means that for the first time front line units will be given time to prepare for a biological attack.

In practice, of course, nothing works that simply. When we filmed the system's first airborne trials, at dawn in September 1994 in the desert at Dugway Proving Ground in Utah, it failed to detect the trail of harmless particles released by a crop-spraying aircraft. It had worked before, we were assured. But if a germ cloud is successfully detected, even this system has a profound limitation: it cannot distinguish one kind of microbe from another. It cannot provide ground forces with a warning of which type of attack to prepare for – and therefore which antidotes to use to negate its effects. That capability will only come in a later version, not scheduled to be ready until 2004. More useful still would be a system which could not only identify the approaching bacteria but also destroy them. One senior officer involved said this would be 'a dream weapon, so you could find the bugs – and zap them.' He confirmed that exploratory research was under way into this, but, given the difficulties of tracking and hitting billions of individual microbes, such a system is described as being 'decades away'. The managers of these projects make no apology for failing to produce instant solutions. In their view, not only are the practical difficulties of coordinating so much technology all too obvious but also the science involved in 'seeing' the invisible, let alone killing it, at a great distance is described as being at 'the cutting-edge'.

Ironically, the trials are being conducted over the very stretches of empty, battered Utah desert, where for decades the US Army had tested its own germ warfare agents, until President Richard Nixon abandoned the programme in 1969. In the same way that designers of nuclear weapons are tackling the consequences of the proliferation of the Bomb, the scientists once involved in devising offensive uses for biological weapons are now engaged in finding a defence against the genie of germ warfare – and they are finding the task much harder.

Their greatest challenge has yet to be addressed: how to prepare for the likeliest use of germ weapons – by terrorists against civilians. One expert in this field, Dr Kathleen Bailey of Lawrence Livermore National Laboratory, believes the need for immediate research into biological defence has become urgent. There could be a massive attack by a terrorist group, she says, 'without us knowing who in fact delivered it.' The West has not prepared for this at all, according to Dr Bailey, even though the evidence suggests that 'I could manufacture biological agent in my own home if I wanted to and then transport it through airport security undetected and deliver it to any country I wish to travel to.' None of the biological defence systems under development is intended to meet the particular threat of terrorist attacks on large targets such as cities. Professor Rosenberg of the Federation of American Scientists criticises even the latest Pentagon efforts, because 'they're not talking about defending the public – they're not talking about defending us.'

The inescapable conclusion is that, without a major research initiative to tackle this threat, Western civilians remain uniquely vulnerable. The microorganisms launched against them may be genetically engineered and previously unknown. Current technology and existing treaties will have failed to stop them. And, worst of all, the diseases may well have no known cure.

In early 1994, as I was writing the chapter on the development of 'non-lethal' weapons, Pentagon commanders were slow to appreciate the potential of what were widely dismissed as 'soft' arms, too laughable and too embarrassing to deploy. That had changed by February 1995. The US Marines sent to Somalia to cover the withdrawal of the UN force were equipped with a variety of weapons, including nonlethal ones: bazooka guns that squirted giant sticky coils to immobilise enemy gunmen; gladiators' nets covered with glue to trap potential attackers; and beanbags that could explode to release thousands of stinging pellets to deter hostile crowds. The concept of imposing one's will without causing casualties seems to be taking hold – but not without critics, inside and outside the military.

One type of nonlethal weapon reportedly taken by the US forces to Somalia was a device meant to dazzle hostile forces. Code-named Sabre 203, this weapon is a grenade, launched by rifle, which explodes with a brilliant flash of laser light to 'temporarily blind or impair the vision of enemy soldiers, reducing their ability to fight.' Yet the researchers who confirmed the details of this weapon, the New York-based Human Rights Watch Arms Project, argue that it has the potential to cause permanent damage to the human eyeball – to blind its victims forever. In a report published in May 1995, Human Rights Watch disclosed that the Pentagon was researching a total of ten laser weapons and the report condemned them as 'unnecessarily cruel and injurious.' One of the systems, a 40-pound portable gun, is apparently powerful enough to burn out human retinas from up to 3,000 feet away. The use of such blinding weapons, the report concludes, is 'repugnant to the public conscience.'

The armed forces that have been exploring the use of such weapons – including Britain, France, Russia, China and Israel – reason that in sensitive situations it is better to deter an enemy sniper or pilot from attacking rather than to kill him. When, for example, the Royal Navy sent warships to the Persian Gulf in 1987 to protect civilian oil tankers from attack by Iraq and Iran, they deployed a 'dazzle gun' to ward off threatening warplanes. The explanation at the time was that to resort to lethal firepower in every case would exacerbate an already tense scene and risk wider war. In addition lasers have become essential tools for target designation and range-finding, and defence chiefs maintain that the lasers used in this role are too weak to cause permanent damage to anyone on the receiving end. Indeed the Pentagon's official line is that none of its present or future laser systems – for whatever purpose – is 'designed or primarily intended to permanently blind enemy combatants.'

Yet Human Rights Watch argues that any laser beam aimed at a position such as an observation post would be amplified by whatever optical device – binoculars or gunner's sight – was being used by the enemy. The intensified beam would 'shoot back to the human retina in less than one second, causing eye damage' that could result in permanent blindness. Such weapons, it claims, are therefore 'anti-personnel'. Further, they cannot be considered to be nonlethal, since their use would weaken the enemy's defences and pave the way for the more effective deployment of other, lethal weapons. The controversy is unlikely to end there. Many proponents maintain that, however dangerous lasers may be, it is better to blind than to kill. And it is certain that future commanders will be under growing pressure to keep enemy fatalities to a minimum. The debate about the precise effects of lasers – and whether they are more or less humane than conventional weapons – is unlikely to undermine their importance to future arsenals, whether truly nonlethal or not.

By contrast, a debate which has attracted widespread attention in the United States does not seem even to have begun in Russia. When the Russian army set out to reestablish the Kremlin's control over the breakaway republic of Chechnya in December 1994, old ways were evidently dying hard. Attempts by the Tsars to suppress the Caucasus had used the same brute force as was applied now. Tanks may have replaced horses and artillery have acquired a longer range, but the priority remained domination at any price. The lesson – that a clumsy and savage operation creates a legacy of bitterness and hostility – seemed to have been ignored. Even by the summer of 1995, pockets of Chechen rebels were still holding out in the mountains and Russians administrators were left trying to justify to surviving Chechen civilians why an estimated 20,000 of their number had been killed and their capital, Grozny, laid waste.

It is conceivable that the new technology of nonlethal weapons, in offering different means, could have achieved a more civilised end. Certainly, if the Russians could have supplanted the Chechen leadership without resorting to massive violence, their chances of rebuilding a durable peace with their subjects would have been far greater. Even now, though, as Russian generals pride themselves on a successful victory, the seeds of further insurrection and violence are being sown in Chechnya and elsewhere in the Causasus.

The problem is that revolutions in military thinking do not come easily, not only in Russia. Senior officers tend to favour the familiar in hardware and procedures; there is so much else that can go wrong. And the older the forces and the better-established the traditions the harder it will be to recognise the value of change. Yet that is what is required now. The accustomed global patterns of military power and of advances in weaponry are undergoing a transformation. We are only at the start of this process but the first signs of its implications and dangers are there for those who wish to see them.

– Brussels, August 1995

NOTES AND REFERENCES

Notes to Chapter 1
1. John Keegan, *A History of Warfare*, Hutchinson, 1993
2. Charles Dick et al, 'Potential sources of conflict in post-Communist Europe', Conflict Studies Research Centre, Occasional Brief no. 15, December 1992

Notes to Chapter 2
1. Richard Rhodes, *The Making of the Atomic Bomb*, Simon & Schuster, 1986
2. Pavel Sudoplatov and Anatoli Sudoplatov, *Special Tasks: Memoirs of an Unwanted Witness*, Little, Brown, 1994
3. Memo to Dean Acheson, acting Secretary of State, 7 May 1946, Harry S. Truman Library
4. Speech to the Centre for Defence Studies, King's College, London, 23 November 1993
5. Igor Kurchatov Institute archives, quoted in *Bulletin of Atomic Scientists*, May 1993
6. Quoted in *The Nuclear Weapons Databook*, vol. 5, Natural Resources Defense Council, Washington, 1994
7. Assessment of Indian nuclear test, US Mission to NATO, 5 June 1974
8. Associated Press, Islamabad, 30 July 1993
9. PTV, Pakistani Television, 7 December 1993
10. Raju G. C. Thomas, Adelphi Paper 278, IISS, July 1993
11. 'The Start treaty and beyond', Congressional Budget Office, October 1991
12. Inter Press Service, Islamabad, 16 February 1994
13. Quoted in Seymour M. Hersh, *The Samson Option*, Faber & Faber, 1991
14. *Bulletin of Arms Control*, no. 12, November 1993
15. Dr Oumirseric Kasenov and Dr Kairat Abuseitov, *The Future of Nuclear Weapons in the Kazakh Republic*, Centre for Strategic Studies, Alma-Ata, published by the Potomac Centre, McLean, Virginia, 1992

257

16. *Jane's Defence Weekly*, 2 April 1994
17. China News Agency, Taipei, 12 April 1994

Notes to Chapter 3

1. Stanley Orman, *Faith in G.O.D.S.*, Brassey's, 1991, p. 39
2. Quoted in *The New York Times*, 3 December 1993, p. A18
3. *Defense News*, 14–20 March 1994
4. Document 1394, Assembly of Western European Union, Technological and Aerospace Committee, 8 November 1993
5. BBC Monitoring, SWB, SU/1744 D/1, 19 July 1993
6. BBC Monitoring, SWB, SU/1744 D/1, 19 July 1993, quoting ITAR-TASS of 12 July
7. SWB, SU/1792 H/1, 13 September 1993
8. *The New York Times*, 9 July 1993
9. *Defense News*, 31 January–February 1994
10. Major Thomas M. Petzold, 'The crisis in Russian basic science', Central & East European Defense Studies Occasional Paper, Supreme Headquarters Allied Powers in Europe, 9 November 1993

Notes to Chapter 4

1. *Whatever happened to Star Wars?*, Horizon documentary, BBC2, March 1993
2. William J. Broad, *Teller's War*, Simon & Schuster, 1992
3. Ibid. p. 251
4. Gregory Canavan and Edward Teller, 'Strategic defence for the 1990s', *Nature*, vol. 344, no. 6268, 19 April 1990
5. *Aviation Week & Space Technology*, 18 October 1993, p. 96
6. *Aviation Week & Space Technology*, 21 March 1994
7. John Dickie, *Inside the Foreign Office*, Chapmans, 1992, p. 277
8. Quoted in Robin Ranger, 'Theatre missile defences: lessons from British experiences with air and missile defences', *Comparative Strategy*, vol. 12, 1993
9. George Lewis, Steve Fetter and Lisbeth Gronlund, 'Casualties and damage from Scud attacks in the 1991 Gulf War', Defense and Arms Control Studies Program, Massachusetts Institute of Technology, March 1993
10. Barbara Opall, 'DoD targets missile nemeses', *Defense News*, 8–14 November 1993
11. *Aviation Week & Space Technology*, 21 February 1994
12. Reuven Pedatzur, 'Israeli defence planning and ballistic missile defence', seminar paper, Defense and Arms Control Studies Program, Massachusetts Institute of Technology, 13 October 1993
13. *Flight International*, 27 October 1993

Notes to Chapter 5

1. Quoted in Robin Ranger, 'Theatre missile defences: lessons from British experiences with air and missile defences', *Comparative Strategy*, vol. 12, 1993
2. Andy McNab, *Bravo-Two-Zero*, Bantam Press, 1993, p. 116
3. BMD Monitor, 18 June 1993
4. *Jane's Defence Weekly*, 15 January 1994
5. *Defense News*, 17–23 January 1994
6. *The Times*, 12 March 1992

Notes to Chapter 6

1. *The Independent*, letters page, 6 July 1993
2. 'GPS performance: an initial assessment by Commander Patrick Sharrett and others, US Space Command', a paper presented to the Institute of Navigation on 12 September 1991
3. *Washington Post*, 15 June 1993, p. A19

Notes to Chapter 7

1. Rick Atkinson, 'Firefight in Mogadishu', *Washington Post*, 30 and 31 January 1994
2. Brian Beedham, 'Democracies have to fight wars of interest and of conscience', *International Herald Tribune*, 19 October 1993
3. *Business Week*, 25 October 1988
4. *City Paper*, Washington DC, 7 December 1990
5. *Wall Street Journal*, 28 November 1990
6. *Aviation Week & Space Technology*, 31 January 1994
7. *Jane's Defence Weekly*, 9 April 1994
8. *STAR 21: Strategic Technologies for the Army of the 21st Century*, National Academy Press, 1992
9. Pacific News Service, 1 October 1986
10. Martin Libicki, 'The mesh and the net', McNair paper no. 29, National Defense University, Washington DC, March 1994
11. *Hemispheres*, Science & Technology Section, May 1993
12. Kawachi Millibioflight Project, ERATO New Projects, Tokyo, 1992
13. Selden B. Crary et al, 'Prospects for microflight using micromechanisms', University of Michigan, paper presented at the International Symposium on Theory of Machines and Mechanisms, 24–6 September 1992
14. Keith Brendley and Randall Steeb, 'Military applications of microelectromechanical systems', RAND, Santa Monica, California, 1993

Notes to Chapter 8

1. Fred Kaplan, *The Wizards of Armageddon*, Stanford University Press, 1983, p. 137
2. *Defense News*, 28 March–3 April 1994, p. 46

Notes to Conclusion

1. Ted Gold and Richard Wagner, 'Long shadows and virtual swords: managing defense resources in the changing security environment', Hicks & Associates Inc. and Kaman Corporation, Washington, June 1990
2. Gregory Canavan, *Applied Research in America*, Los Alamos National Laboratory, 1993

BIBLIOGRAPHY

Bellamy, Christopher, *Expert Witness: A Defence Correspondent's Gulf War 1990–91*, Brassey's, 1993

Beschloss, Michael and Strobe Talbott, *At the Highest Levels: The Inside Story of the End of the Cold War*, Little, Brown, 1993

Broad, William J., *Teller's War*, Simon & Schuster, 1992

Brown, Ben and David Shukman, *All Necessary Means: Inside the Gulf War*, BBC Books, 1991

Connell, Jon, *The New Maginot Line*, 1988, paperback edition by Coronet, London

de la Billière, Sir Peter, *Storm Command: A Personal Account of the Gulf War*, HarperCollins, 1992

Dickie, John, *Inside the Foreign Office*, Chapmans, 1992

Freedman, Lawrence and Efraim Karsh, *The Gulf Conflict 1990–91*, Faber & Faber, 1993

Freedman, Lawrence (ed.), *War*, Oxford University Press, 1994

Hartcup, Guy, *The Silent Revolution: Development of Conventional Weapons 1945–85*, Brassey's, 1993

Hersh, Seymour M., *The Samson Option: Israel, America and the Bomb*, Faber & Faber, 1991

Kaplan, Fred, *The Wizards of Armageddon*, Stanford University Press, 1983

Keegan, John, *A History of Warfare*, Hutchinson, 1993

——*The Second World War*, Hutchinson, 1989

Mack, Joanna and Steve Humphries, *The Making of Modern London 1939–45: London at War*, Sidgwick & Jackson, 1985

McNab, Andy, *Bravo-Two-Zero*, Bantam Press, 1993

Moss, Norman, *Klaus Fuchs: The Man Who Stole the Atom Bomb*, Grafton Books, 1987

Munro, Neil, *Electronic Combat and Modern Warfare*, Macmillan, 1991

Navias, Martin, *Going Ballistic: The Build-up of Missiles in the Middle East*, Brassey's, 1993

Newhouse, John, *The Nuclear Age: From Hiroshima to Star Wars*, Michael Joseph, 1989

Norris, Robert S., Andrew Burrows and Richard W. Fieldhouse, *Nuclear Weapons Databook Volume V: British, French and Chinese Nuclear Weapons*, Westview Press, 1994

O'Connell, Robert L., *Of Arms and Men: A History of War, Weapons and Aggression*, Oxford University Press, 1989

Orman, Stanley, *Faith in G.O.D.S.: Stability in the Nuclear Age*, Brassey's, 1991

Rhodes, Richard, *The Making of the Atomic Bomb*, first published by Simon & Schuster, 1986; Penguin edition, 1988

Rosenthal, Debra, *At the Heart of the Bomb: The Dangerous Allure of Weapons Work*, Addison-Wesley, 1990

Rummel, Jack, *Robert Oppenheimer: Dark Prince*, Facts on File, 1992

Schwarzkopf, Norman H., *It Doesn't Take a Hero*, Bantam Press, 1992

Toffler, Alvin and Heidi, *War and Anti-War*, Little, Brown, 1993

US Department of Defence, *Soviet Military Forces in Transition*, US Government Printing Office, Washington DC, 1991

van Creveld, Martin, *The Transformation of War*, Free Press, 1991

——*Technology and War from 200 BC to the Present*, Brassey's, 1991

van Hamm, Peter, *Managing Non-Proliferation Regimes in the 1990s: Power, Politics and Policies*, Pinter Publishers, 1993

Williamson, Samuel R. jnr. and Steven Reardon, *The Origins of US Nuclear Strategy 1945-53*, St Martin's Press, 1993

Wright, Susan (ed.), *Preventing a Biological Arms Race*, MIT Press, 1990

INDEX